"What hath Christian witness to do with the arts? Well, virtually everything, according to King. The author's assertion is sorely needed and long overdue, particularly in a day when 70 percent of the world's people can't, don't, or won't read. King's lifelong ministry and academic engagement as an active 'musicianary' make her seasoned reflections here a must-read!"

—**James R. Krabill**, Anabaptist Mennonite Biblical Seminary; general editor, *Mission and Worship for the Global Church: An Ethnodoxology Handbook*

"King brings us a very important reveal about why artistic specialists and expression stand central to effective gospel proclamation. Creative, with plenty of stories, culturally sensitive, and filled with insight and life, this book provides much help for how indigenous Christian community formation really happens. Artists, musicians, missionaries, worship leaders, and anyone else who is concerned about the church making sense in her context will find this book to be a must-have. King gives her life for these insights, and now we get her wisdom distilled in ways that will increase our ministry effectiveness. Along the way, too, she affirms all the artistic kingdom servants so often overlooked for the strategic role they play in God's kingdom purposes."

—**Byron Spradlin**, president, Artists in Christian Testimony International

"Inviting the reader on a global spiritual and artistic safari, King has richly and skillfully advanced our understanding about the role, importance, and impact of the arts in its ability to incarnate the good news in cross-cultural contexts. Informed by twenty-two years of missionary ministry in East and West Africa and over two decades of academic leadership at Fuller Theological Seminary, King has adroitly crafted and curated a resource that provides a theological and missional framework for expressive cultural interaction through the arts that becomes a platform that leads to authentic spiritual dialogue and gospel witness."

—**Stan Moore**, president of the executive board, Global Consultation on Music and Missions; B. H. Carroll Theological Institute

"Packed with stories on subjects ranging from Bono to the Senufo, this volume will motivate and inspire its readers to think in new ways about the value of global arts in the church. I especially appreciate King's ten recommendations for needed shifts in our thinking. If these shifts could be implemented today, the use of arts in witness and worship worldwide would change dramatically for the better."

—**Robin Harris**, Center for Excellence in World Arts, Dallas International University

MISSION
in Global Community

SCOTT W. SUNQUIST
AND AMOS YONG,
SERIES EDITORS

The Mission in Global Community series is designed to reach college students and those interested in learning more about responsible mission involvement. Written by faculty and graduates from Fuller Theological Seminary, the series is designed as a global conversation with stories and perspectives from around the world.

GLOBAL ARTS AND CHRISTIAN WITNESS

Exegeting Culture, Translating the Message,
and Communicating Christ

ROBERTA R. KING

Baker Academic
a division of Baker Publishing Group
Grand Rapids, Michigan

© 2019 by Roberta R. King

Published by Baker Academic
a division of Baker Publishing Group
PO Box 6287, Grand Rapids, MI 49516-6287
www.bakeracademic.com

Printed in the United States of America

Library of Congress Cataloging-in-Publication Data
Names: King, Roberta Rose, 1949– author.
Title: Global arts and Christian witness : exegeting culture, translating the message, and
    communicating Christ / Roberta R. King.
Description: Grand Rapids : Baker Academic, a division of Baker Publishing Group, 2019. | Series:
    Mission in global community | Includes bibliographical references and index.
Identifiers: LCCN 2018053562 | ISBN 9780801098857 (pbk.)
Subjects: LCSH: Christianity and the arts. | Globalization—Religious aspects—Christianity. |
    Christianity and culture. | Evangelistic work.
Classification: LCC BR115.A8 K56 2019 | DDC 261.5/7—dc23
LC record available at https://lccn.loc.gov/2018053562

ISBN 978-1-5409-6215-7 (casebound)

19 20 21 22 23 24 25   7 6 5 4 3 2 1

For the Lord of the harvest

To my students, colleagues, and global companions
who witness to Christ's glory and salvation through music and the arts

Contents

Illustrations

Series Preface

A mission leader in 1965, not too long ago, could not have foreseen what mission would look like today. In 1965 nations in the non-Western world were gaining their independence after centuries of Western colonialism. Mission societies from Europe and North America were trying to adjust to the new global realities where Muslim nations, once dominated by the West, no longer granted "missionary visas." The largest mission field, China, was closed. Decolonization, it seemed, was bringing a decline to missionary work in Africa and Asia.

On the home front, Western churches were in decline, and the traditional missionary factories—mainline churches in the West—were struggling with their own identities. Membership was then—and remains—in decline, and missionary vocations were following the same pattern. Evangelical and Pentecostal churches began to surpass mainline churches in mission, and then, just when we thought we understood the new missionary patterns, Brazilians began to go to Pakistan, and Malaysians began to evangelize Vietnam and Cambodia. Africans (highly educated and strongly Christian) began to move in great numbers to Europe and North America. Countries that had been closed began to see conversions to Christ, without the aid of traditional mission societies. And in the midst of this rapid transformation of missionary work, the alarm rang out that most Christians in the world were now in Asia, Latin America, and Africa rather than in the West.

What does it mean to be involved in mission in this new world where Christianity has been turned upside down in less than a century?

This series is directed at this new global context for mission. Fuller Theological Seminary, particularly through its School of Intercultural Studies (formerly School of World Mission), has been attentive to trends in global mission for over half a century. In fact, much innovation in mission thinking and practice has emanated from Fuller since Donald McGavran moved from Oregon to California—as the first and founding dean of the then School of World Mission—to apply lessons about church growth learned in India to other areas of the world. Since that time many creative mission professors have provided global leadership in mission thinking: Ralph Winter (unreached people groups), Paul Hiebert (anthropology for mission), Charles Kraft (mission and spiritual dynamics), and Dudley Woodberry (Islamics), among others.

This series provides the most recent global scholarship on key themes in mission, written for a general audience of Christians committed to God's mission. Designed to be student, user, and textbook friendly, each volume contains voices from around the world speaking about the theme, and each chapter concludes with discussion questions so the books can be used for group studies. As the fields of mission are changing, shifting, or shrinking, the discussions connect the church and the world, East and West, North and South, the developed and developing worlds, each crossing cultural, political, social, and religious boundaries in its own way and knitting together people living and serving in various communities, both of faith and of other commitments—this is the contemporary landscape of the mission of God. Enjoy the challenges of each volume and find ways to live into God's mission.

Scott W. Sunquist
Amos Yong

Foreword

At the height of the Lord's Resistance Army (LRA) in Northern Uganda, I was worshiping one evening in a so-called Night Commuter Camp, full of young children who gathered at bedtime to sleep on rough mats, but together, in an unused school. Their and their family's hope was that by sleeping together they might avoid being abducted, tortured, and enslaved as child soldiers of Joseph Konye. As we gathered everyone together for a brief time of worship before going to sleep, we danced and we prayed like everything depended on it, since it did. Daniel, the twelve-year-old boy standing next to me, seemed especially intent. As each petition for protection and safety went up from the crowd of children, Daniel said, "Amen, Jesus," and thrust his hand toward heaven. In his sweaty palm was a small wooden cross.

Afterward, Daniel explained that this cross was one he had made of cha-cha wood. This hardwood, indigenous to the area, was what Konye's troops used to abuse and torture abducted children, brutally forcing them into submission. Now Daniel, profiled in the shadowy light of the camp—young, believing, vulnerable, confident—held his cha-cha cross in his hand. Of course he did: as he explained, it reminded him that God can turn even death into life.

Daniel's cross may be among the simplest of global arts, and it was surely one of the most profound expressions of Christian witness. On the one hand, it was the "old, old story," soaked in the lives and blood of Christian witness across time and around the world. On the other, it was utterly particular, fresh, and contextual—faithful gospel art made of the substance of Northern Ugandan beauty and pain amid the long and desperate era of LRA trauma and violence.

That cross in Daniel's young hand was one of the most beautiful liturgical implements I have ever seen. Daniel assumed that Jesus's cross was every bit as real and imminent as the hard cha-cha wood he gripped. The presence, identification, and protection of Jesus in suffering, fear, and even death was made palpable to Daniel by this artifact of his home and environment. Emmanuel was in hand.

Dr. Roberta King, in this very fine book and training resource, explains and expounds on the intrinsic connections and meanings that link global arts and Christian witness. From biblical texts and scenes, and in countless cultural angles, means, and mediums, the faith "once revealed" becomes the faith endlessly reembodied and reexpressed, not least through the arts. In this comprehensive treatment of global arts and Christian witness, Dr. King lays out what we may feel we "know" but may not have ever really seen or understood as well as Dr. King makes possible.

Though herself a Caucasian American woman, a resident and professor in Africa for several decades, King moves us all around the world and all through the arts. Everywhere we go on this journey, past and present, she keeps expanding and deepening the themes she is exploring. She provides a lens that challenges and inspires readers about the nature of the gospel and about its power to meet us in context and to transform us in and through the very contexts in which we live.

Here Dr. King provides a rich, nuanced, varied invitation to think creatively and concretely about the God who was in Christ reconciling the world to himself. That same God still speaks and acts today in contexts all over the world, and does so by good news that infuses arts and changes realities as clearly and truly as it did Daniel in Northern Uganda or as it has millions of others around the world. Feast. Learn. Create. Witness. All to the glory of God.

Mark Labberton
President, Fuller Theological Seminary

Acknowledgments

Many *safaris* (Swahili for "journeys") begin at a known point, where people bring what they have and who they are into previously unexplored regions. Armed with a BA in piano performance from the University of California at Santa Barbara, a master of music in music education from the University of Oregon, fifteen years of experience as a church organist, and French horn performance skills, I found myself finally responding to the Lord's prompting to go into mission. Little did I know that was a problem. There were very few, if any, formal positions to serve in the world of missions. Now, after twenty-two years of mission through music and the arts in East and West Africa, and almost two decades on Fuller Theological Seminary's faculty as an ethnomusicologist and intercultural communication specialist, I am grateful for each person and institution that has played a significant role in opening up innovative pathways for witnessing to Christ through music and the arts. Each of them has contributed in significant ways to making this book a reality. Each one is a gift, for whom I am immensely grateful.

Among these gifts is the senior faculty of Fuller Theological Seminary's School of Intercultural Studies (SIS). These include world-renowned missiologists such as Charles H. Kraft, the late Paul G. Hiebert, the late Dean Gilliland, Paul Pierson, Dudley Woodberry, and Sherwood Lingenfelter. I'm indebted to them for their vision and encouragement to explore a new and much-needed arena of missiology, that of ethnomusicology. I am also grateful for their initiative in pursuing me to join them on the faculty of the School of Intercultural Studies—which for me was an amazing turn of events.

WorldVenture, the mission organization with whom I served twenty-two years on the field, is another gift. Their philosophy of fostering people's calling for ministry and mission placement facilitated exploring new frontiers. I'm especially indebted to the late Warren and Shirley Webster, who were always planting seeds for doing mission over the course of my life. It was Warren Webster who first suggested ethnomusicology just as I was discovering its possibilities at Daystar Communications (now Daystar University, Nairobi) in 1978. As executive director, he later championed my serving with WorldVenture.

For the gift of Daystar University in Nairobi, Kenya, I cannot adequately express my gratitude at finding myself in a place where I could learn about, from, and with colleagues and students in worship settings, in the classroom, and in researching the significance of the arts in witness. I am grateful for the privilege of participating in the growth and development of one of Africa's premier Christian universities. I am especially indebted to the former vice-chancellor, professor Stephen Talitwala, for his insights and support of cultural musics and the arts in ministry and mission. He was always a defender of the cause, making space for me to travel annually across the African continent for four to six months each year doing ministry and research for the sake of the gospel.

The gift of talented and committed students at Fuller Theological Seminary is my joy and delight. I'm grateful for the students in the MA in global arts and world religions courses who joined in discussing the deeper issues of music, culture, identity, and the role of the arts in interfaith dialogue and peacebuilding. I'm also grateful for doctoral students who studied ethnomusicology with me, both at the PhD and DMiss level. Through research and fieldwork, they have allowed us to drill deeper into the depths of witness via the arts. I am further indebted to those students and grads who have contributed vignettes to this work. I want to especially thank the Lord for the gift of Sunita Puleo, not only a talented performer, artist, and visionary but also an excellent writer and experienced editor. I'm grateful for her grabbing hold of the value and significance of global Christian worship and witness, first as an MA student in class and then as a first editor of this manuscript. Sunita's counsel in the writing and articulation of complex modes of music and the arts as vehicles of communication is of unlimited value.

I am very grateful for the leadership and encouragement of the former dean of SIS, Scott W. Sunquist, and of Amos Yong, the director of the Center for Missiological Research, who are the series editors of Baker Academic's Mission in Global Community series. Their recognition of music and the arts as a critical dimension in missiology opened the opportunity to publish in what for many is unknown territory. I'm also indebted to the trustees of Fuller Theological Seminary for the gift of a six-month sabbatical that provided space to bring together my materials from across a spectrum of courses and ministry experiences.

Once I began writing, I discovered that I needed an inspirational space in which to write, away from the buzzing sounds of city life. I am grateful to my colleague Bill Dyrness for suggesting that I apply as a reader at the Huntington Library. Sitting in the Rothenberg Library at the Huntington was a gift, and it became a place of retreat and lovely surprises. I'll never forget my delight when I glanced up one day from my writing desk and actually looked at the reference works lining the walls. I was sitting next to the *New Grove's Dictionary of Music and Musicians*. Amazingly, I had inadvertently found the section most relevant for my topic. I am grateful to the Huntington Library for their gift of an excellent library, beautiful gardens, and gracious staff.

I also want to acknowledge my colleagues at Baker Academic for their willingness to take on such a volume in this series. Jim Kinney's listening ear and patience in understanding the direction I wanted to take with the volume have brought deep satisfaction. I am also indebted to Brandy Scritchfield, who has kindly facilitated and made manageable many of the details that I would rather do without.

Finally, and in many ways, this book can be summed up as a global *safari* highlighting how God is making himself known through music and the arts worldwide. I am immensely grateful for God's gift of leading me each step of the way into a calling in mission and an academic career in missiology that moved me beyond the boundaries of my imagination and experience. May God be honored and glorified!

Prelude

My Art, God's Mission?

It was in the midst of worship on a mountain in Galilee that Jesus commissioned his followers to go into all the world and make disciples of all nations, all peoples, everywhere (Matt. 28:16–20). It was also in the midst of worship that God called me to move out in paths similar to those of the early disciples. I love worshiping God and longed to see peoples around the world come to love and worship him too. There was just one major question. How do music and the arts fit in with doing mission? Worship and witness form the bookends of God's interaction in the world today. This two-pronged dialogue with God in our lives lies at the heart of activating the gospel message. I struggled with this as I was first thrust out into mission.

My Story: Leaving on a Jet Plane

As I pressed my hand on the window of the plane to wave a final goodbye to family at Seattle's SEA-TAC airport, the question I had been asking over a long period of time remained at the forefront of my thoughts. Could God use me—a woman and a musician? The mission buzzword at that time was church planting, which rarely, if ever, included music and the performing arts as a medium for making Christ known. If it did, it was thought of as a one-time event, often at evangelistic services. Or one could go on a concert tour. Music and the performing arts were not considered a sustainable approach to doing mission in ways that reached into local communities, cities, and nations.

And yet, as the plane backed out of the gate, a flush of emotion came over me. A phrase haunted me from John Denver's pop song of the day, "Leaving on a jet plane, don't know when I'll be back again." It was a risk, flying off to Nairobi, Kenya, not knowing exactly how I would proceed. Yet at the same time there was a great sense of discovery and adventure. Psalm 73 had challenged me:

> Whom have I in heaven but You?
> And besides You, I desire nothing on earth.
> My flesh and my heart may fail,
> But God is the strength of my heart and my portion forever.
> . . . .
> But as for me, the nearness of God is my good;
> I have made the Lord GOD my refuge,
> That I may tell of all Your works. (vv. 25–26, 28 NASB)

I had claimed these verses as I spoke to my local church at the time of my commissioning service. They certainly expressed my sincere desire to draw close to God. Would I be able to follow through on my commitment? Would I be able to follow in the footsteps of Jesus and make my dwelling among a new people in incarnational ways that would bring glory to him (John 1:14), in ways that would make him known and followed through music and the arts? In the following years, I found myself on a musical safari. I had asked God to show me, and he answered in amazing ways, opening up unexplored pathways for witnessing to his goodness. He continues to lead me into arenas of witness that I never could have imagined when I departed so many years ago for East Africa. Indeed, over the last several decades, God has been raising up musicians and artists who are joining in the task of witnessing to the good news of Jesus Christ worldwide.

Where This Book Is Heading

The world of global arts today has expanded enormously. No longer are the arts limited to the high classical arts. Yet classical arts are still valued. Nor are the arts, when crossing cultures, limited to only traditional music, dance, and drama. Nevertheless, indigenous art forms are necessary and also highly desired. Our highly globalized world of the twenty-first century, with its interconnecting ties—social media, the internet, and YouTube—puts all art forms on the table, open to engaging with societies around the world. World music, for example, "is that music we encounter, well, everywhere in the world.

World music can be folk music, art music, or popular music; its practitioners may be amateur or professional."[1] Noted ethnomusicologist Philip Bohlman argues further that "the old definitions and distinctions don't hold anymore; world music can be Western or non-Western, acoustic or electronically mixed. The world of world music has no boundaries, therefore access to world music is open to all."[2] This translates to all arts in general, into what we are here calling "global arts." Global arts span a vast array, their diversity including music, dance, drama, storytelling, proverbs, and visual arts.

In some ways, such diversity is overwhelming. Both positive and negative aspects arise from the arts going global. On the one hand, they provide unique opportunities for bringing people together. On the other hand, there's a darker side: (1) a loss of cultural identity, (2) a homogenizing of village practices in which global spaces usurp those of the village, (3) exploitation of cultural resources by transnational recording companies, and (4) fusion and border crossing, which enhances some world music and art while also impoverishing others.[3] Yet at the same time such a plethora of arts creates exciting and challenging opportunities for witnessing to Christ.

This volume asks the following questions:

1. How do global arts engage in Christian witness?
2. What is the contribution of global arts to communicating Christ, making him known, worshiping him authentically, and following him faithfully?
3. What are the critical issues and hurdles that need to be overcome?
4. What artistic practices engage people in their everyday lives to hear the good news of Jesus Christ?

Why do we need such a volume? It is important since "the church, the body of Christ, has two basic purposes for its existence: worship and witness."[4] Indeed, the arts in worship play major roles in the life of the church and are readily embraced in many areas. But what about the arts in witness? Historically, this has been very spotty, pursued mainly by those who have a particular interest in the arts. My desire here is to help bring understanding of a powerful resource that God has provided—and that he employs himself—for interacting with his people worldwide. In this prelude I create a basic framework to guide our missional intentions throughout the book as a whole.

1. Bohlman, *World Music*, ix.
2. Bohlman, *World Music*, ix.
3. Bohlman, *World Music*, x.
4. Sunquist, "Church: The Community of Worship and Witness," 281.

I address the interrelationship between worship and witness, look at various psalms in light of the intimate link between the two, and cite a number of historical examples that highlight the need for developing effective practices for global arts in mission. Finally, chapter by chapter I lay out what the book is about.

Worship and Witness in Dialogue

Worship and witness make up two sides of the same coin. They are intimately linked. In worship, God initiates and engages with us. An interactive relationship is developed between God and those who bow before him. We then respond and engage with him in worship and prayer. At the same time, witness flows out of worship, where God calls us to join him in his kingdom purposes. We, his people, move out, initiate, contact, and engage with people in various contexts, both near and far, by communicating the goodness of God that we have experienced in our lives and celebrated in our worship.[5] Or at least that is what the Scriptures imply. However, when observing a coin, we look at only one side at a time. Our focus usually rests on our favorite side of the coin. We ignore or fail to remember what is on the other side. Historically, the church has excelled in using the arts in worship. This has truly been a joy for many people as they relate with God. The other side of the coin, however, is largely ignored, leaving a major "arts-in-witness" gap. Local, regional, and global arts in Christian witness have mostly remained hidden.

Perhaps a more helpful metaphor for worship and witness is that of call-and-response song, a foundational musical form practiced around the world. In it, for example, a lead singer calls out an initial musical thought, to be taken up by a group response. It is dialogical, experiential, and interdependent. If either the leader or the group fails to respond, the song stops, and there is no engagement. Indeed, the call-and-response genre can take many forms, some straightforward and simple, such as singing in exact imitation of the call, with other types of call-and-response developing into a highly complex organizational structure where the call is volleyed between the initiator and the responding singers, who then take up the call.[6] In this way I see worship and witness as a divine call-and-response where God is interacting with us in the midst of worship—asking, inviting, even commanding us to join him in engaging the nations, both near and far.

5. See Sunquist, "Church: The Community of Worship and Witness."
6. For a more detailed table of complex call-and-response patterns as practiced in sub-Saharan Africa, see King, *A Time to Sing*, 65–70.

We find this cyclical twofold pattern of divine call-and-response—worship and witness—practiced throughout the Scriptures. God calls out to us first. We respond with faith and then praise and thanksgiving. Interaction with God calls us further into witness. Engaging with God, where we call out to God in the midst of worship, leads to God responding and engaging with us, speaking to us, dialoguing with us, prompting and urging us into witness. Barnabas and Paul, for example, were called to mission in the midst of worship. As the early church was worshiping and fasting, the Holy Spirit identified and set apart Barnabas and Paul for the work of the Lord, to go out and reach peoples in regions beyond (Acts 13:2).

Furthermore, it is particularly striking that Jesus's last command to the disciples took place within the context of worship. Jesus had told the eleven disciples to meet him on a particular mountain in Galilee. Given the custom of the day, meeting on a mountain immediately implied that they were going to a place where they expected to worship (e.g., the woman at the well spoke of worshiping on the mountain rather than in Jerusalem, John 4:20). Matthew 28 tells us, "When they saw him, they worshiped him" (v. 17). As the disciples are worshiping, Jesus gives his final directive to "go and make disciples of all nations, baptizing them in the name of the Father and of the Son and of the Holy Spirit, and teaching them to obey everything" he has commanded. Jesus then assures the disciples of his continued presence and relationship with them as they are to go out and put into practice what he has asked of them (vv. 18–20). Recognizing that the Great Commission took place in a worship context expands and shapes our understanding of how God interacts with us. An encounter with God leads to worship, in which Jesus tells us of the roles we are to play. He tells us to get up and get going! He tells us to move out and make disciples among the nations, peoples of different regions of the world, beginning at home, in the local areas and regions, including going to "the ends of the earth" (Acts 1:8). When the disciples return to Jerusalem, "they all joined together constantly in prayer" (1:14), a form of worship.

I see two things happening here: first, worship precedes witness, and second, the call to witness takes place in the midst of worship, where one is soaked in worship. The call to witness does not allow us to stay put in one place, to limit our lives to dwelling in the sanctuary. Rather, we are told to go and make disciples, with the ultimate intention of bringing our neighbors back to join in the grand, global worship procession. Our interactions with the living God provide the bedrock for developing a passion for completing the task of making Jesus Christ known, followed, and worshiped. The twofold cycle then continues on.

This twofold cycle in practice, however, is in some ways more of a three-fold cycle. Worship and the call to witness are often confined to the worship event. As we worship God, he speaks to us, telling us to go and make disciples, to witness. It's part of the Christian narrative. I believe, however, that the dialogue between worship and witness, when followed through in ways that push us beyond the walls of the church building, becomes more of a threefold cycle: (1) engaging with God in worship, (2) encountering and dialoguing with God in ways that push us out to witness, and (3) responding to God's call by taking it up and engaging with people about God outside the sanctuary. Such engagement is based on practices of witnessing to who God is, what he has done, and his saving grace. Engaging our neighbors, those near and far, leads to transformative encounters that initiate the most significant relationship in a person's life. Ultimately, engagement with our neighbors leads to encountering God, experiencing God, exploring life with God—all of which leads to joining local Christian communities in engaging with God in worship. In this way the fruit of witness generates enhanced worship, where the worshiping community rejoices in God's dynamic interaction in their midst. Scott Sunquist explains, "When they work in perfect harmony, the witness brings people to faith and brings them to worship the Triune God, and the worship moves people to confession, repentance, and then out to witness."[7]

The psalms offer rich and exemplary demonstrations of God's enhanced cycle of call-and-response—that is, worship and witness fleshed out and put into practice. Let's take a look.

The Psalms in Witness: Three Missional Gems

Throughout the centuries, the psalms have served believers as dynamic expressions of Christian experience and "vibrant portrayals of the divine and human encounter."[8] As one of the largest bodies of poetry-lyrics (an art form) in the Scriptures and located at the center of the Bible, the psalms are "passionately dialogical."[9] They immediately pull readers and listeners, singers and participants, into the inner recesses of a faith community's life of worship as they engage with God. We learn how to talk with God and make the praise and prayers of the psalms our own, pulling them into our own contexts and life issues. We learn from them that God is listening and calling out to us at the same time. Beyond that, "the Psalms make it possible to say things that are

7. Sunquist, *Understanding Christian Mission*, 283–84.
8. Brueggemann and Bellinger, *Psalms*, 8.
9. Brueggemann, *Praying the Psalms*, xiv.

otherwise unsayable."[10] They give us license to raise deep, intimate issues of utmost importance to us. They teach us who God is and what he has done for us, and reveal God's thoughts toward us. And "as Luther understood so passionately, the Psalms are not only addressed to God. They are a voice of the gospel, God's good word addressed to God's faithful people."[11] The offering of praise, thanksgiving, and prayer forms an interlocking, dialogical means of engaging with God.

Three missional psalms I find especially strong in calling for witness to the gospel are Psalms 67, 96, and 98. While so much can be said about each psalm, I want to highlight five key elements that point to witness. These include (1) God's passion for the nations, (2) God's purpose in blessing a people, (3) the significance of "singing a new song," (4) each psalm's rootedness in its cultural context and everyday life, and (5) each psalm's method for praising and declaring God's glory and salvation.

God's passion for the nations. I am struck by how "drawing all nations" to worship and honor the Lord appears throughout the book of Psalms as a consistent theme. With great intensity, Psalms 67, 96, and 98 focus on blessing, praising, proclaiming, and declaring God's intervention in the lives of his people. Such psalms are not compartmentalized away from the main corpus of psalmic literature, but rather constitute a major integrating theme within Psalms and throughout the biblical narrative. In actuality, these psalms reveal God's radical passion for reaching the nations through the example of his involvement with the Israelites. It is striking how Psalms as a whole regularly expresses this passion for the nations, for all peoples, as a driving motivation. Indeed, it seems that the lyrical poets rarely, if ever, forget God's heart for the nations and the Israelites' divine calling to join God in making him known and followed. The psalms convey that one does not either worship or witness, compartmentalizing them from each other. Rather, their interlinking integration is a central lifestyle value. One worships to bless and to call the peoples of the world into praise and worship that acknowledges God's rule to the "ends of the earth" in ways that bring him honor and glory.

In each of these three psalms, the nations form an integral part of the worship dialogue. The psalmists speak to God and reflect on God's blessing in their lives and faith community and on the importance of making God's ways known on earth to lead to "salvation among all nations" (Ps. 67:2). The psalmist calls the faith community to "declare his glory among the nations, his marvelous deeds among all peoples" (96:3), and claims that the Lord has

10. Goldingay, *Psalms 1–41*, 22–23.
11. Brueggemann, *Message of the Psalms*, 15.

Psalm 67

May God be gracious to us and bless us
    and make his face shine on us—
so that your ways may be known on earth,
    your salvation among all nations.
May the peoples praise you, God;
    may all the peoples praise you.
May the nations be glad and sing for joy,
    for you rule the peoples with equity
    and guide the nations of the earth.
May the peoples praise you, God;
    may all the peoples praise you.
The land yields its harvest;
    God, our God, blesses us.
May God bless us still,
    so that all the ends of the earth
    will fear him.

Illustration by Eric Tai

indeed "made his salvation known and revealed his righteousness to the nations" (98:2). Knowing God and his just ways is something that cannot be
kept to one local community. It has to spill out into other communities and
nations. There is no exclusivity here. God's glory is the community reaching
out to include others. Indeed, there is a prayerful longing that "*all* the peoples
praise you, God" (cf. Ps. 67:3, 5). Psalm 67 is particularly focused on praying
that the nations and peoples come to praise God with increased intensity. The
repeated chorus heaps phrases one upon another, calling them to praise that
resounds with ever-increasing volume: "May the peoples praise you, God; may
all the peoples praise you" (vv. 3, 5). Drawing from cultural poetic forms, the
psalm builds to a final grand crescendo, knowing that God's blessing on local
worshipers is intimately linked to God's heart and desire for the nations, "so
that all the ends of the earth will fear him" (v. 7).

Likewise, throughout Psalms 96 and 98, the whole world is urged to come
to worship and praise God. Yet again the ultimate purpose appears to be
making the goodness of God's work among all peoples a global reality—
going global with God's call to faithful worshipers. Israel used these psalms,
known as enthronement psalms, in its life as a worshiping community.[12] As

12. See Brueggemann and Bellinger, *Psalms*, 414, 420.

John Goldingay notes, "Yhwh has an eye on the whole world. Perhaps it implies a missionary commission to Israel."[13] We see this further when biblical scholars judge that Psalm 96:10 enunciates and is "the quintessential 'gospel announcement' of the entire Old Testament, that the nations are summoned to acknowledge YHWH as fully sovereign on earth."[14] The global horizon of this psalm, according to Walter Brueggemann, is already evident in the vista of verses 1–3—"all the earth," "among the nations," "among all peoples." Verses 7–9 further reinforce it with "families of nations" and "all the earth."[15] Witness among the nations is not only a high priority but also an imperative.[16] It emerges out of unselfish worship that focuses on God and his passion for all nations, for whom the global horizon extends to all peoples, even to the ends of the earth.

God's purpose in blessing a people. Unselfish worship and praise come about as a result of knowing the purpose of God's blessing among a particular people, the nation of Israel. Psalm 67, for example, provides one case in point. It is "a prayer for God's blessing to be known in the nation's life in such a way that the world as a whole comes to acknowledge God. The interrelationship of these two ideas thus continues from Pss. 65 and 66."[17] The psalmist declares, "May God be gracious to us and bless us, . . . so that your ways may be known on earth, your salvation among all nations" (Ps. 67:1–2). In other words, we bless God so that we may bless others. "The psalm sees Israel's blessing as designed to benefit the whole world. . . . That is a blessing emphasizing Yhwh's name. . . . And again thereby it draws attention to the universality of God's involvement with the world."[18] The central part of the psalm (vv. 3–5) emphasizes how all the peoples of the world are included in giving honor to God in praise and confessing his sovereignty. Goldingay tells us, "Indeed, they are not merely confessing and realistically acknowledging how things are but rejoicing and resounding: that is, resounding with joy. They know that it is indeed true that God's blessing and delivering of Israel is also good news for them."[19] A genuine celebration of God's blessing extends into the global horizon for each people's benefit. The reason for such celebration in the "broad sweep of praise (v. 4) is that YHWH is a judge who will bring all nations to justice, well-being, and peace."[20]

13. Goldingay, *Psalms 90–150*, 108.
14. Brueggemann and Bellinger, *Psalms*, 415.
15. Brueggemann and Bellinger, *Psalms*, 415.
16. See Kaiser, "God's Purpose for Mission in the Psalter of Israel."
17. Goldingay, *Psalms 42–89*, 299.
18. Goldingay, *Psalms 42–89*, 304.
19. Goldingay, *Psalms 42–89*, 302.
20. Brueggemann and Bellinger, *Psalms*, 290.

The significance of "singing a new song." Singing a new song comes as a result of God's active involvement and blessing among all peoples, acting so powerfully that it calls for a new song. A new song emerges out of dialogue and interaction with the living God, in which many peoples experience God's blessing on them. Its purpose, as in Psalms 96 and 98, is to communicate with God, based on a particular people's new understandings of who God is and what he has done among them. Goldingay surmises that "the implication might then be that for the nations a new song is appropriate because they are now becoming aware of facts about Yhwh that they had not known before. Praising Yhwh will mean singing a song they have not sung previously, a new song that will reflect their 'new orientation.'" This presents a stark contrast to what is actually practiced in worship and witness around the world. When making his point, Goldingay nails it that the psalms repeat the exhortation about "singing a new song" a number of times (and they never say, "Let's sing a golden oldie!").[21] This point has extensive ramifications for witness through global arts.

Psalm 96:1–5

Sing to the Lord a new song;
    sing to the Lord, all the earth.
Sing to the Lord, praise his name;
    proclaim his salvation day after day.
Declare his glory among the nations,
    his marvelous deeds among all peoples.
For great is the Lord and most worthy of praise;
    he is to be feared above all gods.
For all the gods of the nations are idols,
    but the Lord made the heavens.

Illustration by Eric Tai

In addition, Brueggemann argues for a linkage between "new song" (Ps. 96:1) and "tell" (Ps. 96:2 NRSV). "The 'new song' points to a new reality while the verb 'tell' most likely means to tell the news, which in the church is rendered as gospel." He notes further: "The interface of new and gospel means to announce (enact?) the new rule of God. . . . In Christian usage [it is used] to relate the newness of the gospel to the proclamation of the kingdom of God and the utterance of Jesus"[22] (see Mark 1:14–15). Applying this to

21. Goldingay, *Psalms 90–150*, 103.
22. Brueggemann and Bellinger, *Psalms*, 417.

today's ever-increasingly globalized world, singing a new song is dialogical and experiential as the gospel is proclaimed among the peoples in local, regional, and global cultural contexts. The practice of singing a new song changes and morphs in culturally appropriate expressions in order to embrace all peoples in meaningful ways.

The psalms' rootedness in their cultural context and everyday life. The psalms assume their cultural context. Indeed, when the Israelites are displaced and away from home, they feel ill at ease as they lament, "How can we sing the songs of the LORD while in a foreign land?" (Ps. 137:4). The Israelites inherently drew from their local and regional cultural arts within their contexts. That is, psalms functioned as languages that were at their disposal in their everyday lives in order to communicate with God. Three observations can be made here. First, Psalms 96 and 98, scholars think, were regularly employed during festivals and processions at different times of the year. They played a normal part in the Israelites' engagement with God in worship and were naturally accessible to them. Second, the interrelationship between praise and prayer points to practices of spirituality that reveal key values and a worldview in the song genres employed. The genres include psalms of "praise, thanksgiving, protest, trust, and obedience."[23] Goldingay aptly notes that the psalms do not appear in any systematic order. Rather, they are "all mixed up in the Psalter—it does not give us the praise psalms, then the thanksgiving psalms, then the prayer psalms, and so on. The Psalter mirrors and affirms our disordered lives."[24] The psalms defy discrete categories because life and our need for prayer and praise defy compartmentalization. Psalms emerge out of the contexts and crises of our lives as these realities intersect and dialogically engage with God.

Third, Psalm 98 also provides a taxonomy of local instruments intended to bring praise to God. The instruments are not imported; they belong to their local music culture. With great enthusiasm, everything available to the Israelites is meant to explode with joyful praise before the Lord. This moves from shouts for joy to jubilant songs with music. Note that in Middle Eastern practices, music is made with instruments. Singing is not considered music; it is the instruments that make music. This underscores the fact that musical instruments are also to engage in jubilant praise and worship. Indeed, music-making incorporates the harp with the sound of singing (v. 5) and "trumpets and the blast of the ram's horn" along with shouts of joy (v. 6). Notice how "shouts" and the sounds of nature, in contrast to contemporary Western

23. Goldingay, *Psalms 1–41*, 67.
24. Peterson, *Answering God*, 107.

Psalm 98:1–5

Sing to the LORD a new song,
    for he has done marvelous things;
his right hand and his holy arm
    have worked salvation for him.
The LORD has made his salvation known
    and revealed his righteousness to the nations.
He has remembered his love
    and his faithfulness to Israel;
all the ends of the earth have seen
    the salvation of our God.
Shout for joy to the LORD, all the earth,
    burst into jubilant song with music;
make music to the LORD with the harp,
    with the harp and the sound of singing.

Illustration by Eric Tai

definitions of music, are also included in the great crescendos of praise and worship of the king. Thus, in all these ways we see that the psalms, grounded in relationship with God, are rooted in the contexts of everyday life as practiced by Israel.

The psalms' method for praising and declaring God's glory and salvation. We have seen, then, that the psalms testify to who God is and to what he has done in the midst of his people. They set a model for witness through the global arts as they reach out to all the nations worldwide. Through interactive praises and prayer, Israel is dialoguing with God so that his character appears on heightened display before the nations. And artistic engagement accomplishes all this.

In witness, one of the major goals is to introduce people to who God is and how he is ready to become involved in the lives of people worldwide. Old Testament scholars attest that theologically the psalms are "the densest material in the entire Old Testament. . . . There is a greater concentration of statements about God here than anywhere else."[25] When nonbelievers are learning about God, they often need concrete examples of how believers relate with God. The psalms—and, I believe, other artistic forms—model before a

25. Goldingay, *Psalms 1–41*, 69.

nonbelieving world that God is involved with his people. Music and global arts have the powerful ability to raise theological content to the surface that would not otherwise be open for discussion. Additionally, the psalms (and other art forms) provide accessible spaces for individuals and communities to see, hear, and engage in the interactive, dialogical relationship between God and humanity. For Israel, this takes place in the midst of worship, worship that engenders witness beyond national boundaries. Thus, testifying to God and accompanying theological insights are on heightened display in the midst of worship as it pushes out to engage our neighbors near and far.

Not only do the psalms teach us how to praise and pray, but they also set a model for engaging in worship and witness. Knowing God lies at the heart of the psalms as they "speak from God by showing us how to speak to God."[26] In particular, "singing new songs" facilitates processing peoples' encounters with God. Peoples' newly acquired depth of relationship becomes dynamic expressions of Christian experience that testify to the character of God and his missional involvement throughout the world. In a contemporary world longing for meaningful spirituality, the book of Psalms becomes then a "manual for spirituality, for relationships with God,"[27] and thus witness to who he is. As God's Word, the psalms cannot help but "spill over into the larger horizon of other peoples."[28] As a dialogical art form, they offer key guidelines for effectively telling God's story worldwide.

This is good news for missions and churches, for musicians and artists who want to join in effective, dynamic witness. Yet, when put into practice, it is more complex, filled with unimagined potholes that can sabotage our efforts. The following section discusses three of the most common potholes—false assumptions—that lead to unintended gaffes and gaps in witness through the arts.

False Assumptions: Gaffes and Gaps in Employing Global Arts

So, how do we go about declaring God's glory via global arts? If the arts are universal, is there really a need to consider how they should be employed? Isn't it just a matter of plug and play? Surprisingly, in the history of Christian mission, employing global arts in witness has often met with confusion, the hardening of hearts away from the gospel, and, above all, misunderstanding who God is: a God of love and compassion toward all peoples and a God who

26. Goldingay, *Psalms 1–41*, 23.
27. Goldingay, *Psalms 1–41*, 58.
28. Brueggemann and Bellinger, *Psalms*, 291.

desires relationship with us. Abundant gaffes and gaps show up throughout contemporary mission history. Historically, when moving out cross-culturally, large numbers of missionaries were not aware that global arts are context-specific. That is, each cultural group defines, derives meaning from, and employs its art forms in contrasting ways. The intentions behind using the arts in witness were well-meaning, yet a lack of informed approaches to employing the global arts contributed to miscommunicating the gospel or presenting a truncated gospel.

Three initial ways that global arts have been inadvertently misused lie in the areas of meaning, aesthetics, and metaphorical association. First, the relationship between language and musical tones, for example, determines the meaning of song lyrics. Tone languages (in which variations in pitch distinguish different words) are spread throughout the world, especially in Asia, such as Mandarin (and its dialects) and Thai, and across sub-Saharan Africa. Stories are told of how the text of a song such as "Precious Name, Oh How Sweet," when translated into a tone language, had the meaning changed to "Well-done chicken, oh, how sweet." Another lyric, "In heaven, there is no sorrow," meant to give comfort, was heard by the people as "There is no egg on the bicycle!" One missionary working in West Africa realized that the tone of the language made hymns unintelligible. He reworked the melodies of the songs so that they could be sung. On the first day, the church was so excited to have the new hymns. But then they began singing them. They stopped and told the missionary, "We can't sing these hymns! We can understand them. We're not supposed to be able to understand the words when we're in church!"[29]

Second is the area of aesthetics. Everyone loves a good song, right? Yes, but according to whom is the song good? Among the Cebaara Senufo of Côte d'Ivoire, the Western missionary leading the local translation team as they worked on the book of Revelation wanted to give a musical example of God's glory. He sang Handel's "Hallelujah Chorus" from the *Messiah* and was stunned at the lack of enthusiasm that greeted him. The local believers on the team were reticent to speak up and tell him what was going on. Finally, one of them revealed the problem, asking, "Why is all of your music crying music?"[30] What is glorious and beautiful to one person from one particular culture does not automatically transfer over to peoples who have different aesthetic standards. We also see this in churches today between generations

---

29. Examples are part of my personal collection of gaffes and gaps acquired over many years.

30. For a discussion of music communication issues, see King, *Pathways in Christian Music Communication.*

where the aesthetics, or what are called "heart" languages, have changed over a period of time due to the dynamic nature of cultures and societies.

The third area of misuse that has caused enormous misunderstanding is that of metaphorical associations. The use of Western art forms contributed to the overall problem of the gospel coming clothed in Western wrappings. Many people thus translated art forms into the understanding that the Christian God is foreign and not relevant to local peoples. Why should they believe in a foreign god when they already have their own gods to contend with? For example, if the gods speak to a Peruvian people in Peru through their drums, why does the Christian God not speak to them in a similar musical language? The stories do not stop there; they keep going. Sadly, the overabundance of gaffes-and-gaps stories includes all art forms—music, dance, drama, storytelling, proverbs, and visual arts. These few examples highlight the need for learning about global arts with a view to understanding the hidden complexities inherent within the diversity of cultural arts available for making known among the nations what God has done (Ps. 96:3).

What This Book Is About

Throughout this work I argue that witness is dialogical and therefore relational; the arts excel in expressive dialogue, forging relational bonding in profound and persuasive ways. Witness through global arts provides a way of loving your neighbor as yourself and is incarnational. I also seek to show how the global arts tap into the deeper affective dimensions of people more directly than mere informational input alone. They communicate in profound ways and make a transformative impact. Thus global arts not only play an accompanying role to witness in general, but they also themselves preach and proclaim the gospel in multivocal ways with significant impact.

The intent of this book is to address the arts-in-witness gap. The global arts provide cultural arenas for mediating dynamic witness and wholehearted worship. They can move the church into embodied faith and culturally embedded practices that affect spiritual and social aspects of mission. Likewise, the arts possess profound abilities to symbolically capture values, reveal worldview themes, shape identity, and communicate with impact in culturally appropriate ways. While my main focus is on music and the performing arts, along with some visual input, other arts need further development as witness. Readers will be able to build on what I present here. Throughout this work, I point to biblical foundations located in Psalms, historical pathways, and theoretical frameworks for communicating Christ through the arts worldwide.

How This Book Is Organized

Music and the arts are multilayered and multidimensional. Powerful and full of impact due to their speaking beyond words, the arts are meant to be experienced. Writing about them is challenging and limits the extent of their dynamic impact. In order to unpack them, this work unfolds in a series of ever-widening, expanding concentric circles, with each chapter building on the preceding one. Each chapter is not compartmentalized in isolation from the next but rather is interlinked and interdependent. Three broad themes centered on witnessing to Jesus Christ through the global arts provide the book's three-part framework: (1) foundations in global arts and Christ-centered witness, (2) encountering Christ through global arts, and (3) engaging peoples for Christ via global arts. In addition to the text of each chapter, vignettes from the field, diagrams, photos, and my personal stories are integrated with the content as essential means to further unpack the complexities of witnessing cross-culturally through the arts.

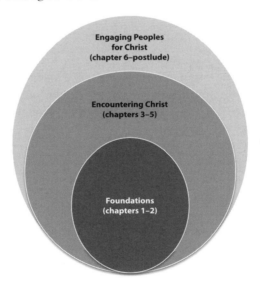

How this book is organized

Foundations in Global Arts and Christ-Centered Witness

The first two chapters present foundations for understanding the essential roles that music and the arts play in faithful witness among all peoples. In chapter 1, I bring understanding about how to negotiate faith and culture.

When working with the arts cross-culturally, one of the first questions that people immediately ask is about culture. I show how the term "culture" is often misunderstood, especially in relation to the arts, and then I point readers to the three dimensions of culture that reveal the arts as expressive culture. The arts, as expressive culture, serve as life processors, languages of communication, and contextualizers. They form the resources and materials through which peoples engage, communicate, and encounter the living God. Creative contextualization, bringing the gospel message into a people's local setting through cultural arts, is taken up in the second half of the chapter.

Chapter 2 looks at music and the arts as expressive languages of communication. I address the misperception that all arts are universally understood. This becomes a hidden yet troublesome reality when witnessing and ministering cross-culturally and across generations. To help us understand and overcome such barriers, I present the cultural building blocks of communication, known as the twelve signal systems. The signal systems provide ways of learning how the arts function and communicate differently among contrasting peoples. I point to significant ways that the arts communicate, and I illustrate how they involve opportunities for negotiating with people for understanding Christ within varying cultural contexts.

Encountering Christ through Global Arts

The next three chapters build on one another as they examine transformative means for encountering Christ in context. Chapter 3 takes us deeper into unpacking cultural issues that launch us into reaching the nations through the arts. Cultural exegesis through music and the arts is a means to listening and learning about people's beliefs, faith, and experiences so that we can be more effective and relevant in our witness. The goal of communicating Christ by employing cultural arts (expressive languages) is to create understanding that overcomes the multiple barriers that have caused people to deem the gospel foreign or irrelevant. One of my greatest delights when communicating through the arts is to hear people say, "You mean that God is *for me*, too?" Drawing from my work among the Senufo of Côte d'Ivoire, I compare and contrast the difference it makes when cultural arts are redeemed for the purposes of the gospel. Then I analyze the Senufo case study and introduce readers to four key concepts drawn from the field of ethnomusicology that help us witness with deeper, transformative impact.

Building on cultural exegesis through the arts, chapter 4 reveals how the arts have always been involved in translating the gospel message. I introduce the reader to the concept of the arts as translatable "cultural texts" for interacting with God. I develop this by first looking at several psalms and the ways in which God interacted with his people in the Old Testament and then show how the psalms are still being translated into cultural texts in relevant modes for the twenty-first century. I present ways contemporary biblical text translation and cultural text translation can join forces for transformed relationships *and* meaningful witness to surrounding communities. The practice of New Song Fellowships, a means of doing holistic translations of the Scriptures in which biblical texts are set to song through group composing with local believers, is explained. Translating cultural texts in tandem with biblical texts leads to translating God's message into the heart languages of a people in holistic ways. Based on "Abraham's Sacrifice and Nyarafolo Drums," a vignette on cultural text translation of the Genesis Abrahamic texts, I demonstrate how music and the arts foster an emerging church's engagement in understanding God's Word in culturally relevant and profound ways.

Chapter 5 takes translating the gospel message via cultural texts to the next level. The creative process of composing songs-in-context weaves together deeply profound lived experiences in light of the Scriptures as people try to make sense of God's presence in their lives. Active theologizing emerges from and fosters following Jesus, even in the midst of life's difficulties and when dealing with both joy and sorrow. The outcome results in witnessing to the goodness of God. A series of vignettes gives compelling evidence of how God is speaking to peoples worldwide through such processes. Two main streams of active theologizing discussed are emerging theologies (first understandings about God) and non-Western theologies of suffering from Ethiopia, Sudan, and China. The chapter closes by identifying key dynamics of interacting with the Scriptures via cultural texts and discussing how creative processes lead to creation of local hermeneutical communities of theological reflection.

Engaging Peoples for Christ via Global Arts

The final four chapters and the postlude present a series of missional practices, outlining and demonstrating incarnational witness through the arts. Missiologists and mission practitioners have long recognized the great potential of the arts. Yet they have not known how to approach them. Chapter 6 brings Christ-centered witness through the arts into everyday life, demonstrating how nonprofessional and professional artists alike can contribute to the mission task. Evelyne Reisacher, noted missiologist in Islamic studies, persuasively speaks to the need for "mission practices that are connected with the everyday realities of people, where people actually live and hurt and hope in local communities. Witness happens in the most ordinary places and in contexts that mission has not yet imagined."[31] With this in mind, the chapter lays out initial pathways of the global arts that foster living Christianly on a daily basis, between the bookends of worship and witness. It first addresses the arts as public witness, providing examples of life-giving songs and music in medical contexts, the visual arts and drama in dealing with trauma and psychological pain, and ukuleles in prison ministry. We then turn to the arts in daily life as a means to growing in Christ, with particular focus on discipling youth and celebrating life cycles through newly created Christian rites.

Chapter 7 continues addressing the arts in daily life by focusing on the role of and methods for telling God's story, especially among oral and postliterate peoples, who make up 70 percent of the world's population.[32] Here I present significant factors in orality for the twenty-first century and highlight how critical storytelling, proverbs, song, and local visual art practices can be in addressing deeply embedded worldview issues. Such practices offer rival stories to people in need of transformation in various spheres of their lives. The chapter outlines key guidelines for telling God's story, with supporting vignettes from around the world.

Chapter 8 turns more specifically to interfaith issues that confront and affect our globalized twenty-first-century world. I explore the contribution of music and the arts in peacebuilding and interfaith dialogue among Muslims and Christians, arguing that bridge building can take place through exchanging and learning one another's art forms. The chapter addresses the questions "How do the creative arts foster loving our religious neighbors?" and "How do believers begin to engage with the newly arrived religious neighbors—for example, refugees and immigrants—coming from the Middle East into the Western world?" Based on my previous research in *(un)Common Sounds* and a recent case study of a church-sponsored benefit concert for Syrian refugees in Southern California, I introduce key concepts inherent in the global arts applied to peacebuilding and interfaith dialogue.[33] These include (1) creating musical spaces of relating, (2) *musicking*, and (3) encountering contrasting music-cultures. These become theoretical foundations for presenting a model of "dialogues of beauty and art" applied to interfaith contexts, specifically among Muslims and Christians. Built around the concept of musicking, the model specifies five dialogical arenas that occur simultaneously in the midst of music-making events. Vignettes and examples from Hawai'i, Israel, Libya, Indonesia, the United States, and Pakistan show how this is being practiced.

31. Reisacher, *Joyful Witness in the Muslim World*, xvii.
32. Jewell, "Winning the Oral Majority," 56.
33. King and Tan, *(un)Common Sounds*.

The next chapter (9) widens the lens to a much broader view of our global world. Globalization is snowballing worldwide. Culture and the arts are directly linked with the processes of globalization. Urban and transnational contexts bring together people in unlikely convergences of gatherings. From transnational festivals in Fez, Morocco, to multicultural, urban Christian gatherings in Australia, innovative relational bonding opportunities are taking place and point to new approaches for making Christ known and followed. As more local art forms, such as hip hop, ukulele playing, and whirling dervishes, go global through the media, a wider divergence of aesthetics and taste is evolving that gives voice, place, and identity to formerly marginalized peoples. The main focus in this chapter is on engaging cities in their hypermulticultural settings. I present a bird's-eye view of cities' thriving musical and artistic diversity, with corresponding shifts in concepts and practices of music and the arts. We first consider the global hip hop phenomenon, its messages of injustice, its theological components, and the significant role that graffiti art has contributed to church planting in the inner city of Los Angeles. The focus then widens further to the diasporas scattered throughout the city area and to the presentation of a schema for forging relational bonds through musical and artistic interaction.

Finally, the concluding postlude speaks to the interactive dynamics between the global arts and Christlike witness. Recognizing that the arts excel in expressive dialogue and relational bonding in profound and persuasive ways, in this chapter I invite you to reconsider and reimagine with me what that means for our expanding horizons in the twenty-first century. The chapter brings together essential markers and guidelines that form a road map for revealing God's glory and salvation to the far ends of the earth (Ps. 67:2). I identify and discuss three essential intersecting pathways in the pursuit of making Jesus Christ known and loved worldwide through the global arts: theological imperatives, shifts in perspectives, and emerging practices. I suggest that when inextricably bound together, like a lifeline, they foster navigating the journey toward Christ in ways that open windows to God's very nature, to encounter and faithfully follow him, and to authentic, wholehearted worship. Working in concert with the Holy Spirit, people are empowered to set out on a journey toward Christ, where they come to gaze on his beauty, seek his face, and, in the midst of brokenness, be overwhelmed with his glory (Ps. 27).

Long ago, as my plane pulled out of the gate heading for Nairobi, Kenya, I thought I was embarking on a journey to discover where and how God could use me, a woman and a musician, longing to serve him in mission. I did not realize that he was sending me on a journey that was at the vanguard of an emerging group of musicians and artists with similar passions. We've come a long way. I invite you to join me in pursuing God's heart for the nations and learning how to join in God's call to make disciples of all nations via the global arts.

Questions for Discussion

1. How are worship and witness interlinked?
2. What do the psalms teach us about the arts and witness?
3. What are the two most important issues that you look forward to learning about in this book?

Part 1

FOUNDATIONS IN GLOBAL ARTS AND CHRIST-CENTERED WITNESS

1

Negotiating Faith and Culture

All roads lead to worship, but how does one get there?

Witness and the arts require negotiating faith and culture. In our heightened globalizing world of the twenty-first century, we are always engaging in witness in contrasting cultural contexts. The global arts form what anthropologists call expressive culture. In this chapter, we begin by addressing the dynamics of expressive culture and their critical significance in contextualizing the Christian faith. We then develop a model of the global arts engaging in dialogue and witness and introduce creative contextualization as a dynamic means for witnessing to Christ via the global arts. With peoples coming together in new ways, everyone from around the world can perform on the same stage. Although understanding and community building are desired goals, they rarely happen. Cultural dynamics play critical roles in fostering deep understanding, as we will see later in the chapter. We turn first to a global festival to initiate discussion of the cultural dynamics embedded within diverse contexts.

My Story: Encountering the Global Arts in Fez, Morocco

There they were, standing, singing out their religious texts, dancing, and performing on the same global stage in Fez, Morocco! From the Sufi tradition, the Al Kindi Ensemble with Sheikh Hamza Shakour and the Munshidins—popularly referred to as the whirling dervishes, of the Damascus Mosque in

Syria—shared the stage with the Tropos Byzantine Choir of Athens, Greece. Craig Adams's Gospel Ensemble, the Voices of New Orleans, shared the stage with Faiz Ali Faiz and his Sufi ensemble from Pakistan, performing Qawwali songs. There was Ghada Shbeir singing second-century Christian songs in the Syriac language—considered by many to be the Aramaic language spoken by Jesus—juxtaposed with the exotic Tuareg singing of the Tartit Women's Ensemble from Mali, traditionally considered Muslim. The list seemed to go on forever. Oh, yes! Even American opera singer Jessye Norman was there, singing "Swing Low, Sweet Chariot," Duke Ellington's "Lord's Prayer," and "Amazing Grace." That one really got me as she sang out, "that saved a wretch like me." I found myself deeply touched and silently weeping as I sat in this Muslim setting.

What was going on? I was astounded to encounter such a dizzying array of musicians (both instrumentalists and singers) performing their faith traditions from the "nations" before the twenty-first-century world—a world full of easy travel, heritage tourism, and digital media. I was even more astounded to see how the peoples drawn literally from around the world experienced the events with great relish and longings for spirituality. How could this be? Christians and Muslims were performing and putting their spirituality and worship practices on visual and sonic display for all the world to see. Indeed, they were on stage, each bearing witness to and sharing their faith tradition, singing in their vernacular languages, incorporating their local expressive cultural arts and practices in configurations that integrated music, poetry, dance, cultural instruments, and appropriate sacred dress in ways that revealed their faith and their spiritual engagement.

It was June 2008. The annual Fez Festival of Sacred Music in Morocco was taking place in a transnational setting, with a goal to bring all the world together as it focused on the three Abrahamic faith streams. Sacred musics from different areas of the world had been taken out of their local worship settings and put on the global stage. I have to admit that I was confused at what was taking place. There I was, out of my comfort zone in a nation reportedly 99 percent Muslim and less than 1 percent Christian and Jewish.[1] The memories of September 11, 2001, and ongoing Gulf conflicts still lay fresh in our minds and psyches. Ultimately, I was astounded at how the world is on the move. No longer a dreamed-for vision, "all the earth and all the peoples" was a reality occurring in our midst. What was going on?

My mind wandered back to John Piper. He became a hero for a number of us Christian artists and musicians in the late twentieth century. Piper boldly

1. "The World Factbook: Africa: Morocco," Central Intelligence Agency, last updated May 1, 2018, https://www.cia.gov/library/publications/the-world-factbook/geos/mo.html.

proclaimed, "Mission exists because worship doesn't."[2] Here I was in Morocco, experiencing something much different. The Fez Festival defies Piper's axiom. Although I understood what Piper was getting at, I had always wanted to tweak his statement. Here at Fez, it was happening right before my very eyes and ears as I related with peoples from the far corners of the world. They were sharing how they worshiped at home in their local contexts.

We run the danger of assuming that when we share Christ through worship arts, we are doing so on a blank canvas of sinful people who have no religion or faith. I doubt that has ever been true. A brief search throughout the Old Testament narrative shows that peoples are always worshiping something or someone, most often idols and false gods. In reality, we need to acknowledge that all the world is worshiping; thus, witness exists to bring about *Christian* worship that honors and glorifies Jesus Christ. Indeed, the nations are already at worship, drawing available art forms from their cultural contexts to negotiate faith and culture. As I looked on, experienced it, and took in more of the Fez events, the foreignness of how the Christian faith appears in non-Western contexts became overwhelming. Have we been too shortsighted? Too blind to what is happening before our very eyes and ears? This has remained one of the major roadblocks in sharing Christ among "all the peoples of the earth." Historically, Christians have shared a message close to their own hearts and brought Western psalms, hymns, and spiritual songs to other countries, resulting in transferring Western cultural Christianity.[3] This has led to a number of problems, especially the foreignness of the gospel and its perceived lack of relevance to peoples within their own cultural contexts. How do diverse peoples experience God within their own cultural contexts? How does one go about evoking meaningful and profound interaction with the God of the universe in ways that resonate in a person's inner regions?[4] How does one negotiate faith and culture?

Cultural Dynamics

Culture involves more than one first realizes. Understanding what culture is and how people live together within their cultural contexts is multifaceted and requires examination of key dynamics. Here we consider competing definitions of culture and three integral dimensions at work within culture that affect our interactions with people.

2. Piper, *Let the Nations Be Glad!*, 35.
3. See Kidula, *Music in Kenyan Christianity*.
4. See Bavinck and Freeman, *Introduction to the Science of Missions*, 240, 242.

Conflicting Definitions of Culture

Everyone knows what culture is—or so they think. Yet we find a plethora of definitions of culture, especially in a globalizing world where the distinctions are becoming more and more blurred. When it comes to the global arts, people often speak of "high" culture when referencing the elite and "low" culture when referring to the masses and popular culture. High culture most commonly refers to the set of cultural products, mainly in the arts, held in the highest esteem by a culture. It is the culture of an elite such as the aristocracy or intelligentsia. In the West, classical music is considered high culture. Many of the performances at the Fez Festival were drawn from Western and Middle Eastern high classical art traditions.

In contrast to high culture, low culture is studied as popular culture in everyday parlance and commonly applies to the masses of less-well-educated peoples. It is made up of a different set of products. These may include gossip magazines, reality television, popular music, escapist fiction, and more. I have often heard popular culture (low culture) referred to as "lowbrow" in contrast to "highbrow" culture,[5] that is, Western classical music. Significantly, popular-culture studies encompass the entirety of ideas, perspectives, attitudes, memes, images, and other phenomena that are within the mainstream of a given culture. In transnational settings, such as the Fez Festival, multiple boundaries of high and low blur and seem to almost vanish. People appear to be coming mostly for the experience. At Fez 2008, after each of the discrete religious traditions performed onstage, we watched and listened to attempts at merging the performance traditions into new configurations, resulting in fairly awkward attempts to create a "hybrid culture"[6] that mixed elements from two or more cultures. While studies of high and low culture are helpful and provide understanding of what is happening within each of these realms in the twenty-first century, they are limited in helping us proceed in relation to Christian witness. We need to move beyond initial, surface-level labels such as high and low culture.

To move into deeper understandings of people functioning within culture, we can draw from cultural anthropology. Paul Hiebert, noted missiologist and anthropologist, offers a helpful definition: culture is "the more or less integrated

---

5. See Thomas Mallon and Pankazj Mishra, "Highbrow, Lowbrow, Middlebrow—Do These Kinds of Cultural Categories Mean Anything Anymore?," *New York Times*, July 29, 2014, https://www.nytimes.com/2014/08/03/books/review/highbrow-lowbrow-middlebrow-do-these-kinds-of-cultural-categories-mean-anything-anymore.html.

6. For in-depth definitions of certain kinds of culture, see "Definition of High Culture, Low Culture, Hybrid Culture and Popular Culture in Depth," eNotes, updated May 2, 2014, https://www.enotes.com/homework-help/definition-high-culture-low-culture-hybrid-culture-468640.

system of beliefs, feelings, and values created and shared by a group of people that enable them to live together socially and that are communicated by means of their systems of symbols and rituals, patterns of behavior, and the material products they make." This definition allows us to move beyond looking mainly at cultural products into considering how people construct culture that fosters living together in community. We know that humans, as social creatures, "depend on one another for survival and a meaningful existence."[7] They thus work at creating shared understandings between themselves, which are foundational to human relationships. Hiebert underscores that human relationships "need a common language and some consensus on beliefs and worldview for communication and coordinated action. Ultimately, their culture is *the home in which they live together*."[8] People feel comfortable when they have a more or less integrated, coherent way of looking at things. Nevertheless, cultures are always changing, especially as groups and individuals within cultures hold different beliefs, views about their world, and values. "The rich, for example, see things differently from the poor and one ethnic group may view the world differently from another. . . . Different communities in the same society struggle to control the society."[9] Each group at the Fez Festival, for example, was performing in the ways in which they felt at home as they approached God and interacted with life. Such diversity required staging both high culture and popular culture. What does each group reveal about their cultural ways of living as they engage in communicating through artistic languages set on global stages? Cultural anthropologists, such as Hiebert, highlight that culture provides the means for navigating life in three dimensions.

Dimensions of Culture

All humans express themselves in three integrated dimensions of culture: beliefs, feelings, and morals (see fig. 1.1).[10] In the cognitive dimension, members of a group or society share a common set of beliefs and knowledge. "Without shared beliefs, communication and community life are impossible. Beliefs link categories into theories of explanation,"[11] such as the origins of the universe and causes of illness. Our cultural knowledge guides us in negotiating all aspects of life, such as how to ride a bicycle, repair a car, make a nourishing meal, engage in interpersonal and international relations, and even

7. Hiebert, *Gospel in Human Contexts*, 150.
8. Hiebert, *Gospel in Human Contexts*, 150 (emphasis added).
9. Hiebert, *Gospel in Human Contexts*, 150.
10. Hiebert, *Gospel in Human Contexts*, 151.
11. Hiebert, *Gospel in Human Contexts*, 151.

how to worship God. It is important to note that there are different methods of storing cultural knowledge. Many cultures store it in writing, such as in books, newspapers, comics, text messages, and the internet. Other cultures specialize in storing cultural knowledge in storytelling, proverbs, song, and various forms of oral traditions that are easily remembered and not dependent on writing. Global arts, such as music, performing arts, and visual arts, store rich cultural information (e.g., creation myths), address understandings of God, gods, and the spirit world, and reveal and comment on life issues. A key to effective Christian witness is to recognize the different ways in which differing peoples access and interact with cultural knowledge.

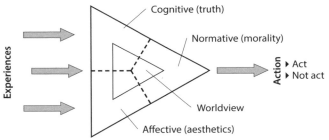

Figure 1.1
Hiebert's dimensions of culture

The affective dimension, intimately linked to the cognitive dimension, deals with people's emotions, such as ideas of beauty and aesthetics, fashion and food, likes and dislikes, and ways of expressing joy, love, sorrow, and pain, to name a few. Cultures reveal extreme diversity in the ways they deal with the emotional side of human life. This is the cultural arena in which global arts excel. Most religions work within their cultural expressive forms as they facilitate meditation, mysticism, and ecstasy through drums and dance, or evoke feelings of awe, transcendence, and fear. One secular American journalist working for a German newspaper at Fez, for example, shared how she was surprised to suddenly find herself weeping as she heard a familiar Christian song, a "Sevenfold Amen," that harked back to her religious days in childhood. The power of the global arts comes from their ability to engage in the affective dimension. Expressive culture moves people beyond the humdrum of daily living, revealing a human penchant for self-expression and aesthetic enjoyment. As Hiebert argues, "It is difficult to imagine what a society would be like without this expressive culture that pervades all areas of life—without art, music and dance, or sports and games; with un-dyed clothes, unpainted houses, and only work to break the boredom."[12] Herein lies a critical key to Christian witness through global arts: here a holistic approach to communicating the gospel can take place simultaneously within both the cognitive and affective dimensions of culture. And there is yet one more integrative dimension to consider.

The evaluative or normative dimension of culture is the arena in which judgments of proper and improper behavior for men, women, and children are fleshed out. Serving as a moral code, this guides people into determining "what is legal and illegal, righteous and sinful."[13] In some cultures, for example, encouraging a person is of ultimate priority and allows for a certain bending of the truth. In other cultures, such as in North America, "it is worse to tell a lie than to hurt a person's feelings."[14]

It is in this evaluative dimension that people decide what they do with the cognitive and affective expressions of cultural information that they are engaging. These three interwoven dimensions of human experience—ideas, feelings, and values—inform our understanding of the nature of humans, their societies, and their cultures. We can't have one without the others. They are pervasively present in every human relationship, though one may dominate until some event triggers the less observable, seemingly muted ones and releases them.

The global arts, as expressive culture, raise to the surface the hidden dimensions so they can be observed and processed into new normative reconfigurations. This is what was taking place on the global stage at the Fez Festival as each group was engaging in expressive culture within its religious tradition. Beliefs, feelings, and values were interacting dialogically as performers and audience members were deciding their meaning for each and every person present. The Fez Festival fostered experiences where peoples simultaneously engaged in all three dimensions of culture: cognitive, affective, and evaluative factors.

The critical factor to note is that all three dimensions are essential in Christian witness. In evangelism, church planting, development work, and cross-cultural worship, we need to know that Jesus is the Son of God who died for our sins. But it does not stop just with the cognitive dimension. We also need the affective dimension—that is, feelings of love for and allegiance to Jesus that ultimately lead us to decide to turn and to follow Christ as the Lord of our lives—alongside the evaluative dimension. Hiebert underscores it well: "We do not proclaim the gospel simply to inform people or to make them feel good. We call them to become lifelong followers of Jesus Christ. So beliefs,

12. Hiebert, *Gospel in Human Contexts*, 152.
13. Hiebert, *Gospel in Human Contexts*, 152–53.
14. Hiebert, *Gospel in Human Contexts*, 153.

feelings, and morals are all important in Christian ministry."[15] The global arts, as expressive culture, are essential in witnessing to Christ and play critical roles in society, including the multiple dynamics of spirituality.

Expressive Culture

Global arts form expressive culture. They foster accessing people within their cultural contexts across almost all domains of life—that is, life-cycle, religious, political, and economic aspects of the culture at large. The global arts as expressive culture reveal, shape, and guide peoples throughout their lives as they integrate cognitive, affective, and evaluative dimensions of various cultural contexts. They provide arenas of experience that excel in expressive and formative dialogue for forging, forming, and engaging in sustained relationships in profound and persuasive ways. They provide a multiplex of languages for interaction and dialogue with people in diverse societies and contexts.

Global arts are universal. However, their meanings and modes of engagement vary according to cultures and contexts within any given society, such as generational differences. They function within all societies—that is, local cultures, global cultures, and regions in between. But they do so in their unique cultural ways of negotiating life. Whether at transnational events such as Fez or singing the psalms under a mango tree in a West African village, the multiple functions of music and the performing arts within society help point us toward meaningful negotiating of faith and culture. On a grand scale, the global arts function in three critical ways for the church in Christian worship and witness: as life processors, as languages of communication, and as contextualizers. We reflect on the unique aspects of each of these in light of the Fez Festival.

Global arts as life processors. The arts take up the narrative strands of people's ways of life and weave them together. This is the negotiation factor. They engage the three dimensions of culture in ways that foster integrating the different dimensions. The Fez Festival revealed how people engage in worship through the arts. Yet, it failed to provide an opportunity for the festival audience(s) to learn the performers' depth of spiritual engagement as they performed. What were the performers thinking and feeling? How were they evaluating their stage performance, revealing *the home in which they live together* and engage in worship? What was happening internally as they shared the stage, watched a different religious performance, and then attempted to perform together? Further, how were the diverse peoples in the audience

---

15. Hiebert, *Gospel in Human Contexts*, 153.

processing and interpreting what was playing out before them? Research into each of these questions is needed. Investigating the arts in culture poses one of the greatest needs in relation to witnessing to Christ within the artistic home-living arenas of diverse peoples.

Global arts as languages of communication. All global arts are embedded within cultural contexts. While the use of spoken languages is universal, their meaning is limited to a range of peoples who have learned to interact via a particular spoken language. Just as spoken languages facilitate communication within social contexts, global arts such as music, performing arts, and visual arts bring together multiple expressive languages that are likewise culturally embedded. They speak simultaneously on multiple levels, both verbal and nonverbal, increasing and enhancing the depth of emotional engagement, profoundly affecting the evaluative dimension. The gospel group from New Orleans, for example, brought together verbal (text), audio (musical sound), kinesic movement (dance), and cultural artifactual elements (appropriate dress and musical instruments) drawn from African American culture as practiced in New Orleans. The Pakistani Qawwali performance group engaged the same expressive elements. However, they drew from the expressive culture as practiced in Pakistan, which includes sitting on the ground, as well as different gestures, vocal qualities, techniques, and performance configurations. The contrast between the two groups showed in stark relief! Depending on which tradition was most familiar to the people in the audience, there was great variance in audience members' degrees of understanding, emotional engagement, and evaluation of what was good and not so good and of its impact on them.

Global arts as contextualizers. On display at Fez were the global arts in relation to spirituality and religion as they have been embedded within their respective cultural contexts. The transnational stage openly displayed contextualized practices usually found within mosques, churches, and temples via cultural performance forms employed for engaging with God.

How might it look if Christian witness arose from within a people's expressive culture in ways that embedded it within the people's ways of thinking and spiritual practices? What are the dynamics that need to be considered? We first need to consider how God has made himself known via expressive culture and, second, to consider key approaches and issues in contextualization of the gospel.

Global Arts in Dialogue: A Contextual Model

In the practice of mission, we often start with the concept that Christianity is incarnational: Jesus came and dwelt among us (John 1:14). Just as Jesus came and dwelt among the Hebrew people, he also made himself at home in their culture, speaking their local language, following religious practices, eating kosher food, and more. He also challenged those aspects of culture that went counter to God's intentions for his people. Jesus lived out his life within the norms of the local society and, at the same time, felt free to challenge other aspects. Since the beginning, as modeled by Jesus, the incarnational principle points to how the gospel is at home in all cultures while at the same time followers of Jesus are not fully at home as they practice a pilgrim faith.[16] They do not naively embrace all of culture. Rather, they give careful attention to God's guidelines for living in a fallen world. As Sunquist argues,

> The incarnational [principle] is an ongoing and purposeful move to be part of a culture; Christianity must be translated into a culture, and the gospel must speak Foochow as well as Spanish, Arabic, and modern Greek. It is this diversity—of the gospel in its many cultural expressions—that Christians must celebrate and that God embraces. At the same time, the pilgrim principle is at work in Christianity. The gospel is (and is only) the gospel of Jesus Christ. It has specific content and meaning, and it comes not to affirm all that is in a local culture, but enters into the culture to lift it up and clean it off.[17]

The global arts, as expressive culture, work within these two dynamics of incarnational witness and pilgrim faith that does not accept all that is part of a culture. It is the gospel that cleanses the sinful elements of a people that work against God and changes the orientation of their expressive culture to one of declaring God's glory and proclaiming his salvation. Global arts specialize in making Christ known and worshiped within diverse contexts. The gospel both affirms and challenges peoples within their cultures, societies, and governments.[18]

A contextual model of the global arts and Christian witness, then, encompasses four arenas that simultaneously interact and dialogue with one another in light of the gospel of Jesus Christ (see fig. 1.2).

These four arenas are word, world, person, and faith community.[19] The Scriptures constantly point to Jesus as the incarnational Word of God. "In the beginning was the Word, and the Word was with God, and the Word

---

16. Walls, *Missionary Movement in Christian History*, 8.
17. Sunquist, *Understanding Christian Mission*, 19.
18. Sunquist, *Understanding Christian Mission*, 19.
19. Missiologists have often referred to the arenas of engagement as word, world, church, and relational dimension as a method for doing mission theology. See Van Engen, "Toward a Contextually Appropriate Methodology."

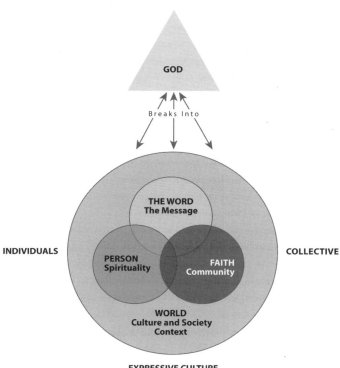

Figure 1.2
Global arts, expressive culture, and Christian witness

was God" (John 1:1). Jesus was with God in the beginning, meaning that he was above human culture and chose to break into it. He became the "light of all mankind" (John 1:4) and shone into the darkness (John 1:5). I find that Zechariah's song poignantly reveals God's hope and plan for salvation:

> Praise be to the Lord, the God of Israel,
>> because he has come to his people and redeemed them.
> He has raised up a horn of salvation for us
>> in the house of his servant David . . .
>
> . . . because of the tender mercy of our God,
>> by which the rising sun will come to us from heaven
> to shine on those living in darkness
>> and in the shadow of death,
> to guide our feet into the path of peace.
>>   (Luke 1:68–69, 78–79)

We see in both John 1:1–5 and Zechariah's prophetic canticle (Luke 1:68–79) that God is indeed incarnational. His incarnation, coming in and living in the midst of his people, is his key practice for loving his people, for whom he sacrifices his all. Therefore, I maintain that culture is not an entity in and of itself, but rather a milieu within which God and his people interact, engage, and communicate, and God's people have opportunities for a dynamic encounter with the living God. "Milieu" here is used in the sense of a set of cultural resources and materials. For example, Jesus spoke Aramaic, the low-culture language of the day; he did not usually speak the high-cultural language of the Pharisees (Hebrew), nor did he speak a foreign language. Neither did he speak the language of the empire or oppressors (Greek). Rather, he spoke the language of the people among whom he wanted most to make himself known. He drew upon appropriate agrarian metaphors, proverbs, and local songs such as those sung as the conclusion of the Lord's table on the night when Jesus was betrayed.

The global arts, then, are embedded in particular cultures and function as life processors that foster God and God's people making themselves known and understood. Culture, to use a visual arts metaphor, is the canvas on which we interact and relate dialogically, drawing from a rich palette of colors and materials for making sense of life, in society and in our relationships (or lack thereof) with one another and most importantly with God. God as the Word breaks into that world, engaging with people, relating with their culture—beliefs, feelings, and cultural norms—drawing on expressive cultural resources and materials that form a complex of dynamic cultural languages. Christ always stands at the center, interacting with and forging relationships with people. Relational dynamics lie at the heart of the gospel; it is because of God's so loving the world that Jesus comes and lives among a particular people (John 3:16).

It is important to note that Christ came into a fallen, broken world. This broken world has lost its intended purpose of communion with God. It consists of broken elements or culturally expressive languages employed in ways that steal God's glory and relationship with his people. This takes place when expressive culture is exploited in ways that lead to wicked, perverse, and broken lines of communication, including stolen relationships of worshiping God that instead promote appeasing other "deities." Sherwood Lingenfelter argues powerfully that "Paul suggests that human beings are in a prison, a cell of disobedience: 'God has imprisoned all human beings in their own disobedience only to show mercy to them all' (Rom. 11:30–32). In Galatians 3:22, paraphrasing Psalm 14:1–3, he observes that 'the whole world is a prisoner of sin.' God has penned up all people in their self-created cells of culture, including Jew and Gentile, pagan and missionary."[20]

Yet that does not make people living "at home" in their world unredeemable. People can still experience liberation, redemption, and freedom in Christ as they are "redeemed from the empty way of life handed down to you from your ancestors . . . with the precious blood of Christ" (1 Pet. 1:18–19). The gospel challenges peoples' social order and beliefs as they turn and become "a chosen people, a royal priesthood, a holy nation, God's special possession, that you may declare the praises of him who called you out of darkness into his wonderful light. Once you were not a people, but now you are the people of God" (1 Pet. 2:9–10). The global arts as expressive culture, when set right before God, make the cultural playing field available as restoring and redeeming agents for declaring his glory, announcing his kingdom, and proclaiming his salvation. They constitute the languages of communication and of making oneself known and understood within diverse contexts. God reveals himself to all the world and converses with all local and global contexts. Ultimately, in the new Jerusalem we see the kings of the earth "bring their splendor" into the city of God. He values what his redeemed people have to offer in worship (Rev. 21:24).

Contextualizing the Gospel and the Arts

The challenge before us in Christian witness via the global arts is finding a map for traversing cultural contexts. Enter contextualization. "The idea of contextualization is to frame the gospel message in language and communication forms appropriate and meaningful to the local culture and to focus the message upon crucial issues in the lives of the people."[21] Key dynamics of setting the gospel in context need to be negotiated with care. We need to ask critical questions. How does one move beyond outright rejection of culture or wholesale acceptance of culture in nuanced ways? How do we contextualize the gospel in ways that bring honor and glory to God? What are culturally appropriate methods of evangelism? What are familiar and meaningful methods of local learning patterns suitable for discipleship?

The implications for contextualizing the gospel in relation to Christian witness are vast, and they raise numerous thorny issues. Among the most immediate aspects to deal with, we need to free forms from past negative associations that do not honor God. Yet it is important to vigilantly pursue

20. Lingenfelter, *Transforming Culture*, 16.
21. Lingenfelter, *Transforming Culture*, 12–13.

dynamic expressions of Christian experience. Not to contextualize the gospel message means running the danger of the gospel becoming irrelevant and of developing syncretistic ways of practicing Christianity, ways that do not bring peoples into meaningful encounters with God. We turn now to considering how to go about contextualizing the gospel in ways that critically engage the arts, avoiding both outright rejection of culture and uncritical acceptance of culture.

Creative Contextualization

I believe global arts are available to do what I call creative contextualization of the gospel. That is, the arts as expressive culture provide the social arenas, languages, processes, and products necessary for doing contextualization. Doing creative contextualization together with local peoples acknowledges the importance of drawing from available cultural art forms, but it is not a slave to taking over a form exactly as it is. Merely inserting the Christian message or a Scripture text on top of the form most often leads to syncretism. What appears to be Christian on a surface level can become just a cover for continuing pagan practices without transforming people's ways of thinking, their engagement with God, and how they live. The result? No culturally appropriate "new songs" emerge that reveal deep encounters with God. Examples abound. In parts of Latin America, religious statues and sacred spaces appear to be Christian, yet the people are still worshiping the same spirits and gods that they did before the Christian faith was brought into their context. The former pagan worship goes underground and continues to enslave the peoples.[22] In other places, we find people talking the right talk without walking the walk, in full allegiance to Jesus Christ. This is merely surface-level contextualization. Too often we are "unaware that these beliefs and practices are rooted in deep worldviews that make up what we think *with*, not what we think *about*. This includes the categories and logics we use, the root metaphors and myths that order our understanding of the world, and the fundamental assumptions we make about beauty and morality."[23] Surface-level contextualization does not go deep enough and ignores the complexity of addressing the life issues of a people at worldview levels. It has not allowed God to break into a people's world and begin the transformation process.

In our haste to make the gospel known quickly, we have brought what we know and understand about God without realizing that we must also work

22. See Vernon J. Sterk, "The Dynamics of Persecution" (PhD diss., Fuller Theological Seminary, 1992). See also Yamamori and Taber, *Christopaganism or Indigenous Christianity?*
23. Hiebert, *Gospel in Human Contexts*, 99–100.

at the deeper levels of a people's worldview. There is much more to the global arts that so easily engage and entertain us; they play critical roles in addressing these deeper levels. We need ways of doing contextualization that allow us to work beneath the surface, to think in new ways that allow people to understand and follow Jesus Christ at deeper levels. Hiebert's approach to doing critical contextualization offers a powerful way to work with the arts at deeper levels and in ways that promote people's living godly lives in the midst of a broken world.

The Need for Critical Contextualization of the Arts

Global arts employed in Christian witness need to critically contextualize the arts as people seek to negotiate faith and culture.[24] Critical contextualization encompasses a process that addresses old beliefs, rituals, stories, songs, customs, proverbs, art, and music—the stuff of expressive culture. In the practice of mission, we have multiple examples of three ways to do contextualization: complete rejection of the old culture, complete acceptance of it, or critical, selective acceptance.

First, rejection of contextualization denies anything and everything that pertains to the old culture. Wholesale rejection of culture arises out of a concern that the old customs are so intimately linked with pagan tradition that they must be completely tossed out. This involves a misunderstanding that the people who carry the Christian gospel into non-Christian cultures are bringing a gospel that has not been tainted by their own cultures. This is totally false. All cultures have elements of contamination in them, including Christianity in the West. Rejection of contextualization makes the supposed "Christian" form a top priority, assuming that the "Christian" form from the West carries the meaning as intended. Confusion enters into the equation. Foreignness and alienation result and keep people from turning toward Christ. Significantly, "It is this foreignness and not the offense of the Gospel that has often kept people from following Christ. We must be careful not to confuse the two."[25] Consequently, the old beliefs, rituals, and artistic products (songs, proverbs, storytelling) go underground, resulting in syncretism beneath the surface. It leads to nominalism and a lack of life transformation.

The second way, uncritical contextualization, completely accepts the old. Based on respect for a people's culture and concern about issues surrounding the foreignness of the gospel, the contextualization pendulum swings to the other extreme. Those who advocate uncritical contextualization can be overly

24. Hiebert, "Critical Contextualization."
25. Hiebert, "Critical Contextualization," 288.

enamored with the particular culture in question, placing it on a pedestal. While their respect is admirable, they overlook the reality of institutional and corporate sins, which exist along with personal ones. Hiebert notes that "to overlook this is to bar sin at the front door of the church, but to allow it in at the back. The Gospel calls both individuals and societies to change."[26] There are indeed elements in every culture that counter and go against what Christ calls us to. Uncritical contextualization ignores this side of the issue, also resulting in syncretism and neo-paganism.

The third approach provides correctives to both wholesale rejection of contextualization and uncritical contextualization. Critical contextualization fosters "communicating the Gospel in ways the people understand, but in ways that challenge them in their personal and corporate lives with God's call to discipleship."[27] It deals with old beliefs and practices in a conscious and intentional process that explicitly examines practices "with regards to meanings and functions in the society, and then [evaluates them] in the light of biblical norms."[28] Critical contextualization is based on a process that affords a local group of believers dynamic and sustainable ways and means for living in Christian discipleship within their particular contexts. A community of believers self-critiques their local customs in light of the Scriptures. This leads to the creation of reinvigorated practices that turn people to honor and glorify Christ. Such newly re-created local customs speak into a people's worldview and foster living as Christians within their unique contexts. The process is dynamic, providing a method for adapting to changing societies, whether local, regional, global, or transnational.

A strength of the critical-contextualization approach is that the process recognizes and honors the people of a culture, who know the meanings of their customs better than outsiders. It fosters believers' embedding their faith into their context as they reconfigure and shape the ways they live out their Christian lives. Agreed-upon spiritual practices come to be owned by the community and are relevant and meaningful. Such a practice of discernment fosters their functioning as a hermeneutical community that can be sustained as new issues and situations develop. Theologically, it puts into practice and reinforces the concept of the priesthood of all believers as it draws from and involves all believers, no matter their level of training or literacy. In essence, it takes the Bible as the definitive and final authority. The people do exegesis as they learn to ask, "What did the text mean in the context in

26. Hiebert, "Critical Contextualization," 289.
27. Hiebert, "Critical Contextualization," 289.
28. Hiebert, "Critical Contextualization," 290.

which it was written?" Hermeneutics follows, as they then ask, "What does it mean in our situation?"[29] Finally, as both old and new issues arise, the growing church has a method that keeps bringing it back to God and his Word.

My Story: An Example of Critical Contextualization in Practice

There they were: standing, singing out their religious texts, playing complex rhythms on the drum, dancing, and performing at the front of the Daystar University closing ceremonies for the Christian Music Ministry course in Nairobi, Kenya (East Africa). The three-week course had focused on studying and setting Colossians 3 to song, based on critical contextualization applied to the arts. Among the twenty students and six faculty members, we spoke some twenty-six African and European languages. The year was 1999, and the political atmosphere was rife with confusion and fear. We had all heard two loud booms just before the beginning of the graduation banquet. Reports were trickling in that the United States embassy in the center of Nairobi had been bombed. Some students had come from downtown and seen it, while others were observing the rising smoke. Rumors were coming in that more than four US embassies in East Africa had been bombed. Nobody knew what was really going on. The ambiguity of the situation pervaded the atmosphere, both in the city of Nairobi and on the Daystar University campus. And yet there we were, celebrating at a graduation luncheon what God had taught us. The vice-chancellor of Daystar, holder of a PhD in engineering from Leeds, England, was seated next to me at the head banquet table.[30] I had especially selected the Ugandan group—an Anglican priest, his new bride, and one church elder—to sing a Ugandan version of Colossians 3:12–14. Not only was it an excellent song, but their mother tongue was the same as the vice-chancellor's. The three of them sang as a hermeneutical community, declaring,

> Therefore, as God's chosen people, holy and dearly loved, clothe yourselves with compassion, kindness, humility, gentleness and patience. Bear with each other and forgive one another if any of you has a grievance against someone. Forgive as the Lord forgave you. And over all these virtues put on love, which binds them all together in perfect unity. (Col. 3:12–14)

29. Hiebert, "Critical Contextualization," 293.
30. In Kenya, the position of vice-chancellor is roughly equivalent to the president of a university.

The vice-chancellor leaned over to me and proudly said, "That's my language." I answered, "Yes, I know." And then he made a profound statement: "That touches me deep down and cleanses me from the inside up!" Reaching the deeper levels of this highly positioned university president and deeply spiritual church leader lay at the heart of what we had been working toward. It was the fruit of putting critical contextualization into practice in ways that could ultimately lead to the transformation of a people in relation to the living God.

In the following chapter, we will explore how this type of critical contextualization in the arts can be a superb vehicle for the gospel to move across cultural borders. It is important to understand the raw materials of communication and the signal systems available to us as we enter into effective witness.

Questions for Discussion

1. What is the meaning and role of culture in our lives?
2. What are the distinctive features of global arts as culture?
3. What needs do you see for creative contextualization of the arts in your own faith community's worship and witness?

2

Communicating Christ through Global Arts

What songs and arts are the best ones for sharing Christ?

Understanding how the arts communicate in diverse contexts requires moving into new cultures. Immersion among a people and experiencing how they interact with one another via the arts is essential to becoming aware of differences in communication patterns and impact. It is one of the first steps in becoming competent in navigating among peoples and their arts worldwide. To launch our discussion, we begin with the challenging experience that propelled me into witness through the global arts.

My Story: First Days in Nairobi

I will never forget my first Sunday in Nairobi, Kenya.[1] Uninformed stereotypes of African worship filled with dynamic rhythms on drums and local instruments washed through my mind before I entered the church. As I stood to sing the opening hymn at Nairobi Baptist Church, I was astounded to find myself singing

1. Nairobi is East Africa's world-class city, the capital of Kenya, a former colony of the United Kingdom. Nairobi is known for its thriving economy, high-rise buildings, and rapid population growth. The city appears to embrace as much of the Western lifestyle as possible. Nairobi, and Kenya in general, is also known for its explosive expansion of Christianity; worshiping faith communities are abundant throughout the city (see Downes, Oehrig, and Shane, *Summary of the Nairobi Church Survey*).

43

"A Mighty Fortress Is Our God," a fine, theologically sound, German reformation hymn composed five centuries earlier.[2] The tempo seemed particularly
slow, especially to me—as a church organist I prefer to keep the tempo brisk. I
also couldn't help but wonder whether there was a fortress in Kenya and how
people in the congregation related to such an image. I later discovered there is
indeed a fortress, Fort Jesus, in Mombasa on the Kenyan coast. The fortress
was built in the late sixteenth century by Portuguese traders to protect their
trade route to India and their interests in East Africa.[3] I mused, "Lord, did you
bring me halfway around the world from the West Coast of the United States
to sing this hymn that seems so out of context?" What did this hymn have to
do with my new friends in Christ there in Nairobi in 1978? I left that formal,
British-influenced worship service feeling a bit perplexed, yet I enjoyed meeting
my Kenyan brothers and sisters in Christ: men in three-piece pin-striped suits
and women dressed to the max and wearing the latest three-inch heels.

Later that evening I attended church just down the road with a few Daystar University students, including a Presbyterian pastor dressed in his white-
collared clerical shirt. We started by singing "What a Friend We Have in
Jesus," a favorite hymn long associated with missions, and then moved on to
a current Western contemporary chorus of that time, "Heaven Came Down
and Glory Filled My Soul." The atmosphere seemed to lighten up a bit. Then
it happened—the musicians moved from playing the Hammond organ and
brought out a drum and *kayamba* (a traditional flat-board bamboo shaker
from the Kenyan coast). The room became electric. Smiles erupted on faces
and bodies began to move, especially the shoulders, as people glided with
small steps back and forth to the right and left. They were fully engaged in
embodied worship, declaring in Swahili:

> *Nimehaidiwa Mfalme mwema* (3×)
> *Hata ni kifa ni tatawala tena.*

> I have been promised a king who does not disappoint (3×)
> that even after I die, I will still live.[4]

The whole church seemed to move together as one body; corporately, they
felt fully at home in singing their praise to God. Here was the "singing of

2. The words are a paraphrase of Psalm 46 and thought to have been composed between
1527 and 1529.
3. "Brief History of Fort Jesus," Mombasa-City.com, accessed May 17, 2018, http://www
.mombasa-city.com/history_of_Fort_jesus.htm.
4. Translation from Kiswahili into English by Rev. Paul Mpishi.

a new song," *a dynamic expression of Christian experience* that explored new arenas that I had never experienced before, but somehow the song rang genuine and authentic.[5] Communication dynamics were flying in new directions; I wanted to know more. I especially wanted to know what it meant for Christian witness.

How do we begin to understand the ways in which the global arts communicate? In this chapter, I look first at the global arts as expressive languages of communication. How are music and the arts universal? How are they not universal? How does this relate to two major goals of communication, and what do they imply for Christian witness? Second, I discuss the raw cultural materials of communication: the twelve signal systems used in the creative process. How do these signal systems serve as vehicles for communicating messages in light of the global arts? I also offer four key considerations to keep in mind as we employ these culturally embedded signals for making Jesus Christ known. Finally, we reflect on theological implications for loving God and loving our neighbors through the arts.

Global Arts as Expressive Languages of Communication

Each and every art is an expressive language that communicates. On my first Sunday in Nairobi, I experienced the universal phenomenon of music and the singing of "psalms, hymns, and songs from the Spirit" (Col. 3:16). I also experienced the reality that culture influences art forms, their performance, and experiential engagement. Cultural art forms reveal varying degrees of difference in communication dynamics and meaning. Each of the four songs in the Nairobi service arose out of an historical and cultural context. Indeed, they constitute part of a body of worship resources that draw from God's people around the world. These songs were fresh expressions of dynamic encounters with God in their respective local origins: in sixteenth-century reformation Germany, in nineteenth-century Ireland,[6] in evangelical Anglo youth culture of the 1970s United States, and in newly emerging praise songs in Kenya in the late 1970s. These songs represented the "new songs" of a particular group of believers in their time period, context, and particular life situation. It is intriguing to me, as an ethnomusicologist, to observe and experience the broad diversity of music available to people for engaging with God, and the

5. It was a pivotal moment that jump-started me on a lifelong journey to understand the intersections between Christian spirituality and expressive culture.

6. "Joseph Scriven, 1820–1886," *STEM Publishing*, accessed May 17, 2018, http://www.stempublishing.com/hymns/biographies/scriven.html.

different ways people grab hold of these types of music and bring them into their own contexts. This naturally raises questions regarding the differing meanings and relevance of various types of music in diverse contexts.

Music and the Arts Are Universal; Their Meanings Are Not Guaranteed

What did each of the four songs above mean to the people singing them? What past experiences did the people bring into their interpretation of them? How did the songs resonate and speak to them? Communication theory offers helpful ways to answer these questions. It points out the importance of distinguishing between transmission and communication. *Transmission* occurs when a signal, such as a radio or cable signal, is sent out with someone hoping that it is picked up and heard. For *communication* to take place, a signal must be transmitted and also received. Even then, if it has reached the ear, we are not sure whether it has reached the mind as it was intended. Transmission is just one of several steps in the communication process. Communication goes further than transmission; it takes place when the sound or message is received, reaches the mind, is processed, *and* is understood as intended. So, were the songs on that Sunday morning transmitting or communicating? For whom? And to what degree? A "new song" in one context does not automatically transfer its original meaning into another setting.

Meaning is dependent on the person or group of persons interacting with the song or art form in their particular context. A young music student at Daystar University in Nairobi, for example, brought to class an Africanized version of "In the Sweet By and By," a song that had become a part of his tradition. I had asked the class to arrange the hymns they sing using Kenyan music styles related to their mother tongues. After we learned to perform the song in the Kamba language and in a Kamba musical style, I asked what the song talked about. The student answered, "Oh, that is that sweet bye-bye song. We sing it at funerals." As we looked more closely at the text, it became apparent that the student did not understand the original lyrics of the song. His response was "Oh, we often don't understand what we are singing, we just clap and dance to it." He was expressing a desire to identify with being a Christian; he considered it part of a Christian funeral ritual. His response thus reflected the way it had become part of a local Christian rite, in spite of people not understanding the original intent of the lyrics. Here we have an example of how music is universal, but not a universal language. While everyone can engage in singing or performing a song, its meanings are not universal. Meanings differ depending on the culture and context. In other words, the same song will have different meanings to different people, both within a given culture and especially across cultures. So, music is found universally and travels worldwide but does not communicate in the same ways as it travels. Each person processes it on his or her own terms.

The transmission of music and performing arts, therefore, does not guarantee agreed-upon comprehension, full communication in which a message is understood as intended or in similar ways. This causes many misunderstandings between people, including the carriers of the gospel message. There's more to music than reaches the ear. And there is more to the performing and visual arts than beauty, as wonderful as that is. When it comes to Christian witness, we need to evaluate whether we are effectively communicating or only transmitting the gospel message. In order to communicate, we need to establish the goals and purposes of communication.

Two Major Goals of Communication

Indeed, all of life is communication. It is ubiquitous and taken for granted. "Every day, everywhere, people are communicating."[7] This makes communication a vast and complex topic. Creating understanding and interactive engagement with and among people comprises two of the major goals required in effective communication of the gospel message. In order to create understanding, communication needs to be interactive. It "requires the active participation of [at least] two people sending and receiving messages."[8] Both parties are actively participating in the communication event as they are simultaneously sending (encoding) and receiving (decoding) messages in their attempts to create understanding and build relationship. Communication is not a one-way shot in the dark. Rather, it seeks to stimulate relational interaction so that people can build degrees of commonness, agreement, and understanding, thereby to feel at home with themselves and the people in their social group. It is a two-way process.

In order to create understanding, communication also requires involvement in the lives of people. It does not happen overnight. As Donald Smith argues, communication is "a constantly broadening involvement that finds and builds more and more commonness, more areas of sharing. . . . It is people moving together into widening areas of common joys, problems, and answers."[9] I am convinced that the expressive languages of the arts generate dynamic interaction among peoples and offer powerful ways of creating understanding, both of which are integral in Christian witness. As seen in Jesus's interaction with

7. Neuliep, *Intercultural Communication*, 10.
8. Neuliep, *Intercultural Communication*, 13.
9. D. Smith, *Creating Understanding*, 24–25.

the Samaritan woman in John 4, in Christian witness our two major goals are to create understanding and to evoke relational interaction that brings people into dynamic relationship with the living God and with faith communities. Music and the arts, when practiced with intention, offer powerful ways of engaging with people in almost all aspects of life.

What lies at the foundations of music and the arts to make them vehicles of communication? What allows these expressive languages to communicate? We turn to the most basic units in expressive culture that generate interactive communication, known as the twelve signal systems of human communication. Each of these twelve systems functions like a language on its own terms; yet at the same time each one intimately interconnects with at least two or more of the other signal systems.

The Twelve Signal Systems and Global Arts

The global arts excel in incorporating both verbal and nonverbal patterns of communication, as is normative of all communication in general. Song, visual arts, and drama, for example, bring together different sets of signs and symbols in unique, creative ways. While sometimes heavily drawing on verbal signals, such as in songs that contain both lyrics and audio sounds, the arts are especially adept and profound in the nonverbal arenas. Indeed, communication scholars have become fascinated with identifying unique and distinctive nonverbal elements of communication in order to better understand the significance and impact of each system in the communication process.

The twelve signal systems, as identified by Donald Smith, provide an expanded taxonomy of verbal and nonverbal signals, with an explanation of their interrelationships, meant to help us understand the complexity of communication. They comprise signs and symbols that draw from and make up the cultural elements of our messages and dynamic interactions with one another. Signals are made up of anything that can convey information, such as words, body motions, shapes, and patterns of light. They refer to an object or an idea, usually drawing from the environment of a particular context. Spoken and written languages are unique in that each of their signals is made up of an "arbitrarily selected and learned stimulus that represents something else,"[10] and these signs are often identified as symbols. Both signs and symbols, terms I am using interchangeably since both signal information,[11] are the vehicles

10. Neuliep, *Intercultural Communication*, 13.
11. For a full treatment of signals and symbols, see Neuliep, *Intercultural Communication*, 247–328.

"by which the thoughts and ideas of one person can be communicated to another person. Messages are constructed with verbal and nonverbal symbols. Through symbols, meanings are transferred between people."[12] The people receiving the message are the ones who determine the meaning.

The twelve signal systems are the observable parts of culture, the most basic units in communication. They make up the primary materials in all human communication and can be described as follows:[13]

1. **Verbal.** The verbal signal system is the most commonly recognized system. There are more than five thousand spoken languages worldwide, and then there are dialectical modifications on top of that. For example, the way English is spoken around the world varies greatly. Countries that were once a part of the British Empire speak a variation of the Queen's English, which contrasts with American English, as spoken in different parts of the United States. But not all the world speaks English! Languages have their unique sounds, grammar, and syntax, and are important in shaping how we see and think about the world.[14] Hence, Bible translators negotiate for the intended meaning of God's Word as they enter into different languages worldwide. Jesus modeled the importance of entering into a people's language when he chose to speak the everyday language of the people, Aramaic. He modeled and demonstrated the importance of speaking in the terms and thought forms that the people knew. Singing in a foreign tongue, for example, affects people differently than singing in their mother tongue. Both are possible. However, the question of meaning is paramount.

2. **Written.** The written signal system is based on the verbal language that is used. It allows people to transmit information without the limitations of time and space. Written symbols representing speech vary among the many languages of the world. For example, here is John 3:16 in Nepali: हो, परमेश्वरले संसारलाई यति साह्रो प्रेम गर्नुभयो, कि उहाँले आफ्ना एकमात्र पुत्रलाई दिनु भयो। परमेश्वरले आफ्ना पुत्रलाई दिनु भयो त्यस द्वारा उहाँमाथि विश्वास गर्ने कोहीपनि नाश हुने छैन, तर अनन्त जीवन प्राप्त गर्नेछ। These symbols appear quite mysterious to an uninformed eye! Musical notation is another type of written system that has assigned symbols to represent the audible sounds of music in relation to one another. A vast range of methods have been developed for notating music, including staff notation, *solfege* based on tonic sol-fa,

12. Neuliep, *Intercultural Communication*, 13.
13. For a list of the technical terms, see Neuliep, *Intercultural Communication*, 279–315.
14. See "Sapir-Worf Hypothesis," in Neuliep, *Intercultural Communication*, 247–48.

sargam in India,[15] and *slendro* in Indonesia. In assessing the worldwide value of communicating via the arts, it is important to note that more than 70 percent of people do not read or do not choose reading as their dominant means of communication. For these people, known as oral learners, the arts lie at the core of their daily lives and religious activities.

3. **Numeric.** Individual numbers and number systems are used to carry meaning, in terms of quantity and/or metaphorically. For example, three is an important number for Christians in its representation of the Trinity; many Westerners consider the number thirteen to be bad luck; many Chinese dislike the number four since its verbal sound is close to the word "death," and yet, for other Chinese in various religious ideologies, four can signify fortune and good luck.[16] The arts incorporate numbers in various ways, often quite subconsciously. For example, as far back as the ninth century, in Western classical music an augmented fourth (tritone) was considered by many, including the church, as the Devil's triad or Devil's interval.

4. **Pictorial.** This signal system, comprised of two-dimensional representations, is the special domain of artists, who reflect their cultural perceptions of their environment. "By use of symbols, with realistic and abstract representations, a philosophy is expressed, emotional response is aroused, and specific messages are carried—to those who know the symbolism of the originating culture."[17] In other words, just as in music and other arts, there is no universal language of visual arts, since there is no universal art alphabet. Rather, artists draw from their available cultural elements and materials to symbolically represent what they have in mind within their setting. For example, Western artists often use bridges to represent connecting separated groups, while Chinese artists would more likely use a bridge to indicate death and the transition from one life to the next.

5. **Artifactual.** Three-dimensional representations make up the artifactual system. Art objects, such as sculptures and carvings, are used for deliberate symbolic communication. Musical instruments are worldwide artifacts that lend to the creation of music. They often carry multiple levels of metaphorical significance. For example, the Middle Eastern *oud* (lute) is traditionally viewed as the major leader or ruler of the

15. For an overview of musical notation, see "Musical Notation," Wikipedia, updated April 12, 2018, https://en.wikipedia.org/wiki/Musical_notation.
16. Swee Hoon Ang, "Chinese Consumers' Perception of Alpha-Numeric Brand Names," *Asia Pacific Journal of Marketing and Logistics* 8, no. 1 (1996): 31–47, https://doi.org/10.1108/eb010268.
17. D. Smith, *Creating Understanding*, 148.

Photo by Scott Sunquist

Figure 2.1 Crucifixion batik from Bali

small classical Arabic ensemble called the *takt*, both in terms of sound and metaphorically. The Senufo people of Côte d'Ivoire (West Africa) perceive the wood-frame *balafon* (xylophone) as a metaphor of family kinship patterns. The lowest (and largest) key represents the mother and indicates a matrilineal society. The adjacent key is symbolic of the father. All other keys are the children.[18]

6. **Audio.** This signal system employs nonverbal sounds and silence with a great number of generative possibilities. From tones of voice, such as a nasal to diapason tonal quality, to a sonic palette that extends to the

18. Personal fieldnotes, 1987.

Figure 2.2 Senufo *balafons* and drums "singing" the gospel

sounds of pipe organs, clashing cymbals, synthesizers, and electronic music—the audio system pervades much of our lives. The verbal system combines with the audio system to create spoken languages. Someone's tone of voice carries much of a message. Psalms 149:1, 3, and 150:3–5 demonstrate the ways in which both music and individual sound symbols combine to praise the Lord.

7. **Kinesics.** The kinesic system includes body motions, facial expressions, and posture. Motions speak loudly, even without any verbal component. Indeed, when speaking, we use body motions unconsciously. Preaching arts, drama, and dance function heavily in this signal arena. Their gestures communicate specific information, but as in the case of the other signal systems, the same signals differ in meaning from culture

to culture. An acceptable dance gesture in one culture, such as putting the hands on the hips among a particular Ghanaian language group, is quite offensive in a neighboring language group in Ghana.[19]

Vignette 2.1

Chapos, Mandazis, and Ballroom Dancing

Julisa Rowe

Artists in Christian Testimony International, Kenya Director

To illustrate the power of signal systems to reflect cultural values and world-view, the play *Eight Cow Saint* was performed in two very different ways.[a] Performed by Kenyans, one performance was done as written, in a Western style, with the troupe in coordinated black outfits with colored shirts, Western-style aprons, and props such as a loaf of bread, wedding veil, and bouquet. The music was typical of American musical theater and the actors did ballroom dances, in couples, as a part of a wedding scene. The other production contextualized the play by using Kenyan-style clothing, *kangas* (Kenyan fabric), and props such as *chapos* and *mandazi* (African breads). In the wedding scene the actors separated into two lines, men and women, dancing separately, not touching, and singing in a Kenyan musical style.

The first production (written in a Western style) revealed an innate foreign-ness in the way the actors presented the whole piece. This included not only the signal systems but also the whole outlook of the players—their expectations of a woman in marriage (as written in the script), their looks, how they expressed themselves (verbal phrasing of ideas), and how they interacted with each other (the whole interplay of characters physically, verbally, and attitudinally). Audience reaction clearly favored the latter (contextualized) production, largely on the basis of the artifactual, tactile, and musical signals used. As one audience member said, "The costumes showed a village setting that was us [as opposed to Western costumes that talked about a village but didn't show it in what they wore and how they acted]." The second production was hailed as "very Kenyan," with the perception that much more time and effort were spent on the scripting. Interestingly, the script was exactly the same; only the signal systems changed.

[a] *Eight Cow Saint* is a short musical play by Karen Lund and Samuel Vance. It tells the story of a girl looked down on by her village until a visiting merchant gives eight cows for her to be his bride, and she begins to reflect her true worth. The story is taken from a Filipino folktale

19. Hanna, "Dance Movement."

(although it could easily be an African tale), but the village characters are somewhat European, and the setting is of a traveling group of players telling a story. The story fits many non-European countries, though, beginning with the symbolic cultural significance of cows to indicate the value of the bride.

8. **Optical.** The optical system references the use of light and color. Different degrees of light and dark communicate different meanings. The use of gas lanterns or candles can indicate a lack of electricity, such as in a rural village of Côte d'Ivoire; or, if used in a clandestine political meeting held in the evening in Kenya in the 1980s, can be seen as threatening to the local government; or, if used in a candlelight dinner in the West, can be understood as an invitation to a romantic evening. Without saying a word, the degree of light communicates the intent. Light and color are fundamental aesthetic elements in the visual arts, such as in the work of Van Gogh. Specific colors also communicate messages across cultures. The color red varies immensely in its meaning when moving across cultures. In Eugene, Oregon, red symbolized the unappreciated cult living just beyond the city borders during the 1980s. The Red Cross organization, on the other hand, uses red in association with saving and working with people in distress. In Kenya, a red, white, and black beaded Digo flute, a *chivote* from the Digo people living on the coast of Kenya, displays the village spirits. For the Maasai, red is considered sacred and ceremonial and can also mean danger or bravery.[20]

9. **Tactile.** Touch and the sense of feel make up the tactile system. Holding hands is practiced differently across cultures. In parts of traditional Africa, it is not proper for a man and his wife to hold hands in public, while in the United States a husband and wife holding hands indicates that the relationship is thriving. The extended hand of a Maasai elder touching the top of a child's head indicates blessing.

10. **Temporal.** The use of time, the temporal system, occurs in three distinct ways. The units of time vary across cultures. For example, in northern Europe, meetings are arranged down to the minute, sometimes seconds when it comes to a train departing on time. In France, to depart on time means that a train departs within a range of five to ten minutes. The Cebaara Senufo of Côte d'Ivoire measure time based on the position of the sun in the sky during that time of day. This is seen in their greetings: "Greetings on the sun at its highest point," meaning "Hi at noontime." Other temporal uses include when to arrive at an important

20. Rev. Paul Mpishi, email correspondence with author, March 14, 2017.

meeting, precisely on time (Western) or about thirty minutes beyond the scheduled time (many parts of Africa). In relation to the arts, we find a stark contrast between the length of songs in different cultures. In some cultures, brevity can indicate that the message is not particularly significant. It is rare to find a very short song in Africa, in contrast to the three-minute worship chorus in Western worship services.

11. **Spatial.** The utilization of space includes personal space, working space, and living space. Culture determines whether a person is sitting or talking too close to another. Friendly conversation for North Americans is comfortable at about thirty to thirty-six inches apart, while in Latin America, eighteen inches indicates a comfort level appropriate for friendliness. If one pulls away, unconsciously the other person can easily interpret it as being unfriendly. Grand work spaces and small, cramped offices both indicate the status of the employee or employer. In relation to the arts, Western choirs require adequate space between singers, while singing with shoulders touching is normative in inner-city choirs in Nairobi. Music, dance, and drama events occupy different spaces, as dictated by cultural norms.

12. **Olfactory.** Finally, taste and smell make up the olfactory system.[21] The Scriptures are rich with language about incense, the sweet savor of a burnt offering, and spices (Exod. 29:18; 30:23–24, 34–38). At the Last Supper, Jesus instituted what has come to be known as Communion, where eating bread and drinking wine serve as symbols of Christ's body and blood. Festivals and Christmas events almost always include food. *Global Rhythm*, a transnational magazine about global musics, includes discussion of cultural foods as a regular feature in addition to its reporting on world musics.[22]

Engaging the Signal Systems

The signal systems are the dynamic, raw materials that allow people to share human experience. While the signal systems of communication are universal, cultural groupings shape and manipulate them in different ways. Hence, meaning is context-specific. "Usage of these signal systems in a commonly accepted way knits a diverse group of people together."[23] They can foster bonding and enhanced relational interactions. Or the opposite can take place:

21. See D. Smith, *Creating Understanding*, 144–60.
22. See "Food," *Global Rhythm*, http://www.globalrhythm.net/food.
23. D. Smith, *Creating Understanding*, 160.

signal systems can cause division among groups if they are not used in the same way. Since the signal systems are the observable parts of culture, learning to identify them and their usage helps one function effectively among differing peoples, across generations, and in new cultures. The global arts powerfully engage each of the twelve signal systems in differing configurations that communicate in profound ways. It takes "knowing the basic components of communication within any culture, and how they fit together,"[24] for one to meaningfully and effectively practice Christian witness through the arts worldwide.

We Rarely Use One Signal System in Isolation

Verbal and nonverbal symbols—signal systems—are intricately linked and combine to create a resultant message. Each of the global arts is configured through different combinations of signal systems. Preaching and oratory arts combine the use of words (verbal), appropriate dress and objects (artifactual), vocal tone qualities (audio), gestures and expressions (kinesics), the length of a sermon (temporal), and the place where the speaker stands (spatial). Drama combines many of the same signal systems as preaching, yet does so in strikingly different ways. Music—song in particular—draws on the verbal and predominantly audio signal systems, often including the artifactual when including musical instruments. When studying musics across cultures, we discover that musics of different cultures incorporate even more signal systems, such as dancing and drama, both heavily kinesic-dominated art forms. African musics, for example, incorporate music, dance, and drama together, combining in a multimedia richness that creates memorable occasions. Indonesian art forms, such as the *gamelan*, dwell heavily on artifactual elements, with a huge set of xylophones and gongs, plus masks and puppetry, and the kinesic elements of stylized dance—all combining in rich mythological storytelling.

The combination of signals results in the total message that is being expressed. When the signals complement one another in culturally appropriate ways, more information can be transferred, and the combination dramatically increases the impact of the message. The various media likewise emphasize different signal systems. Books and newspapers primarily use the written system, but often include the pictorial and even optical, when color is included. Radio is based on verbal and audio, while television adds pictorial, and film adds on optical with the use of darkness and light and rich cinematography.

24. D. Smith, *Creating Understanding*, 160.

Figure 2.3
The more believable signal systems

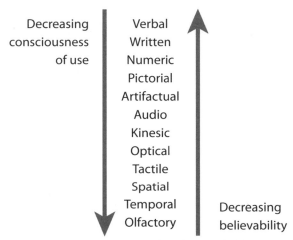

Decreasing consciousness of use

Verbal
Written
Numeric
Pictorial
Artifactual
Audio
Kinesic
Optical
Tactile
Spatial
Temporal
Olfactory

Decreasing believability

Adapted from Donald K. Smith, *Creating Understanding: A Handbook for Christian Communication across Cultural Landscapes* (Grand Rapids: Zondervan, 1992), 163. Used with permission.

The internet has captured our attention and dominates many people's lives by incorporating a rich configuration of signal systems that generate broadening involvement with people. The global arts, with their rich combinations of signal systems, offer enhanced opportunities for dynamic, interactive Christian witness when carefully and thoughtfully planned.

Additionally, the incorporation of more signal systems results in greater retention of information that has been communicated. Such multisensory learning increases memory. Chinese wisdom from the fifth century BCE taught: "I see and I forget; I hear and I remember; I do and I understand."[25] This is still true today. Similarly, educators report that after two weeks we tend to remember 10 percent of what we read, 20 percent of what we hear, 30 percent of what we see, 50 percent of what we see and hear, 70 percent of what we say, and 90 percent of what we say and do.[26] Note that the progression from passive to active involvement plays a critical role in increasing retention. This arena holds tremendous implications for effective Christian witness and will be more fully developed in the following chapters.

25. Commonly credited to Confucius, Chinese philosopher and reformer (551–479 BCE). For the original text and its translation, see Geany, *On the Epistemology of the Senses*, 143.

26. D. Smith, *Creating Understanding*, 162. For a more recent scientific study, see Ladan Shams and Aaron R. Seitz, "Benefits of Multisensory Learning," *Trends in Cognitive Sciences* 12 (2008): 411–17, https://doi.org/10.1016/j.tics.2008.07.006.

It Is Possible for One System to Contradict the Other Systems

This is where misunderstandings between people often surface. As long as two or more systems support one another, people believe the message to be sincere. The problem comes when the signals contradict each other; the recipient thinks the person delivering the message is insincere, thus undermining the reception of the message as intended. The principle holds that the less consciously used system carries greater weight and is thus more believable than systems used more consciously—that is, the verbal and written systems. The less consciously used signals lie in the nonverbal arenas: audio, kinesic, optical, spatial, and olfactory. This means that one may be saying something sincerely, yet the receiver of the message reads the nonverbal signs differently, such as tone of voice (audio), gestures (kinesics), eye contact (kinesics), or distance between people (spatial). This discrepancy usurps the intended message.

Awareness of the way the less consciously used systems carry greater believability helps us understand the profound impact made by many of the global arts. When gestures, clothing, and tone of voice do not support the verbal message, the message is distorted. This happens on a regular basis when working cross-culturally or across generations. While songs, for example, can be sung around the world, their import is ultimately determined by audio and kinesic signals, and whether or not they are used in culturally appropriate ways. There is also truth to the adage that "actions speak louder than words." This can be observed in the Scriptures, for example, in Psalm 50:16–17, when God asks,

> What right have you to recite my laws,
>   or take my covenant on your lips?
> You hate my instruction
>   and cast my words behind you.

All Systems Have Two Levels of Information: The Rational and the Emotional

In addition to carrying more or less believability, some signal systems carry more emotional information, while others carry higher loads of rational input. These tend to parallel the more believable and less consciously used systems as discussed above. "The written is heavily rational, but emotional response to writing is nevertheless present; in some cultures, the message will be believed because it is written or printed. But in other cultures, it will be disbelieved precisely because it is printed."[27] In most cultures, tactile, spatial, temporal,

---

27. D. Smith, *Creating Understanding*, 163.

and olfactory systems carry much emotional information. Misuse of space or touch can cause people's tempers to flare without them understanding why they are becoming angry.

It is critical to recognize that both reason and emotion are necessary in effective communication. They are interlinked in their impact, which does not result from either one or the other. Historically, Protestant Christians have placed a high priority on the rational spoken and written word. Because Protestant Christians have not acknowledged its importance, the emotional arena has typically been inadequately addressed, sometimes unintentionally usurping the intended message. As communicators of the gospel, we have missed out on numerous opportunities for persuasively communicating at deeper levels of emotion and believability. Incorporating the global arts as an integral part of Christian witness offers helpful correctives for overcoming walls of misunderstanding, foreignness, and latent historical bitterness accumulated over long periods of time. Used in culturally appropriate and relevant ways, arts can foster open attitudes toward Christ. Their strength to communicate in the affective dimensions of culture contributes immensely to communicating Christ.

My research among the Cebaara Senufo of Côte d'Ivoire, for example, revealed that Scripture songs drawn from indigenous music styles and appropriated in culturally relevant ways influenced the way believers and nonbelievers responded to their messages.[28] The nonbelievers were attracted first to the culturally rooted musical sounds and found themselves drawn into the circle dance, where the lead singer was "preaching"—declaring God's glory and proclaiming his salvation. The contextualized music style opened them up to joining in the music event and listening to the message that hung in the air as part of a song event. The Christians took it a step beyond. The culturally appropriate music style allowed them to immediately engage more directly with the text. They joyfully experienced the songs of God's Word as if they were hearing God speak words and instruction directly to them. Understanding of the Christian faith emerged at deeper levels, as the songs wooed them to more faithfully follow Christ. The pathway of their songs started first in the affective arena and simultaneously fostered processing their faith in the cognitive dimension.[29] In the world of the Cebaara Senufo people, the message rang true and authentic as the songs communicated in more believable ways for understanding the truths of the gospel.

28. King, *Pathways in Christian Music Communication.*
29. King, *Pathways in Christian Music Communication,* 176–92.

Culture Influences the Signal Systems and Their Function, Use, and Meaning

This point cannot be overstated. The signal systems are embedded within cultural contexts that shape and determine the ways people express themselves, interact with one another, and interpret the transmitted messages. As James Neuliep argues, "The cultural context in which human communication occurs is perhaps the most defining influence on human interaction. Culture provides the overall framework wherein humans learn to organize their thoughts, emotions, and behaviors in relation to their environment."[30] Thus, the signal systems differ in their functions and meaning across cultures, resulting in a variety of ways they are used, ways they foster interaction with one another, and ways the message is understood. If we want to clearly communicate an infinite message to finite human beings, our use of the global arts in Christian witness must take into account this cultural variability. Cultural literacy and cultural competence in engaging the signal systems of a people's expressive languages build the foundation for making the message and person of Jesus Christ known and understood for who he is.

Conclusion: Loving God and Loving Our Neighbors through the Signal Systems

Where is God in the midst of all this? We need to remember that we are God's creation, made in his image. He knows how we are made and how we communicate within and across cultural contexts. In the twelve signal systems, God has provided us with rich materials and resources for communicating with him, growing in relationship with him, and also declaring his glory and proclaiming his salvation to others. He longs to engage with us in holistic ways, both cognitively and emotionally, that lead us to decide to faithfully walk with him throughout life.

In Luke 10, an expert in the law asks Jesus what he must do to inherit eternal life. Jesus responds with a twofold answer drawn from the expert's own tradition and belief system. He tells him, "Love the Lord your God with all your heart and with all your soul and with all your strength and with all your mind" and "Love your neighbor as yourself" (10:27). Note that first of all God wants to be loved on all levels: with all our heart, with all our soul, with all our strength, and also with all our mind. In other words, he wants to know us on deep emotional levels—heart, soul, strength—as well as on the

30. Neuliep, *Intercultural Communication*, 48.

rational level, the mind. He does not limit our relationship with him mental information about him. Rather, he desires for all of our very being to be committed to him, both the rational and the emotional.

Here in Luke, Jesus is harking back to the Old Testament command known as the Shema (Deut. 6:5), where the children of Israel are told to love God with all their heart, soul, and strength. Scholars point out that the symbolic use of the heart (*leb, lebab*) does not refer to just the emotional seat of a person, but rather refers to "the determinative center of the person, the inner being—almost the whole person." The heart may also include "the aspect of the person that thinks about things, forms attitudes, and makes decisions."[31] These are the very communication dimensions that we have been discussing: cognitive, affective, and evaluative. Note also that following the Shema in Deuteronomy 6, the children of Israel are told how to implement loving God with all their hearts and with a set of culturally appropriate signal systems. That is, they are to talk about God's law (verbal) while sitting, walking, lying down, and getting up (kinesic); bind ties on their hand and foreheads (arti-factual); and write (written) them out as well (Deut. 6:6–9). In other words, use everything available for offering loving commitment to God; use every signal system that meets the goals of communication. We see God's desire for the people to know him throughout life in ways that foster a broadening involvement and a growing relationship of intimacy with him. We are first of all to love God in ways that are authentic to ourselves.

Yet Jesus, in speaking to the expert of the law in Luke, does not stop with loving God alone. He pushes further into loving our neighbors as we love ourselves. This second command is revolutionary when considering the global arts in Christian witness. When it comes to loving our neighbors in terms of the arts, our goal is to work within a people's cultural, expressive languages (signal systems) in ways that foster loving God with all their heart, soul, strength, and mind. They should not have to use a different set of expressive languages to love him.

Like Jesus, we need to move into a people's culture and work within their expressive languages and signal systems so that the people in that context may come to love God with all their heart, soul, strength, and mind. Then they will know that God loves them as they are—fully created in his own image.

The signal systems have provided us with basic tools for understanding a people and their communication patterns. The next step is to learn how to exegete the music and art cultures of those among whom and with whom

31. Goldingay, *Psalms 42–89*, 700.

we seek to call all peoples to praise and honor him. That is the topic of our next chapter.

Questions for Discussion

1. In what ways are the global arts universal? In what ways are they *not* universal?
2. How do the global arts engage the twelve signal systems?
3. What is the importance of shaping Christian witness and worship in light of culture and the twelve signal systems?

Part 2

ENCOUNTERING CHRIST THROUGH GLOBAL ARTS

3

Exegeting Cultures
through Global Arts

*You mean I can be a Christian and not
have to take on another culture?*

Cultural exegesis is often a missing element in communicating Christ, a lack especially true for music and global arts. As we discuss cultural exegesis, we need to keep two considerations in mind: the psalmist's call for all peoples to praise him and the broader dimensions of Christian witness that go beyond words. These form theological underpinnings for pursuing the exegesis of cultures via a people's artistic practices.

Psalm 67 makes it very clear that God's blessing on his people has a higher purpose. That purpose is to make God's ways and salvation known on earth—among all peoples. As a result, all peoples throughout the world will praise him. This purpose applies not just to the people closest to us, but extends throughout the world. God's desire to be known among all peoples is totally and thoroughly comprehensive. Throughout Psalm 67 we find this inclusiveness of all peoples reiterated.

> May the peoples praise you, God;
>   may all the peoples praise you.
> The land yields its harvest;
>   God, our God, blesses us.
> May God bless us still,
>   so that all the ends of the earth will fear him. (Ps. 67:5–7)

The task of reaching all peoples is expansive and all-encompassing, whether in transnational events that bring people together from all regions of the world or in international cities with their different segments of society. Whether separated by economics and social class or living shoulder to shoulder with other ethnic groups in a bustling urban area; whether living in distinctly separate villages or in uniform suburban towns—all people are included in God's agenda to reach them with his love and salvation. In each and every context and among each and every people, music and the arts play important integrating roles that bond peoples together in ways that foster community and a relationship with God. Music and the arts promote engaging with people; music and the arts promote engaging with God. The two are bound up with each other.

The equation we consider here can be depicted as shown in figure 3.1. In other words, global arts launch experiential spaces wherein expressive languages, in dynamic interplay within their cultural contexts, foster people's engagement with one another and also with God. They serve as vehicles of communication that both reflect a people's culture—their history, values, beliefs, and *ways* of thinking—*and* influence a people's decision-making and lifestyle choices.

Figure 3.1
Global arts: experiencing, expressing, engaging

Global arts + Christian witness

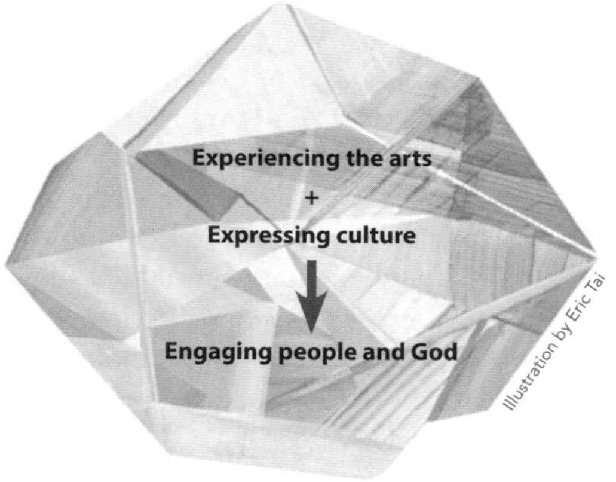

Experiencing the arts
+
Expressing culture

Engaging people and God

Illustration by Eric Tai

What Is Christian Witness?

Christian witness is a matter of communicating Christ. It creates understanding of who Jesus Christ is in ways that allow people to choose to faithfully follow him. Christian witness requires dynamic interaction and a broadening involvement with people in helping them understand God's love for them as mediated through Jesus Christ. Rather than a linear process, it proceeds like a circling spiral toward a growing relationship with the Triune God.

In essence, Christian witness involves both speaking and serving. It entails giving a clear verbal message of the gospel, telling our stories of God's work in our lives, and living in ways that point to the good news of Jesus Christ.[1] Yet we also need to expand the idea beyond the verbal means for communicating the message of the gospel. In addition to the cognitive dimension of our faith, we also need to communicate more intentionally into the affective arena, which works at the deeper levels of our humanity. Often, persuading takes place in the affective arena for what we are processing cognitively. Thus, we need to holistically pursue engaging people through the multiplex of signal systems configured in culturally relevant ways—such as the global arts—ways that make the gospel message distinctly relevant and understandable.

Christian witness is dialogical and interactive. Its ultimate intention is to be transformational. Christian witness begins by listening to the beliefs, faith, and experiences of others. Throughout the process, we are always ready to speak of our own faith, hope, and practices. We achieve this mainly by actively participating with diverse peoples in social contexts, seeking broadening opportunities for not only speaking of but also living out the hope that is within us. When we engage in Christian witness cross-culturally, we are called to take further risks by participating in learning languages—the verbal language plus the full range of expressive languages that foster increased involvement with people. I maintain that the global arts, as expressive languages practiced within their particular cultural contexts, promote opportunities for listening, asking, and interacting with people. In the midst of engagement through the expressive arts of a people, we are relating with them within their own communicative worlds, building trust and credibility as bearers of the gospel message.

The purpose of this chapter is to engage in cultural exegesis of music and the arts as a means of listening to a people's beliefs, faith, and experiences. Such exegesis helps us to understand a people and where they are coming from. It asks, What do we learn about a people through investigating their cultural music and arts? One of the greatest barriers to effective gospel communication worldwide is that the Christian faith comes across as foreign and irrelevant. This often happens because of the ways it comes clothed in Western garb to non-Westerners, or in old-fashioned garb to the younger generation,

---

1. For an excellent development of these practices, see Sunquist, *Understanding Christian Mission*, 281–310.

Figure 3.2
Map of the African continent

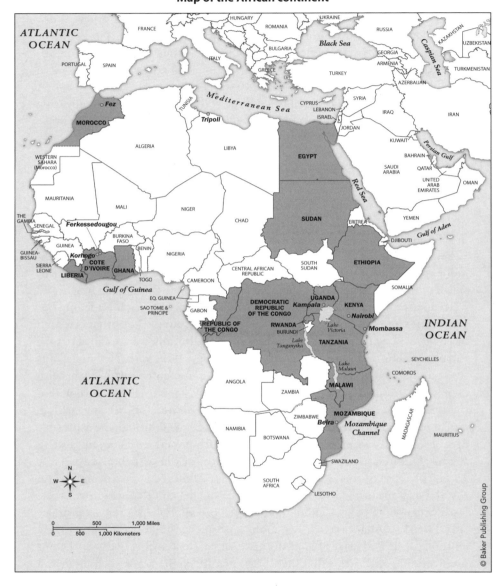

such as millennials and postmillennials in the West. In this chapter I argue
that learning about a people through their cultural arts gives us a means for
understanding them and engaging in effective modes of communication. Issues

of identity and employing culturally appropriate and relevant art forms can lead to people saying, "You mean I can be a Christian and *not* have to deny my culture and people?" I maintain that every culture has differing constellations of art forms that contribute to gaining cultural knowledge about a people, and this knowledge helps us effectively communicate within their world. Here we pursue cultural exegesis through the lens of ethnomusicology, a discipline that investigates the interplay between human creativity and culture.

Come with me now to West Africa, more than a ten-hour flight from Nairobi, to one of the "ends of the earth"—the north of Côte d'Ivoire and a little-known people called the Senufo. This is one of the places where God is making himself known through music and the arts among the far distant villages. It is the place where I have had the longest sustained contact, doing ethnomusicological studies over a period of eighteen years. Here I have also had the privilege to learn from Senufo believers of innovative ways to proclaim God's salvation and declare his glory, and at the same time I have also grown in my faith. Expect to experience a world of music and the arts that contrasts greatly with the Western world yet also offers us insight into Christian witness today in our own contexts.

My Story: The World of Senufo Music and Art in Christian Witness

The small mud-and-thatch house could hardly hold the nine of us. Yet we felt a gentle and accepting rapport among us as we sat on the wooden benches from the village church. One woman, her hairdo taking on the shape of her white scarf, was explaining how songs had helped her in "walking the Jesus road."[2] Suddenly, she lifted her voice and sang one of the believers' songs. The group intuitively sang back the response. I was amazed: all eight Senufo believers were totally caught up in the group interview, talking about the role of Senufo Christian songs in their lives. She cut the song short and explained: "When my heart is troubled and I sing, then I find joy once again. It's the same joy as if one was preaching words from the Bible. Songs really help me!"[3] After three hours of engrossed discussion, I asked to turn off the tape recorder. They granted permission but made one request. Could they please have a copy of the tape? For them, discussing their songs together had been an act of worship.

This woman's experience stands in stark contrast to the early days of mission work among the unreached Senufo. The first evangelical witness among them began in 1947 and was fruitless for the first five years of ministry: not one

2. "Walking the Jesus road" is the Senufo term for following Jesus as a Christian believer.
3. Story adapted from King, *Pathways in Christian Music Communication*, 12.

profession of faith. Like the Catholics who had arrived in 1902, missionaries found the Senufo highly resistant to the gospel. The conundrum appeared to be that new believers would have to leave their fetishes and stop sacrificing to the spirits, a pagan practice that helped them maintain balance in their daily lives.[4] By 1958, though, a small group of Senufo Baptist Christians had started to form, due in part to missionaries' asking for a hearing with local chiefs in ways that respected their traditions. As was typical of so many places, the missionaries introduced Western hymns that were translated into Senari, the language of the Cebaara Senufo.

The worship was terrible, in fact a disaster! The people were not at all at ease with the translated hymns. They sang with great timidity, if at all. Many slept. It was said that "the song service really was quite dead, . . . so, by the time a person got up to preach, he really had lost his congregation."[5] Many preachers concluded that it would be better *not* to sing at all and just go straight into the message. The people could sing *after* the message if they wanted to. In addition to the distasteful, unacceptable sounds of the music, the meanings of the song texts were incomprehensible. The transmitted messages destroyed the intended meaning; they were not communicating anything that made sense to the people. The Senari language is a tone language, in which tones contribute to the meaning of a word. One example of what the people were hearing was "Our Houses Are Cursed Being Sick" rather than the intended text, "Our Dwelling Places Are in Heaven."

The situation became desperate. Finally, one missionary challenged the people at the end of his sermon, "Can't you sing something about what God has done for you?" With that, a believer stood and began singing in their unique call-and-response style. It was amazing to see how immediately "the group just picked up the response. . . . It made your flesh creep." Senufo believers had moved from little or no engagement in the singing to immediate, total involvement. This sparked a spontaneous emergence of new songs that drew from their own music system. The missionary had stumbled on a critical key in Christian witness. He had unknowingly allowed the local believers to tap into their cultural communication patterns. He freed up local believers to develop a song style that overcame the foreignness of the gospel. It allowed them to engage with God and with one another as a faith community; "walking the Jesus road" had moved into Senufo land.

Christian witness was taking place naturally. Not only was the content of the message now comprehensible; they were also developing rites and practices

4. See King, "Stepping Stones toward Senufo Christian Songs."
5. Harold Van den Berg in King, *Pathways in Christian Music Communication*, 64.

that engaged believers and nonbelievers alike. For example, as believers were singing their faith songs in the field, nonbelievers working in the same area found themselves moving closer as they tilled the ground. They just had to hear what the songs were saying. One farmer finally asked where the singers were learning such songs. Invited to a midweek service, he accepted Christ and ultimately became a leading pastor in the region. Meanwhile, the highlight of the annual women's conference became the final night, when the women brought out the new songs that God had given them throughout the year. The new-song event was intended for the women, yet believing and nonbelieving men alike could not stay away. As the lead singer sang out the message and the conference women did their slow, shuffle-like circle dance, the men captured the new songs on cassette recorders to take back to their villages. The songs were on the move throughout the Senufo region.

Two strikingly different practices that emerged and became regular features of church life among the Senufo are *Noéli*, all-night Christmas celebrations that take place in the villages from January to March, and testimony songs of twenty-plus minutes about God's intervention in people's lives. Key to such innovations is the gifting of local artists and musicians, who naturally draw from the cultural stuff, the signal systems of music-making practices acquired over a lifetime. Nɔnyimɛ, a convert and former sorceress, for example, knows Senufo cultural practices at a depth that makes her songs and song-leading profound and powerful. Singing in the open air at *Noéli*, for example, Nɔnyimɛ leads out in her clear, strong voice, at the center of the circle dance that surrounds her in concentric circles. Two or three *balafons* and *njembe* drums lay the multipart sonic foundation, above which she declares her sermon-in-song. With shuffling feet stirring up the dust, while those who want to more precisely hear every word move closer via the rhythmic dance steps, she sings out her message based on shifting pentatonic scales typical of the Senufo. Her song, based on the faith chapter in Hebrews 11, opens with a well-known cultural proverb now applied to the Christian Scriptures. She sings out her opening statement:

> People, grab hold of faith!
> Faith is like an egg. If it escapes and falls, it breaks.
> People, grab hold of faith![6]

She then begins citing from Hebrews 11, noting in particular how God raised up Enoch and how he pleased God. Nɔnyimɛ then begins preaching on

6. King, *Pathways in Christian Music Communication*, 212–13.

how "you cannot please God without faith," and she addresses the sins that local believers are doing that do not please God. These include "looking at the world," "bad behavior," "looking at the good-looking men of the world," and "looking at the beautiful women of the world." After each line, she brings the text back to the proverb "Faith is like an egg" as it becomes the response the people will sing back to her. The response serves as a means of contemplating what she has just preached to them. The credibility of the singer-songwriter is important as she leads out. Nɔnyimɛ, as a singing evangelist who calls people to faith, has a wealth of sociocultural capital. That she is a former sorceress who now walks the Jesus road witnesses to the fact that she no longer lives in bondage to the spirits. It is indeed possible to leave the pagan pathways and walk the Jesus road. She embodies in her presence the hope of freedom from the spirits that hold so many Senufo people hostage. Her life in itself serves as a witness to the power of Jesus Christ over demons and spirits. The power of her conversion combined with her songs of witness draws people from all over the region when they hear that she is going to sing at *Noéli* or be present in Sunday worship. This is incarnational witness through music and the arts at its finest.

"Can't you sing something about what God has done for you?" This simple yet profound question from a desperate missionary had unwittingly tapped into keys for unlocking social structures and their indigenous communication systems through local art forms. The local culture makes its embedded forms readily available for reconfiguration in ways that create understanding and interactive participation with the gospel message. The question asked in desperation also invited Senufo believers into offering meaningful praise to God within their own cultural context. Another "nation" started down the road to praising and worshiping before the Triune God. What can we learn from the Senufo story?

Looking and Learning through an Ethnomusicological Lens

What was going on among Senufo believers that shifted contextualized music and the arts into major methods of Christian witness and resulted in opening up rather than closing off receptivity to the gospel message? Western communication patterns of singing hymns were blatantly ineffective. One could have falsely concluded that the Senufo people were not at all musical.[7] Yet a

---

7. This, in fact, is what happened among a number of the ethnic groups in Kenya. I have had many students who claimed that their people could not sing well. In reality, what they meant is that they did not sing Western hymns and Western music well.

Figure 3.3 Senufo believers praising God in their local context

panoply of music constantly surrounded Western missionaries with the local soundscape of *jegele*, *kaanrige*, and *djembe*-type drums playing all night at funeral ceremonies.[8]

In addition, local visual arts, such as hand-spun, woven cotton cloths with traditional paintings of the spirit world were readily available for accessing the worldview of the people.

Sculptures of masks appeared at key rituals of the *poro*, the Senufo secret society that shapes social norms. Both music-making and visual arts were taking place as a normative feature of life among the Senufo. Due to their lack of knowledge about how to exegete a society via the arts, the missionaries were ignoring, at their peril, what was taking place right under their noses. They falsely assumed that *all* Senufo music and art forms were pagan—as they were, at the time, since the Christian faith had not yet made any inroads into the society. The uninformed conclusion held that they were not redeemable. The watershed moment of asking for the people to sing their own songs,

8. *Jegele* is a Senufo seventeen-key, wood-frame xylophone, known more widely in West Africa as the *balafon*. *Kaanrige* is the metal scraper that defines the basic rhythm in addition to the set of drums, which create sophisticated multipart cross-rhythms.

Photo by Roberta King

Figure 3.4 Senufo images of both their physical world and their worldview, on hand-spun cotton

however, tapped into inherent social structures and communication patterns indigenous to the world of Senufo music and related arts. The missionaries needed a way of learning about a people and making sense of what was going on through music and the arts that would help them meaningfully engage with the people. The lens of ethnomusicology, a discipline just in its infant stages at the time of early witness among the Senufo, offered a means for making sense of what was happening, for gaining understanding of a people. What, then, is distinctive about ethnomusicology and its contribution to exegeting culture?

Ethnomusicology provides perspectives and methods for understanding the intersection between music and culture. Edward T. Hall, a noted cultural anthropologist who pioneered the study of nonverbal communication, argues that "culture hides more than it reveals."[9] The discipline of ethnomusicology specializes in investigating music and related performing arts—that is, music, dance, and drama—in relation to culture at many of the hidden levels. This includes the full gamut of signal systems, verbal and nonverbal communication arenas of any cultural context. Through cultural exegesis of a people's music and art, we can work toward understanding Hall's hidden dimensions of culture that contribute to understanding a people. Ethnomusicology recognizes a constellation of variation found among peoples worldwide and considers all peoples and their musics valid and worthy subjects of inquiry. Timothy

9. Hall, *Silent Language*, 39.

Rice defines ethnomusicology as "the study of why, and how, human beings are musical."[10] He notes that "musical" does not refer to musical ability or talent; "rather it refers to the capacity of humans to create, perform, organize cognitively, react physically and emotionally to, and interpret the meanings of humanly organized sound."[11] In other words, it focuses on people and how they interact with one another via music and the arts within their particular contexts.

The universal aspect of music is that all humans, whether musicians or not, are musical: we all have the capacity to make and understand music. All peoples have some form of music-making that takes place within cultural settings and through which they interact. Ethnomusicology has traditionally focused on studying the social and cultural aspects of music and dance in local and global contexts. In so doing, it recognizes and validates all peoples and their music-making, whether Western or non-Western, whether local, global, or transnational, and whether classical, popular, or urban, as valid and worthy of study. Rice argues that "making music" needs to "include not only playing music but also how people 'make' music perceptually, conceptually, and emotionally, as well."[12] In other words, how are the people interacting with the music and with one another? What are they doing with music and the arts within their very beings and within their societies? These are key considerations in relation to Christian witness. The study of any and all musics has in common a range of methodologies that ethnomusicology employs to do cultural exegesis.[13] Among them we have ethnographical and qualitative research methods drawn from anthropology. Beginning to understand a people through their music can be daunting and overwhelming. The differences may exceed our aesthetic tastes, limitations of musical experience, and understandings about music. Yet music-cultures offer us the observable parts of culture that we can begin to investigate.

The Music-Culture Concept Focuses on How People Are Involved with Music

The concept of a *music-culture* helps us learn what and how people are making music. As Jeff Todd Titon notes, "Musical situations and the very concept of music mean different things and involve different activities around the globe."[14]

10. Rice, *Ethnomusicology*, 1.
11. Rice, *Ethnomusicology*, 1.
12. Rice, *Ethnomusicology*, 6.
13. Stone, *Theory for Ethnomusicology*.
14. Titon, *Worlds of Music*, 4.

Senufo peoples living in the north of Côte d'Ivoire, for example, live a large part of their daily lives out of doors, working in the fields and walking to the market. They have developed music-performance events that take place outside, that do not make great distinctions between performers and the audience, and that require a high degree of participation. It is expected that everyone will join in music-making to some extent, by just hanging out at the event, joining in the dance, and/or responding to the call of the lead singer. Both the women's conference new-song event and the *Noéli* Christmas celebrations reflect this. They organize both time and space in ways familiar to the people and transform cultural practices into culturally appropriate and relevant events. These events take place within their world of music and the arts—on their terms.

The broad concept of music-culture refers to a "group's total involvement with music: ideas, actions, institutions, material objects—everything that has to do with music."[15] This allows us to address questions about the music and all the culturally embedded beliefs and activities associated with it. The Senufo concept of music differs drastically from the Western hymns that had arrived part and parcel with the gospel as transmitted through Western missions. Poorly translated and lyrically incomprehensible words combined with strange and foreign melodic lines to form hymns that promptly put the people to sleep. Senufo songs, on the other hand, are largely made up of complex sets of calls-and-responses based on their own music theory. They incorporate movement and clapping and are usually performed in a circular format. Confining Christian worship to a small rectangular building as brought by Western missionaries did not provide a natural worship setting. Senufo music-culture offered ways in which they felt at home as they interacted with one another through song and dance performed in a circular arrangement. Worship and witness become more effective when they recognize and develop from within a people's music-culture.

Understanding the music-culture concept is critical for practicing effective Christian witness through music and the arts among all peoples. Moving beyond the Senufo, a broad array of music-cultures exists. Some are found among small groups, such as family traditions, or are bounded by a particular community—an ethnicity, a geographical region, or a nation. Other music-cultures can be identified by musical genres, such as a hip hop music-culture, a jazz music-culture, a classical music-culture, a barbershop quartet music-culture, or a popular music-culture. One of the first questions Fuller Theological Seminary students grapple with in my classes is "What is music to you?" The diversity of personal definitions is astounding. It's amazing to

15. Titon, *Worlds of Music*, 4.

hear the range of answers that reveal the multiple music-cultures each student brings with them into the classroom and how they engage with music.

Studying a people's music-culture is vast and complex. We know that all cultures have music. A definition broad enough to encompass music world-wide delineates music as "human sound communication outside the scope of spoken language."[16] When moving into any new cultural context, or even in studying our own music-culture, the first questions we should ask about a particular people's music are these: What is music—in this culture? How do these people define music? What is allowed? What is considered aesthetically pleasing? What are the rules or implicit theories that guide the process of making music? Exegeting music-cultures leads us to understanding music from an insider's perspective and provides a key to effectively communicate and witness.

What follows are selected foundational concepts we need to keep in mind as we exegete culture in order to effectively witness to the gospel. An analysis of the events in the Senufo case study presented in this chapter serves as one example.

Identity is asserted through music. Music is intimately linked with identity. It gives voice to and establishes a people across multiple domains. Music can "signify many aspects of identity, including nationality, place, ethnicity, race, class, religion, and gender."[17] Once Senufo believers began singing culturally appropriate songs, for example, an emerging identity of what it is to be Senufo *and* Christian began to take shape. New ground was opening up. Rather than the gospel vaguely offering something perceived as irrelevant, the underlying message now proclaimed that the Christian faith opened a new pathway for the Senufo. Jesus as the Word made flesh could now move among them. He had become someone they could follow within their own cultural milieu and social structures. Identity asserted through Senufo Christian songs forged a pathway for following Christ. It gave voice where none had previously existed by distinguishing itself from the long-established animistic and folk Islamic paths that reigned in the area. Music thus constructed the identity of a fledgling Christian faith community and acquired layers of meaning through its sound and settings. The multiple channels of text, tune, dance, instrumental practice, and performance style contributed to further layers of meaning. Senufo Christian songs shaped and became a symbol of Christian identity.

Music and the arts most often work in tandem. Music is not always compartmentalized away from other arts. Rather, music and the arts often intertwine and make up constituent parts of what may be considered "music" by

16. Nettl, *Study of Ethnomusicology*, 25.
17. Shelemay, *Soundscapes*, 421.

outsiders to the culture. Even though some music stands alone, it more often incorporates dance, theater, visual arts, and literature in culturally unique ways. This yields a holistic way of dealing with life as it draws from a fuller range of signal systems in a manner of thinking familiar to people. Music in sub-Saharan Africa is most often practiced as the integration of music, dance, and drama. We can also see this in Senufo Christian songs as they continued developing over a period of time. Clapping and dancing—what Western missionaries chose to call the "Christian shuffle"—are distinctive features in Senufo song. They eventually made their way into the believers' performance practices. Research showed that both dancing and clapping were critical features that bore testimony to their faith in the Christian God. In fact, some even indicated that if a believer was *not* dancing or clapping in the midst of sung worship, then there was sin in that person's life. Not dancing or clapping signified a broken relationship with God. The deep function taking place here identifies a Christian believer: people reveal their relationship with God via dancing and clapping. In other words, the music form puts their Christian identity and faith on full display before the community as they are engaging with God in embodied musical worship.

The performance aspects of music-cultures vary from culture to culture. In addition to combining music and related arts in varying configurations, performance styles can also differ. Thomas Turino identifies two contrasting fields of artistic practice: participatory performance and presentation performance. He defines *participatory performance* as "a special type of artistic practice in which there are no artist-audience distinctions, only participants and potential participants performing different roles, where the primary goal is to involve the maximum number of people in some performance role."[18] Participatory performance is the standard practice of the Senufos. They focus on the *doing*, not a final product. Significantly, participatory music-making "leads to a special kind of concentration on the other people one is interacting with through sound and motion and on the activity, in itself and for itself."[19] Participants are establishing and fostering relationship. Such participatory music-dance provides a strong force for social bonding. *Presentation performance*, on the other hand, is more typical of classical art traditions. It refers to situations where "one group of people, the artists, prepare and provide music for another group, the audience, who do not participate in making the music or dancing."[20] Learning to identify differing performance styles

18. Turino, *Music as Social Life*, 26.
19. Turino, *Music as Social Life*, 28.
20. Turino, *Music as Social Life*, 26.

can affect receptivity to the gospel in significant ways. Working within the framework of these two basic styles of performance fosters engaging with people in normative ways that are meaningful to them.

The role of music in daily life, its use and functions, is essential in understanding a people. Throughout this book we have seen that music and the arts are used in multiple ways. Depending on the context, musical situations and events involve different activities worldwide: from work songs to songs that engage a people's life-cycle events, as well as economic, religious, and political occasions. Drawing on these observable parts of music-cultures, we can begin asking questions in order to learn more about a people—their ways of life, needs, and spiritual practices.

Most studies of the use of music are descriptive and based on participant observations of the researcher.[21] The functions of music, however, take place at deeper cultural levels, below the surface. These are those hidden aspects of culture that elude us. Timothy Rice argues that music is not just the product of ordered sound but rather is a "resource in aid of various psychological and social goals." One of its major functions is to "integrate society around common, shared behaviors and values."[22] Learning about the functions of music requires garnering deep-level cultural knowledge and its interpretation. This means relying on the perspectives of "insiders" to help "outsiders" understand what is going on. It requires interviewing the music participants, musicians, and event participants about how they experience and engage with the music.

Vignette 3.1

"What Is Music to You?"

Birdsongs, Heavy Metal, and Classical Orchestral Pieces

I asked students at Fuller Theological Seminary what music was to them. Coming from a Kenyan, a Canadian, and a Korean immigrant, the following three statements reveal diverse, contrasting perceptions, levels of identity, and impact in life.

Music and Birdsongs (Rev. Gideon Mbui, Kenyan MA in Theology graduate)

To me, the meaning of music is as vast as the media, tunes, shapes, and genres in and through which it is expressed. I would say music is any intentionally organized or ordered/streamlined sound/noise. But I still find this definition

21. Miller and Shahriari, *World Music*, 219.
22. Rice, *Ethnomusicology*, 45.

rather limiting, as I am not sure whether birds or other animals such as frogs are intentional in their music-making, yet I consider their noise as a version of music, or at least singing.

I would not claim to have a fixed taste as far as musical genres go; I consider myself quite liberal in my preferences, which range from country, reggae, blues, contemporary (e.g., Congolese Lingala), and folk tunes (rather unconventional rhythms and melodies). To me, whatever genre is pleasant to the ear and fits with the particular mood I find myself in at any particular moment carries the day, particularly if it blends with and enhances my personal times of worship.

Music is central in worship since it helps the worshiper to truly express oneself in a more profoundly authentic manner. Evidently, "music says what cannot be put into words and often adds to words what cannot be merely spoken."[a] And this is true for witness as well.

Music and Heavy Metal (Melody Frost, Canadian MA in Intercultural Studies graduate)

The definition of music is culturally conditioned: "Our own concept of what distinguishes music from noise is more or less the same as that of our overall 'culture,' . . . an environment that conveyed to us general notions about the distinctions between the two."[b] What I, as a Caucasian Canadian woman, have been raised to understand as music varies from what a man from rural Japan, for example, considers music.

My favorite music genre is heavy metal. The genre grew on me during high school after my best friend introduced me to a few bands. I began listening to the likes of Underoath; Oh, Sleeper; Haste the Day; and August Burns Red. What sealed the deal was seeing these bands in concert; the energy and layers of sounds captivated me. When listening to this music, I contemplate beauty, creativity, emotions, theology, the lyrics, or nothing but relaxation.

Music is important in worship and witness because it reaches into the core of a culture and transmits heartfelt expressions to God. Understanding music-cultures, which encompass musical sounds and styles as well as people's engagement with music,[c] is valuable in relational ministry. To appreciate a music-culture is to appreciate how a people can make music unto God.

Music and Classical Orchestral Pieces (MinAh Oh, Korean American Master of Theology student)

To me, music has always been a great tool to express myself. When I first moved to the States, I had a tough time learning the new language and the culture. I often felt isolated, lonely, and depressed because it was so hard for me to make friends and there was nothing that I could control. However, I was able to overcome this difficult period through music. I was able to express as well as discover emotions and feelings that were inexpressible in words. The more I spent time listening to and making music, the more I felt that I belonged and I had a purpose in this world. Years later, when I accepted Christ, I finally realized that music had subconsciously taught me that there is something or someone greater than I. Looking back now, I know God used music in my life to prepare my heart to receive him.

I love classical music, especially orchestral pieces. Orchestral pieces always make me aware of God's beauty, majesty, and harmony. I believe that through music humans can sense truth and reality holistically. It is a gracious gift from God that is an essential element in worship and witness. Miller and Shahriari write, "Music helps us enter our humanity more fully, by embracing the most mysterious things about us and about our lives in time and space."[d] Music is one of the greatest instruments that God has given us to worship him and share his love with others.

[a] Terry E. Miller and Andrew Shahriari, *World Music: A Global Journey* (New York: Routledge, 2006), 8.
[b] Miller and Shahriari, *World Music*, 2.
[c] Roberta R. King, Jean Ngoya Kidula, James Krabill, and Thomas Oduro, eds., *Music in the Life of the African Church* (Waco: Baylor University Press, 2008), 7.
[d] Miller and Shahriari, *World Music*, 18.

This is especially true of researching music's functions in religious and spiritual realms. Ethnomusicologists have noted that "humans seem to believe nearly everywhere that singing, over and above ordinary speech, is necessary to communicate with gods, ancestors, and spirits."[23] Again, we found this happening among the Senufo. The people expected to interact spiritually through song. As I investigated the role of culturally appropriate songs among the Senufo, for example, to my amazement I discovered that their Christian songs function "like the Word of God." This major discovery happened because part of my research included working with singer-songwriters in setting Scripture to song. The newly composed songs moved quickly among the believers. The response to the songs revealed that they functioned like the Word of God in three ways (see fig. 3.5).

First, the people spoke of how the songs are instructional by telling how they "teach us to the depths of our hearts" and "counsel and advise" us. Second, they "bring back joy" when one's "heart is troubled or they are distressed."

23. Rice, *Ethnomusicology*, 48.

Figure 3.5
How Senufo songs function like the Word of God

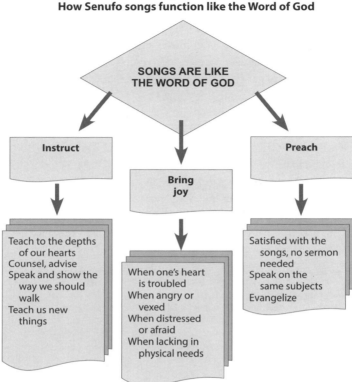

From Roberta King, *Pathways in Christian Music Communication: The Case of the Senufo of Côte d'Ivoire* (Eugene, OR: Pickwick, 2009), 184 (fig. 22). Used by permission of Wipf and Stock Publishers. www.wipf andstock.com.

Finally, the songs "preach!" Once they have sung songs based on Scripture, they are satisfied and have no need of a sermon!

Musical instruments play symbolic roles of integration and identity formation. The huge variety of musical instruments throughout the ages has played critical roles in "how people make music meaningful and useful in their lives."[24] Here it is important to recognize scriptural precedents of musical instruments playing integral roles in the lives of God's peoples as found in both the Old and New Testaments. Two stories of the origins of musical instruments come from Genesis. First, Jubal, the son of Cain, is identified as "the father of all who played stringed instruments and pipes" (Gen. 4:21). The second instance stems from Jewish tradition, in which, in the story of the binding of Isaac (Gen.

24. Wade, *Thinking Musically*, 27.

22), Abraham finds that the horns of the ram God provided for the sacrifice were left behind. Tradition has it that Abraham rescued these horns and made them into the *shofar*, which became the Jewish people's central ritual instrument. Philip Bohlman notes that "the sounding of the *shofar* gives meaning to time and history, and it sonically represents Jewish identity, which remains traceable even today to the first musicians in *Genesis*."[25] Furthermore, Psalm 150 includes a taxonomy of Jewish instruments that calls on the sounding of the trumpet, harp, lyre, timbrel, strings, pipe, and clashing/resounding cymbals to join in the grand crescendo of praise to the Lord. The breadth of cultural instruments implies that all are purposed to praise the Lord.

The use of musical instruments in Christian witness and worship has provoked numerous areas of contention, in both the Western and non-Western worlds. Not only do they sonically represent a people's identity and give meaning to time and history, but they also carry spiritual associations. In non-Christian contexts, instruments are used to "give voice to a sacred spirit"[26] and sometimes invoke spirits as part of a people's worship. This raises theological questions surrounding redeeming musical instruments found within such societies. Senufo believers went through a process of discussing whether or not the *balafon*, culturally associated with pagan worship, was acceptable. Slowly they began incorporating the *balafon* as a regular part of their Christian worship and witness. They began with only one *balafon*, and over a period of time added two more, typical of cultural music ensembles in the region. I will address more of the issues surrounding redeeming musical instruments later. It is interesting to note here that the term *balafon* literally means "the wood that speaks." Ultimately, Senufo believers adapted and redeemed their *balafons* for "speaking" the gospel with enhanced clarity.

Doing Musical Ethnography as a Practice of Christian Witness

By entering the world of Senufo music and art via the lens of ethnomusicology, we have demonstrated key perspectives that help us analyze and begin to understand how peoples engage with one another, how they make music meaningful, and how music functions as a means of identity formation, social integration, bonding, and multivocal communication. Experiencing music and the arts provides numerous opportunities for bearers of the gospel to engage with people as a major means of witnessing to Jesus Christ. In other words, investigating and learning about cultural musics and related arts *is* communication; it *is* Christian witness.

25. Bohlman, *World Music*, 10.
26. Wade, *Thinking Musically*, 38.

Historically, missionaries understood this concept as early as 1578, when the Huguenot missionary Jean de Léry studied the music of the Tupinambá living in the region of what is known today as the Bay of Rio de Janeiro. Motivated by missionary zeal, he studied the music of the Tupinambá, transcribed their melodies and texts used in specific rituals, and worked at fleshing out the contexts of those rituals.[27] In the process of studying the people's music, Léry discovered himself "growing closer to the music of the Tupinambá, undergoing an aesthetic conversion of his own, from an initial stage in which Tupinambá songs were meaningless to a point in which he felt a closeness, even a recognizable kinship."[28] Bohlman surmises that Léry underwent a transformation of his person. Through studying the music of the local people, Léry modeled and set up a means for gaining broadening involvement with a people, a major goal of effectively communicating the gospel. He likewise demonstrated how to go about learning the insider's perspective, and in the process, he himself was identifying with people. In doing so, he demonstrated God's love and affirmation of the Tupinambá as a people.

Léry models for us the process and effects of becoming bimusical. Becoming *bimusical*, a goal in ethnomusicological research, helps one gain entry to a people, bonding and moving one closer in relationship. It means understanding a people and their music-making more from an insider's (emic) perspective. Furthermore, as ethnomusicologists have learned, "successful fieldwork is impossible without the friendship and cooperation of those with whom ethnomusicologists study."[29] Learning about a people by studying their music builds relationships with people at levels not attained through the mere exchange of words. It provides excellent beginning contact points and builds sustainable friendships for doing mission and ministry over a longer period of time.

Musical ethnography, discovering and documenting a world of music,[30] is one of the hallmarks of the discipline of ethnomusicology. While the ideal is to spend long periods of time living among a people, building trust and friendship, and learning the local language and music-making, scholars have begun recognizing that the methods involved can also be practiced in our own backyards. Thus, the method can be applied in any context where music-making takes place. Music events, such as weddings, funerals, and festivals, present occasions for doing participant observation and informal interviews that engage people and allow you to discover how they are assigning meaning

27. Bohlman, *World Music*, 2.
28. Bohlman, *World Music*, 3.
29. Rice, *Ethnomusicology*, 43.
30. Titon uses the phrase "world of music" as a synonym for the music-culture concept. See Titon, *Worlds of Music*, 1–34.

to the music and how it functions in their lives. Documenting and keeping a log of all the music you hear, recording audio and video, and describing an event—all contribute to understanding a people in the midst of daily life.

Musical ethnography can also pursue the study of rituals, including religious rituals. Within any music event are some key components to observe, document, and participate with. These include (1) the musical sound itself; (2) the performers—including singers, instrumentalists, and dancers; (3) the audience; and (4) the time and space of the event.[31] Observing the twelve signal systems in a music event helps to guide observations and document music events, including Christian worship worldwide. Christian witnesses, including short-term and especially long-term missionaries, have excellent opportunities for conducting deep-level, sustained research that can make a difference in kingdom issues.

Conclusion

Ethnomusicology and doing musical ethnography are valuable for ministry in the way they look beyond musical sounds to explore how a people relate to music and what it means for their society. Ethnomusicology provides exegetical tools for learning about a people's beliefs and faith, and how they experience life. By looking at music through a Christian ethnomusicological lens, one can enter a ministry context and better understand how the gospel will be best received. It is also an essential part of translating the gospel story into meaningful, contextualized worship and witness. We turn next to the role of the arts in translating the message, which includes translating the biblical text into accessible forms by using a people's expressive languages.

Questions for Discussion

1. What can we learn about a people by researching their cultural music and arts?
2. Identify three core concepts from ethnomusicology that affect how we communicate Christ through the global arts. What are their implications for Christian witness?
3. Watch the first five minutes of the movie *African Queen*, starring Humphrey Bogart and Kathryn Hepburn (available on YouTube). Discuss where and how similar cultural gaps might be taking place today.

31. For an excellent introduction to doing musical ethnography, see Titon and Reck, "Discovering and Documenting a World of Music."

4

Translating the Message
via Global Arts

What do the arts have to do with translating
biblical texts for diverse contexts?

Ever since the disciples sang with Jesus in the upper room, music and the arts have played significant roles in translating the gospel message. First-century Christians did not stop speaking their language, nor did they stop fully participating in their cultural practices. Rather, they translated their newfound faith into the cultural languages and practices available to them. The apostle Paul, for example, demonstrates the natural extension of drawing from all languages of communication available within local cultural contexts when he advises the Colossians, "Let the message of Christ dwell among you richly as you teach and admonish one another with all wisdom through psalms, hymns, and songs from the Spirit" (Col. 3:16). He further emphasizes the arts as communication vehicles when telling the Ephesians to "be filled with the Spirit, speaking to one another with psalms, hymns, and songs from the Spirit" (Eph. 5:18–19). Paul considered it a normal practice to communicate God's message translated into multiple cultural forms. Lamin Sanneh argues that "the disciples came to a clear and firm position regarding the translatability of the gospel"[1] into all spoken and expressive cultural languages for

1. Sanneh, *Translating the Message*, 1.

the sake of God's purposes. In other words, the gospel message is universal, and every culture is valid and worthy of receiving the gospel translated into its own cultural languages. As the apostle Paul demonstrated, full cultural translations of the gospel, including music and the arts, form part of becoming a *new creation*. The translatability of the gospel extends beyond words to the expressive languages—music and art—of every culture.

The purpose of this chapter is to demonstrate how the global arts, as cultural texts, complement and expand translation of the biblical text in ways that enhance, clarify, and undergird its message. The gospel message is universal, but the ways in which God's message is communicated will vary according to cultural languages in diverse contexts, as verbal, written, and expressive languages dynamically interact with and support one another. Translating the biblical text must go beyond verbal and written translations alone. A more comprehensive translation extends into the expressive languages of a culture. Spoken and written languages are only two of the twelve signal systems functioning within a culture. Joining together as allies in translating the message of the gospel fosters increased receptivity to the gospel. It dramatically enhances Christian witness. We first address the translatability of the psalms as found originally in the Old Testament and their continuation into the twenty-first century, followed by an extended case study in translating the Scriptures among the Senufo via a New Song workshop.

Translatability of the Message: Cultural Texts and the Psalms

The translatability of God's interaction into human contexts extends to both the verbal/written texts and the cultural texts of each people group. The term "cultural text" here is used to distinguish music and the arts from verbal/written texts as a means of discussing the translatability of the message in more expansive ways.[2] In this section, we will consider the psalms in contrasting contexts: first, the original Old Testament context and, second, these psalms in two different twenty-first-century globalized contexts.

---

2. While language and culture are intimately linked, I am distinguishing cultural texts from verbal/written texts in order to address expressive languages so interlinking the form and the message that they become a "text" of their own. Meaning lies in how people interpret the message and the form interwoven together. Or, as Marshall McLuhan first proposed, "The medium is the message." There is a symbiotic relationship between the message and the medium, such as song and art forms. The "medium embeds itself in any message" that is transmitted and thus influences how the message is perceived. See "The Medium Is the Message," Wikipedia, updated February 24, 2018, https://en.wikipedia.org/wiki/The_medium_is_the_message.

The Psalms in the Old Testament

The psalms, as we have observed earlier, serve as models for dynamic expressions of interacting with Yahweh. In his call for singing a new song, the psalmist is translating lived experiences with God into his local cultural art form. As one of the major outcomes, the new song witnesses to God's involvement in a people's life.[3] The psalmist states it succinctly when he declares,

> He put a new song in my mouth,
>   a hymn of praise to our God.
> Many will see and fear the LORD
>   and put their trust in him. (Ps. 40:3)

Here we see that new songs arise out of life experiences. They provide a means for people to declare and testify to what they have gone through. The depth of the experience calls for incorporating more than just words. A new song also moves the experience from a personal one into the public domain for all to hear. People have a deep desire not only to express themselves, but also to share their story in ways that will affect others. The psalms translate the story into a cultural form, a new song, that heightens and intensifies the weight of the story. We find this in Psalm 40:1–3, where the psalmist boldly declares how God intervened in his life. He cried out to God with great intensity. God listened and rescued him out of extremely difficult circumstances. Amazingly, he has found himself on firm ground in a new place. The new song becomes "a sign of new orientation"[4] that holds a new understanding of God's trustworthiness. The psalmist cannot contain his joy. He credits God for putting a new song in his mouth. It is a song of witness that will cause others to take note, come to see who this God is, and put their trust in him. In the psalms, new songs bear witness to God's faithful interaction with humanity. As newly translated cultural texts, which interlink form and message, the songs move beyond their original private source into the public domain. They establish a broadened foundation for enhanced witness to God's intervening in the life of his people.

The Psalms in the Twenty-First Century

The translatability of the psalms continues on into the twenty-first century. It is taking place in smaller, monocultural peasant societies, in multicultural

---

3. The psalms regularly reference new songs and challenge us to also sing new songs (see Pss. 96:1; 98:1).
4. Brueggemann, *Message of the Psalms*, 128.

cities, and in transnational contexts with an incredible plethora of language groups. In each people group, important dialogical partnerships take place when verbal, written, and expressive languages work in tandem with one another to translate the message. For example, in Kampala, the capital city of Uganda, high-level, young professionals come together for weekend retreats to compose songs that draw from their cultural roots. They are fluent in the international popular music played on FM music stations out of the United Kingdom. They know and sing contemporary Christian music, Western hymns, and pan-African Scripture choruses. Yet all these do not fully satisfy their thirst for singing praise to God in their own musical mother tongues—with songs that are culturally rooted. There comes a moment in their gatherings when they say to each other, "Now take me home!" This pivotal moment means that they then sing their faith in their own musical language and worship God in ways in which they find themselves at home. They enter into a process of doing their own cultural translations for singing their adoration to God. They want to extend the musical menu to include deeper levels of their identity.

A transnational example is the partnership forged between Eugene Peterson, the translator of *The Message*,[5] and Bono, international rock star and lead singer for the Irish band U2. Although they have worked independently from each other, they both are translators in their distinctive areas of specialty. Peterson translates on the written language level, while Bono translates Peterson's newly translated psalms into a global cultural form, rock music. The dynamic, fresh expressions contained in Peterson's translations of the psalms resonate with Bono and U2 on deeper levels than they previously experienced. The psalm translations speak to them on a heart level. The band has incorporated the reading of the psalms as a regular part of their preconcert ritual; this encourages them as they go into concert stadiums packed with thousands of people. They compose "new songs," based on various psalms, that are contemporary musical translations (cultural texts) and make up part of their concert repertoire. The new songs, as dynamic expressions of Christian experiences, reach out and witness to a vast, international audience.

Bono and Peterson each delight in the other's work. Bono acknowledges that the psalms had not spoken to him so poignantly until he read Peterson's translations in *The Message*. Peterson, on the other hand, delighted in U2 songs such as "Forty," a translation of Psalm 40. Peterson happily notes that "Bono is singing to the very people I did this work for. I feel that we are allies in this. He is helping get me and *The Message* to the very people Jesus spent

---

5. *The Message* is a modern English paraphrase of the Scriptures.

much of his time with."[6] In this way translating the biblical text becomes an ally with cultural translation beyond spoken language, leading to the creation of new songs that resonate with younger generations in deep ways. U2's new songs enter into the globalizing world of rock music and speak through the expressive languages embedded in global culture.

But this is not all. Bible translation of the Scriptures into mother tongues needs to be addressed more directly. While the globalizing world is spinning with multitudes of possibilities to find commonness, a plethora of diverse language groups around the world have no translation. Missiologists project that translating the Scriptures will continue into the future, with the availability of translated Scriptures into local languages and related literacy movements constituting major ways that the kingdom is spread.[7] The process of translating the Scriptures in settings where they have never been translated is complex. In the translation process, linking arms between the Scriptures and the arts creates alliances that generate holistic and more comprehensive translations. Each benefits the other. In order to understand the complexity of the process, we return to the Senufo peoples of Côte d'Ivoire. Having done an initial exegeting of culture through the arts, as discussed in the previous chapter, major work still remains to make the gospel message available to the people in ways that profoundly affect them.

My Story: A Case of Bible Translation and the Arts

They insisted! They wanted to sing the Scriptures in *their* musical mother tongue, their "heart music."[8] I could hardly believe that I was back in Côte d'Ivoire again. I had worked with the Cebaara Senufo over a period of five years and figured the Cebaara could continue on without me. But now, the Nyarafolo Senufo[9] believers, perhaps fifteen to twenty in number, wanted not only to work on translating the Scriptures into the vernacular, but also

---

6. Fuller Studio, "Bono and Eugene Peterson on the Psalms," accessed May 17, 2018, https://fullerstudio.fuller.edu/bono-eugene-peterson-psalms.

7. Sunquist, "Historian's Hunches," 285.

8. Heart music can be defined as "the musical system that a person learns as a child or youth and that most fully expresses his or her emotions. A person's heart music may include several different music systems." Brian Schrag and Paul Neeley, quoted in "What Is Your Heart Music?," *International Council of Ethnodoxologists*, November 16, 2017, https://www.worldofworship.org/library/what-is-your-heart-music.

9. The Senufo-speaking peoples of West Africa are spread across the north of Côte d'Ivoire, southeast Mali, southwestern Burkina Faso, and along the Ghana–Côte d'Ivoire border. Thirteen distinct languages comprise what is generically referred to as the Senufo language. See King, *Pathways in Christian Music Communication*, 51.

to worship and praise God through their own Nyarafolo songs, in their own culturally rooted song styles. They had been singing the Cebaara Christian songs and found that they did not clearly communicate the Christian message. Two main reasons topped the list: First, the translation team had discovered the tone system of the Nyarafolo language worked in ways opposite from the Cebaara tonal system. This meant that the verbal message of the songs, when wed with the Cebaara melodies, made the songs simply unintelligible for the Nyarafolo. Second, my new Nyarafolo friends said there was a "sweetness"[10] in their own songs that was lacking in the Cebaara songs.

Translating the gospel message meant translating not only their spoken mother tongue, but also their cultural forms, their expressive languages. They could not compartmentalize language from their expressive languages. They wanted to work within their own music-culture. As the invited outsider, I could not yet distinguish between Cebaara and Nyarafolo music; it all sounded "Senufo" to me. Here was an opportunity to collaborate together and investigate further into the song-making process. And so we began a journey that took us into unexplored regions of translating the Bible and cultural arts.

Together we developed New Song Fellowships—a process for groups to compose new songs based on newly translated Scriptures. We started by bringing together the Nyarafolo believers for a New Song workshop. They settled on an adapted storytelling song form suited to narrating Scripture passages in a call-and-response form, similar to the Cebaara. In the first workshop we recorded twelve new songs based on one to two verses from the Scriptures.

Amazingly, this small beginning, with only a dozen songs, made a huge impact and over the course of the year revealed the power of translating both the biblical text and the musical style. The songs began to be known in town. On one occasion, for example, a song was needed to sing at a flag-raising ceremony, a new custom for the small town of Ferkessedougou. Someone suggested singing one of the new songs from the Nyarafolo believers. After it was sung, the local townspeople exclaimed, "Tchieh! You mean the god you are singing about is for us? We thought he belonged to the Cebaara!" Witness to the good news had started making inroads into the world of the Nyarafolo through composing new cultural songs based on translated Scripture. Bible translation and the arts were working hand in hand in meaningful ways and gaining new territory. Nyarafolo identity as believers in Christ had gained a foothold in the local setting.

Over the years, my missionary colleagues and I learned that local translation teams and New Song Fellowships share in many similar tasks. They

10. "Sweetness" is the Senufo aesthetic equivalent for "beauty" in the West.

work hand in hand, contributing to each other for meaningful communication among a people. Linnea Boese, the translation team leader, explains: "The Bible translator faces two distinct challenges while searching for the right expression to effectively communicate a concept. One is to clearly describe a completely foreign notion; the other is to effectively reveal a connection between what comes from so long ago and far away to ideas currently held by the receptor people."[11]

Finding connections between foreign concepts and currently held ideas became particularly evident in the midst of a Nyarafolo New Song Fellowship workshop focused on the Abrahamic narrative, Genesis 12–22. Journey back with me to listen in on some of the deep theological processing that took place.

Vignette 4.1

Abraham's Sacrifice and Nyarafolo Drums
(It's about Worship)[a]

Roberta R. King

It is Ramadan in Ferkessedougou, Côte d'Ivoire, a season of all-day fasting for Muslims.[b] The local soundscape is a swirl of pulsating, throbbing rhythms of the famed Senufo wood-framed *balafons* piercing the evening air and signaling all-night funerals.[c] They play in counterpoint with a pair of *njembe* drums. Add in the bleating of goats assembled in the town square awaiting their sacrificial role at the celebration of *tabaski*, the Muslim version of the story of Abraham and his son Ishmael (rather than Isaac). Motorcyclists, returning home from a long day of work in the fields, layer a droning buzz to the growing swell of sound. The multisensory atmosphere of music, life, and ritual provide an amazing backdrop for the ten-day New Song workshop. Some thirty-five Senufo believers from the Nyarafolo, the Minyanka, the Djimini, and the Shenara gather in this multicultural West African town. They are eager to begin and declare, "We are here to learn how to sing in the language of our ethnic group. We are thirsty for it; we know that we have great richness there."[d]

Scene 1

The daily composition process begins as they hear the newly translated Scriptures read and explained. The four groups discuss the text together as they

11. Linnea E. Boese, "Canaanite, Israelite and Nyarafolo Worldviews: A Meeting of the Minds in the Pentateuch" (unpublished essay, Plymouth, Michigan, 2005), 1.

seek to make sense of the new concepts before dividing into language groups to make their own songs.

The group discussion centers on Genesis 12:1–3. We focus on God's blessing in contrast to Senufo concepts of blessing. The participants explain, "Blessings [in our culture] come from family, older ones. It's a prayer to ask God to cover them with good(s)."

Yusuf, a Shenara from Mali, continues:

> To get the blessings, you have to satisfy the desires of your parents (relatives). You have to respect the parents. Other gods, spirits, give blessings and curses. They can do good and bad. They also demand that you respect them, do as they say. We have more fear of God, because he can make you die. . . . [We] don't want a bad relation with him.

Moïse, a Nyarafolo, then takes it one step further:

> When we were born, we were told we had to follow our parents; doing that was God's way, and no other way could replace it. But in [God's] Word it shows that our parents' way and God's way are different. Worshiping the spirits, as our parents did, there is no blessing there, although our parents think that there is. . . . We want to make it clear in our songs that God's blessings is not like that, to make life bad for us and take away our joy.

A shift in the understanding of God's blessing in the people's lives has taken place.

Scene 2

A few days later, the discussion centers on how the Nyarafolo culture appears to surface in Scripture when Sarai sends Hagar to Abram (Gen. 16).

Moïse: Sarai did not stay proud, but did what she could to be helpful.
Abdulai: Yes, she did a good thing, a selfless thing!
Sikatchi (a Nyarafolo): God must have worked powerfully in her heart so that she could have this attitude!

After much discussion, they begin to change their minds. . . .

Moïse: Sarai wanted to help arrange things for God, whereas God was able to take care of things himself!
Sikatchi: The Nyarafolo custom is much like this. It's scandalous to see in the Bible. The custom is that if a woman gives another woman to her husband, usually the woman becomes the titular wife and the other

is chased away—How did a Nyarafolo custom get into the Bible? Whose culture came first—the Israelites' or the Nyarafolos'?[e]

Scene 3

Another day, the discussion turns to "pagan" versus "Christian" instruments. In the midst of doing cultural translation, while interacting with the Scriptures, key questions and assumptions are raised.

Yusuf: We have many drums but are not authorized to use them all in church. . . . Sometimes they are used for worshiping a certain fetish; also used for encouragement in agriculture [fields, millet harvest]; so they are taken as "worldly," to be abandoned. . . .

Moïse: There is a Christian dance that is approved [called] *tirer-revenir*, *samak-abo*. Other dances are not approved. . . . What is a truly Christian dance? . . .

Sikatchi: Were some instruments used to praise God before they became worldly, or vice versa?

Yusuf: What is the origin of instruments?

Scene 4

Later in the workshop week, the most profound biblical lesson emerges. With the bleating of the goats ringing out on the other side of the wall reminding us of the Muslim story of Abraham, the four language groups hear a new chapter in the biblical story of Abraham for the first time, each in their own language. Their encounter of Abraham of the Old Testament confronts and challenges their deeply held notions of God. They understand immediately that a sacrifice is required as Abraham goes up the mountain with Isaac. At first, they outright refuse to set this part of the story to song; they cannot bring themselves to witness to a god who demands such an abhorrent act.

Moïse, the lead Nyarafolo translator, comments: "One expects that [kind of awful command] from the 'charlatans' and other fetishers but not from God!"

Surely, this cannot be the same God of the New Testament that they have come to know and revere. Yet, amazingly, before knowing the end of the story, they reason that it is God's Word that they are hearing. They must remain obedient to him and reluctantly agree to continue with the story as they negotiate for understanding more about God. What could be happening that God would require such a detestable act?

Moïse explains how the discussion progressed: "When the substitute sheep is provided, the testing finally makes sense, and it is understood that God is not bound by our ideas in the kinds of testing he may send our way. The tension in the story, the way Abraham does not fully reveal the purpose of the trip to his son, also strikes at the heart; people do not want division between father and son. So, the resolution is very comforting."

Yet the Nyarafolo also ask: "Why would God wait until the very last minute? Then one sees that it was a test of whether Abraham truly feared God, how far his faith would go. . . . Abraham's binding of Isaac on the altar shows that he has chosen God, . . . trusting him."

The significance of God providing the sacrificial sheep does not escape them. This is indeed *something new*; they conclude that a musical equivalent that adequately matches and supports the profound implications of the story is required. The song calls for everyone to listen to this *new thing* about God that they have just recently come to understand. It touches them to such a depth that they hark back to their deepest indigenous song roots. Text and tune emerge together with an authenticity that grounds them in their Senufo worlds.

Abraham Took His Son and Went to the Mountain
(Composed by KONE Nayergue Moïse)

Call: He took his son and went to the mountain,
Abraham took his son and went to the mountain.
Response: Abraham took his son and went to the mountain.

Call: This is something new; men and women, listen!
Response: Abraham took his son and went to the mountain.

Call: So they started the walk along [the path]. When they had gone a long way, Isaac said, "Father Abraham, please let me ask:
I ask you, where is the fire? I ask you, where is the knife?"
Response: Abraham took his son and went to the mountain.

Call: Abraham said, "My son Isaac, be quiet, and let's go on.
God will provide the sheep."
Response: Abraham took his son and went to the mountain.

Call: When they arrived—listen, my friends!—
This is a new thing, listen: Abraham tied up Isaac!
Response: Abraham took his son and went to the mountain.

Call: And God said to Abraham, "Don't kill the child!
Abraham, let your son go! Today I know that you fear me."
Response: Abraham took his son and went to the mountain.

Call: So, Abraham seized the sheep; he caught the sheep and killed it to worship God.
Response: Abraham took his son and went to the mountain.

Call: My dear ones, come! If God talks to you,
accept what he says, listen to him!
Response: Abraham took his son and went to the mountain.[f]

The lyrics explain *something new* about God that needs to be heard and understood. Translation specialist Linnea Boese notes how the thematic chorus "resonates immediately with the Nyarafolo worldview: men do take a son to a mountain to offer sacrifice to a god. The song show[s] faith in the High God. Nyarafolos do not sacrifice to him, only to lesser ones that seem interested in their affairs. . . . The message was clear: Yahweh is to be worshiped!"[g] But the song-composing process cannot stop with just the text. They need to draw more deeply from the Nyarafolo music-culture in order to adequately communicate the significance of the story. They turn to the issue of rhythm and musical instruments.

Although the Nyarafolos have attained a genuine Nyarafolo song style, they are still borrowing the seventeen-key Cebaara *balafon* (see fig. 2.2) that has become a part of Christian worship in the area. This *balafon*, however, is not compatible with the melody and text. The teaching of the song is so profound that they first search for a rhythm adequate enough to communicate the depth plumbed by the story.

> Reaching back to traditional Nyarafolo music, the group decides on a particular rhythm played on the traditional drums called *pire* (Nyarafolo drums used for agricultural competitions). Not yet having such a drum available to them, they borrow *djembes* to get the needed accompaniment. The group participants are really excited during the workshop to compose a song that reaches further into their particular ethnic music. Through it, deeper significance and weight pervades the performance of the song, speaking powerfully in combined verbal and nonverbal dimensions that Yahweh is drawing even closer into their world with a very important message.[h]

When the traditional *pire* drums were finally obtained, Boese observed that "Nyarafolo music came alive. Whenever they sang at an event, a crowd would gather. Nyarafolos said, 'This group is bringing back our music!' Suddenly the demand for Nyarafolo gospel music increased dramatically."[i]

[a] Adapted from Roberta R. King, "Toward a Discipline of Christian Ethnomusicology: A Missiological Paradigm," *Missiology: An International Review* 32 (2004): 293–307.

[b] A large portion of the Senufo people follow Muslim teachings, first introduced as early as the sixteenth century. See Karen Faye Willetts, "The Senoufo: The Tiembara of Korhogo" (unpublished manuscript; Advanced Ethnology: International Linguistics Center, 1979), 10.

[c] A *balafon* is a seventeen- to twenty-one-key xylophone set on a wood frame, held with a strap over the shoulders of the player, who is free to walk and move while playing.

[d] Linnea Boese, "Fieldnotes from the Abraham New Song Workshop" (Ferkessedougou, Côte d'Ivoire, 2002), 1. The workshop was conducted in French with simultaneous translation into the four participating Senufo languages. The fieldnotes are a compilation of these discussions by my

colleague Linnea Boese, who drew on her knowledge of both Nyarafolo and French and finally translated them into English.

ᵉ Linnea Boese, "Fieldnotes," 3.

ᶠ In writing about musical examples, it is difficult to offer a full experience of the music without audio components. For a fuller understanding of Nyarafolo music, see the webography under "Côte d'Ivoire."

ᵍ Linnea Boese, email correspondence with author, October 24, 2016.

ʰ Roberta R. King, "Encountering Abraham in Africa," in *Conversations at the Edges of Things: Reflections for the Church in Honor of John Goldingay* (Eugene, OR: Pickwick, 2012), 142–53, here 152.

ⁱ Linnea Boese, email correspondence with author, October 24, 2016.

So, What's Going on Here?

The "Abraham's Sacrifice and Nyarafolo Drums" case of Bible translation and the arts (music) exemplifies the close, interdependent linkage of music, language, and culture. As far back as the fifth century, the Roman philosopher Boethius wrote, "Music is so naturally united with us that we cannot be free from it even if we so desired."[12] Boethius's argument rings true today as well. Cultural music and the arts work in tandem with meaningful translation of the Christian message, each one contributing to the other. They connect closely in meaningful translation of biblical Scriptures and simultaneously influence the cultural translation process of composing contextualized songs and art forms that deepen and expand dynamic communication of the gospel message. In this case, translation is taking place on at least three levels: (1) translating the biblical text, (2) translating cultural texts, and (3) translating for transformed relationships. Let's consider how this was working itself out in the midst of the Abraham story.

Translating the Biblical Text

In the midst of translation, a toggling always occurs between the original, "outside" text and the local concepts already within the receiving cultural context. "Language and culture," Lamin Sanneh notes, "are essential aspects of Christian transmission, especially where these interact with the themes of cross-cultural appropriation"[13] in diverse contexts. In other words, one must find the appropriate terms within the receiving people's cultural context in order to achieve understanding. Newly translated Scripture texts require back translations[14] in order to check what is understood. Back translations check

12. Quoted in Storr, *Music and the Mind*, 8.
13. Sanneh, *Translating the Message*, 1.
14. The practice of translating back into the original language to check for accuracy of meaning.

Photo by Linnea Boese

Figure 4.1 Nyarafolo traditional *pire* drum ensemble

how the receptors interpret what they are hearing or reading. The New Song Fellowship workshop provides spaces for processing the biblical text on more than just a cursory level. Of particular note is the group discussion of the text that allows for the surfacing of multiple meanings and deeply embedded cultural terms, perspectives, and practices.

Music-making and the arts make a major contribution to the translation process by discovering culturally significant key terms for shaping and nuancing translation of the biblical text. For example, in composing the song based on Abraham taking Isaac up the mountain (Gen. 22), three key terms surfaced, each heavily loaded with cultural significance in Nyarafolo thought and customs: mountain, sacrifice,[15] and sheep. They view the key term "mountain" (*nyagurugo*), for example, in a way similar to Hebrew thought. "It connotes strength and protection, due to being seen as high and hard (a rock), and

15. "Almost every people group in Africa seems to have had some form of traditional sacrificial system. . . . The animal . . . had to be carefully chosen. . . . The animal offered had to be of a uniform colour. While the exact colour preferred differed from group to group, black, red and white were the most common colours for sacrificial animals. . . . The animal needed to be perfect in every respect, with no birth defects or injuries." Samuel Ngewa in Adeyamo, *Africa Bible Commentary*, 1502.

is the most important of the various places where sacrifices are made."[16] A mountain is naturally seen as a place where one can have connection with the spiritual world. Upon hearing that a father and son are taking fire and wood to a mountain, the Nyarafolo listener immediately understands that a sacrifice will take place.[17] Sacrifices are practiced daily among Senufo peoples in order to gain equilibrium with the spirit world. Thus, they immediately pick up the implications. Finally, in a truly important sacrifice, as opposed to lesser sacrifices, they regard a sheep as the animal to use.[18]

Additionally, the New Song creative group process fosters negotiating for understanding the new concepts and how God's Word relates to them. As the storytelling builds, the implicit expectation of what is to come builds tension as the text confronts local concepts about God and misperceptions about biblical passages—for example, Abraham and Isaac in light of contrasting Muslim traditions practiced in their local cultural rituals. As Kwame Bediako argues, "Scripture and culture are like merging circles, gradually coming to have one centre as we increasingly recognize ourselves in Scripture and Scripture becomes more and more recognizable as our story."[19] This merging of culture and Scripture shows clearly in the two questions raised when discussing Sarai's sending Hagar to Abram for bearing a child (Gen. 16). Sikatchi asked, "How did a Nyarafolo custom get into the Bible? Whose culture came first—the Israelites' or the Nyarafolos'?" For a people who believe in a creator God who is high, distant, and not directly accessible, accepting a God who knows them in their daily traditions causes a major paradigm shift.

Translating Cultural Texts

Well-translated biblical texts are required when working on translating the gospel message into meaningful, culturally appropriate art forms that undergird God's Word moving into a people's world of lived experience. This is one side of toggling between translating the sacred written text and culturally expressive languages. On the other side we need cultural translation of the performing arts (i.e., music, dance, and drama) into local music-cultures for developing culturally appropriate forms that adequately carry the message.[20]

16. Interview notes: Linnea Boese, email correspondence with author, October 19, 2011.
17. It is also very common to "take fire" in the form of some burning coals to the field during work or to another village or camp; this is another way in which the story resonates as normal action.
18. Lesser sacrifices are composed of chickens and rice, for example.
19. Bediako, "Scripture as the Interpreter of Culture and Tradition," 4.
20. Postmodern scholarship has turned to studying music, drama, and dance as texts themselves. Miller and Shahriari summarize the new approach: "Whereas modernism taught that (capital T) Truth could be established, what is now called *postmodernism* teaches that 'truth' is

In other words, oral, nonverbal cultural forms, called *cultural texts*, must be translated just as much as languages. Translating cultural texts facilitates working *with* culture and creating new culturally appropriate forms and products *within* the cultural milieu where people find themselves most at home. For many peoples around the world, oral forms such as song, dance, and drama are essential means for hearing the Scriptures.[21] Indeed, these may be their only means of hearing the biblical text. Others who have learned to read still prefer oral forms for processing new information.

Just as language and culture are intimately linked, art forms are culturally embedded and function at deep levels of culture, further complicating the translation process. Philip Bohlman, commenting on how cultural translation is the "disciplinary vernacular of the everyday for ethnomusicologists," highlights the complexity and argues that cultural translation "requires active negotiation between multiple symbol systems."[22] Sadly, cultural translation is the arena wherein Protestant missions has been the weakest, and many scholars consider it "perhaps the area of greatest deficit for evangelical missionaries."[23] When it comes to Bible translation and the arts, the goal driving the translation of cultural texts is to foster local songs and art products that support and enhance God's Word being made alive within a people's lived experience. God comes close and dwells among them in meaningful and spiritually powerful ways. Biblical text translation and cultural text translation need to forge ahead together in harmony rather than working in opposition to each other.

A brief cultural analysis of vignette 4.1 demonstrates how translation of cultural texts negotiates multiple symbol systems that further enhance understanding of the gospel message and affect local social dynamics. The interdependence of text, melody, rhythm, and musical instruments—each one a symbol system in itself—reveals the multivocal nature of translating cultural texts, that is, musical forms. The Nyarafolo's concern for finding an adequate rhythm to communicate the significance of God's providing a sheep for the sacrifice reveals that the *balafon* was in reality a foreign instrument for

relative and has little validity beyond the person attempting to establish it. Instead of 'describing facts,' postmodern scholars seek to 'interpret texts,' a text being anything, including a book, painting, sculpture, or a piece of music." Miller and Shahriari, *World Music*, 55. The method here is helpful in approaching music and the arts as cultural entities in and of themselves.

21. Estimates indicate that 70 percent of the world's population are oral learners. Jewell, "Winning the Oral Majority," 56.

22. Philip V. Bohlman, "Becoming Ethnomusicologists: On Cultural Translation," *Society for Ethnomusicology Newsletter* 41, no. 2 (March 2007): 5, https://cdn.ymaws.com/www.ethno musicology.org/resource/resmgr/newsletters/41_2_mar_2007.pdf. Bohlman notes further that, as ethnomusicologists, "we are called upon to enact translation as musicians, ethnographers, literary scholars, and cultural theorists."

23. Pocock, Van Rheenen, and McConnell, *Changing Face of World Missions*, 348.

the Nyarafolo and limited the comprehensive cultural translation of the new song. The *balafon* neither fit the Nyarafolo language structure nor carried a depth of associative metaphors that resonated with the people. It seems that the *balafon*, meaningful among the Cebaara, carried the taint of foreignness for the Nyarafolo and in reality was undermining the biblical message they were seeking to communicate.

Questions about incorporating local, traditional musical instruments and dance have historically addressed only whether the instruments are pagan and/or satanic. These are indeed critical issues that need to be considered and discussed by local communities. A theology of and process for redeeming local instruments and dance has yet to be fully developed. Cebaara Christians, however, offer an initial model in the way they have brought one of their traditional instruments, the *balafon*,[24] into their Christian worship. Through communal reflection on theological concepts and cultural practices, they worked through the *balafon*'s negative and satanic associations. These discussions then led to making adjustments to the instrument to get rid of these associations. Their reasoning in the redemption of this instrument included acknowledging that God is the creator of the wood, calabash, and hide used to construct the *balafon*. They had *balafons* made that did not include the chicken sacrifice that was a normal part of the construction process. They also expanded the number of keys on it so that they could more clearly communicate God's message.[25] They made such adaptations in community, and they point to a *translation of cultural texts* that work toward creating *new songs* that can effectively affect Christian witness and worship in local communities. In the cultural translation process, thoughtful and discerning instrument redemption needs to address the "satanic" issue, yet also go beyond it by addressing root issues intertwined in its use and function. Not doing so limits and puts at risk the potential for making the Word come alive in deeper, impactful ways within a people's music-culture.

Translating for Transformed Relationships

The ultimate goal for collaboration between translation of biblical and cultural texts is to provide a more comprehensive translation of the message so that new songs affect a people to "see and fear the LORD, and put their trust in him" (Ps. 40:3). New Song Fellowships provide cultural arenas for addressing a fuller range of the dynamic interplay between people of varying spoken languages, expressive languages, and cultural contexts.

24. *Balafon* is a general term for the wood-frame xylophone spread across West Africa, in particular the Manding Kingdom (see fig. 2.2). The Cebaara term for their *balafon* is *jegele*.
25. See King, *Pathways in Christian Music Communication*, 112–16.

Figure 4.2
Bible translation and the arts: a cyclical process

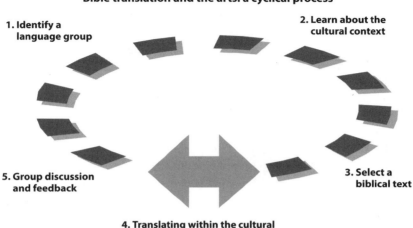

1. Identify a language group

2. Learn about the cultural context

3. Select a biblical text

4. Translating within the cultural context via local music and arts

5. Group discussion and feedback

In the case of vignette 4.1, New Song Fellowships brought together four emerging Christian faith communities to engage in translating the message appropriate to their lived experiences. Moving beyond verbal-cum-written translations to also translate cultural texts—music, dance, and drama—fostered more comprehensive translation that works *with* the intent of the gospel message to gain relevance within each linguistic world of local believers. Extending the translation process to the expressive languages helps to fill in the gaps and functions at deeper cultural levels that move the message beyond surface-level understandings. Hence, in the midst of the process, each language group was growing in deeper understandings of the Scriptures, growing in relationship within their group, and often developing better associations with the other Senufo language groups as the Scripture and resulting new songs were presented and discussed in the larger group setting.

Thus, translating cultural texts in tandem with Scripture texts provides cultural experiences that shape "the way human experience impacts the nature of the respective people's processing information in a way that makes sense to them."[26] New Song Fellowships provide culturally appropriate experiences that foster processing information that makes sense as it naturally plays into people's customary ways of interacting in life. The process promotes gaining access to what the people need to know in order to faithfully follow the God of Abraham, and ultimately to follow Jesus Christ. It plays into the ways they *think* and thus

26. Dan Shaw, email correspondence with author, April 7, 2017.

affects everything they do. As such, New Song Fellowships create cognitive environments that simultaneously interact at all levels of culture: cognitive, affective, and evaluative. The interactive, dialogical swirl generated through group discussions and song composition produces an environment where new connections can take place. The songs become *new* in orienting the people in their Christian walk, in showing how to *walk the Jesus road* as followers of Jesus.

In the midst of translating the gospel message, relationships are formed, and a musical bonding takes place as emerging faith communities evolve into potential hermeneutical communities for engaging with God's Word and with one another via the group composing process. As Paul Hiebert stresses, "The church . . . is to be a true community of people seeking to follow Christ and serve one another. Only then will it become . . . [an] 'authentic Christian community,' a hermeneutical community that strives to understand God's message to it and bears a witness to the world of what it means to be a Christian, not only in beliefs but also in life. The church as a body is a 'new order.'"[27] Singing new songs engenders fully embodied Christian witness via translating God's message to his peoples.

Vignette 4.2

Arts as Witness among Ojibway Youth of Manitoulin Island, Canada
(Hip Hop, YouTube, and Ojibway Local Customs)

Melody Frost
MA in Intercultural Studies

The Ojibway people in Wiikwemkoong Unceded Territory (Wiky) proudly live on unceded land in Canada. Since its chiefs never signed land over to the Canadian government, Wiky arts, being relatively unaffected by Western culture, flourish. Dancing, singing, and drumming, which carry both aesthetic and spiritual significance, are prominent forms; others include oral traditions such as storytelling. A push from Ojibway elders has challenged Wiky youth to retain their Native roots, which forces teenagers to navigate their own culture, the mainstream influences found online, and Jesus Christ.

Generally, both elders and youth desire connection to their traditional culture. The elders teach the youth to value Native culture, but youth also seem to be stepping up and self-identifying as Native in the face of social/political celebration (e.g., powwows) and challenge (e.g., the Dakota Access Pipeline).

---

27. Hiebert, *Critical Contextualization*, 192.

However, since very few Ojibway elders follow Jesus, few are teaching youth to be Native *and* Christian. In addition to these two factors, the youth resonate with hip hop and YouTube, which can be but are not exclusively God-honoring. The Western missionaries are more comfortable connecting with Ojibway youth through elements of Western youth culture, but this leaves students wondering where their own cultural traditions fit into worship and witness.

I observed this struggle when I visited a local youth group in April 2015. Through the evening, a leader blasted hip hop by Christian artists, students pulled out iPods and traded music videos on YouTube, and others strummed pop tunes on a beat-up guitar. I inquired whether they sing corporately or know Ojibway Christian musicians. Their replies: not really. The students evidently love music, yet no link exists between Ojibway music and worship or witness to the glory of God.

As observation follow-up, I held ongoing conversations with Skylar Manitowabi, a Native young adult who has been following Jesus since 2012. Skylar expresses his gratitude for the Western missionaries who recognize music as a catalyst for relational ministry. He acknowledges, however, that a more excellent way to disciple Native people, from elders to youth proud of their culture, is through Native arts and traditions. Rather than merely translating English hymns or dipping into global youth culture, faithful witness accords with God's desire to honor, redeem, and transform Ojibway culture—including their music—for his glory.

An example of drawing from traditional art practices comes from the Aboriginals of Australia as told by Peter Brook. In his serving as an EthnoArts consultant, indigenous art forms play critical roles in translating the Scriptures and bringing the gospel message into the local context.

Vignette 4.3

Aboriginals Contextualizing the Scriptures through Painting

Peter Brook
MA in Intercultural Studies, Theology and the Arts
Wycliffe Australia EthnoArts Consultant

Contemporary Australian Aboriginal arts have become famous globally since painting was introduced by schoolteacher Geoffrey Bardon to the indigenous community of Papunya in the early 1970s.[a] Painting has become a powerful medium for expressing daily life, passing on traditional lore, and connecting spiritually with the ancestors and homelands. An active group of artists exists in most Aboriginal communities in the western and central desert areas, and a high proportion of them are professing Christians. Many community members cannot read, and the arts help them engage with Scripture in meaningful ways. For several years in the small Alyawarr-speaking community of Epenarra, 335 miles (540 km) northeast of Alice Springs, a group of approximately ten Christian women has been sporadically contextualizing the Scriptures through painting. These paintings are then shared in church services. Together with local missionaries, who are involved in discipleship within the community, my wife and I provided the art materials and the space for these women to devote focused time to painting just prior to Easter. Spreading a tarpaulin out on the cement floor of the church building, the women sat and worked on paintings for several days, despite temperatures reaching 113°F (45°C). A couple of artists who do not go to church were invited by some of the women to come and join them, and it was exciting to see them interact with the Scriptures as they painted. The women created a body of paintings using local pictographs, communicating the gospel message especially for their upcoming Easter convention. They also intend to share their paintings in church services, funerals, and other community events.

[a] See Vivien Johnson, *Lives of the Papunya Tula Artists* (Alice Springs, Australia: IAD Press, 2008), xiii.

In this painting (fig. 4.3), the women depict a Christian's journey from the old Adam to the new Adam through baptism at the foot of the cross. The three arches at the top are the Triune God: Father, Son, and Holy Spirit. The horseshoe shapes represent people (the shape made when one sits in the dirt). This iconography is generally used by Christians in the region and was originally developed by the Warlpiri people south of Epenarra. It has now become a visual language that many indigenous Christians use regardless of the oral language they speak. In a sense it has become a creole for vernacular visual language.

Conclusion

In conclusion, the book of Psalms, Paul's admonitions to communicate via the arts, and vignette 4.1 all point to the translatability of the gospel by

Figure 4.3 A Christian's journey from the old Adam to the new Adam (acrylic on canvas)

incorporating a full range of available cultural vehicles. Holistic translation of Scripture texts must extend beyond words to embrace the expressive languages—music and arts—of every culture. Not to do so hinders Christian witness. Sanneh, in *Translating the Message*, effectively argues that Christianity, from a very early stage, has always practiced "culture as the natural extension of the new religion, and therefore views cultural failure as ultimately detrimental to Christian success."[28]

The term "cultural" encompasses the arts as well. It is paramount that Bible translation and the arts come together in translating the gospel message. As vital partners, they actively negotiate between multiple symbol systems working together to bring meaningful understanding of who God is and how he enters into each people's world. The process of translation is of ultimate importance, as are the sought-after final products. As we have seen, New Song Fellowships provide spaces for engaging newly translated biblical texts in light of cultural values and beliefs that arise in the midst of translating cultural texts. In working toward developing cultural products, the process itself is transformative as it draws on local peoples to directly interact with and dialogue about the biblical text. Biblical text translation and cultural

28. Sanneh, *Translating the Message*, 7.

text translation join forces for transformed relationships that bond believers together in faith communities *and* give witness to surrounding communities.

In the midst of an increasingly globalized world with constantly moving people, there remains a longing to return "home" to one's cultural roots and places of deepest interactions. Cultural texts, translated for carrying God's message, become resources for theologizing a people's encounters with God and daily struggles. We further address this topic in the following chapter.

Questions for Discussion

1. What is the contribution of cultural texts to translating the message of the gospel?

2. Identify three of the most critical reasons for translating cultural texts as part of the Bible translation process. Support your reasoning.

3. Why does Bono's song "Forty" bring joy to Eugene Peterson, who translated Psalm 40 in *The Message*? What other collaborations do you see happening between translating the biblical text and cultural texts? How can your church or mission encourage such collaborations?

5

Theologizing with Global Arts

What does it mean to follow Jesus in my local context?

Songs of testimony recount a people's first encounters with the living God, who has broken into their immediate world. Such songs reach out to others and play critical roles in helping to bring more people into a living relationship with God. They reveal how new believers are beginning to see the world and live out their newfound faith. Some early steps in active theologizing are beginning to take shape in such narratives.

For example, Xiao Min, a Chinese peasant woman and house-church Christian from Henan, sings out a song of testimony from a prison cell. While this chapter focuses mainly on sung theological textual content, the pentatonic melodies that arise around her as Xiao Min lifts her voice reveal a natural drawing from local cultural musical practices that contribute to the songs' dynamic impact among listeners.[1] Singing as part of an ongoing dialogue with her prison inmates, she begins by raising questions surrounding creation:

1. For examples, see "Xiao Min Singing," Women of Christianity, March 26, 2011, http://womenofchristianity.com/xiao-min-singing; "The Canaan Hymns (English Version)," YouTube, https://youtu.be/xa1saiWejjo; *The Cross: Jesus in China* (Petaluma, CA: China Soul for Christ Foundation, 2003), DVD; and *Love of the Cross (Selection of Canaan Hymns)* (Petaluma, CA: China Soul for Christ Foundation, 2004), CD-ROM.

Why do leaves die and grow new buds?
Why do spring, summer, fall, winter resurrect in cycles?
Why cannot I see the wind and the air?
Why do the sun, moon, and stars suspend high in the sky?
All of this—and many, many more
Has become a difficult riddle in my heart . . .

I heard people say,
Go, and seek after the true God.
He will give you all the answers
Because He created the heavens and the earth.
Knowledge, wisdom, and everything is in Him. . . .
How I rejoiced when I found the mighty Most High,
The One who answered my many, many riddles.

He revealed to me the value and meaning of existence.
Life became abundant and beautiful.
No longer wandering in the wind,
No longer hesitating between crossroads,
I found life and beauty,
I found a passion that attaches.

Friends, do you also have these riddles?
Please come and know the Most High!
He is not far from you,
Right next to you.
He dwells in your heart of faith.[2]

What is Xiao Min revealing here? Powerful in natural allegory, Xiao Min's
song raises issues about the riddles of life and shares from her own experience of finding the Mighty, Most High—God the Creator—in whom all wisdom and knowledge resides. Reminiscent of Paul's words to the Athenians,[3]
Xiao Min's song interprets God's creation in a way that points to the reality of his being and that undergirds God's purpose in creation. She invites listeners to come and know him, explaining, "He is not far from you,
right next to you. He dwells in your heart of faith." These are stunning new

2. Canaan Hymn 25, "My Song," in Sun, "Songs of Canaan."
3. "From one man he made all the nations, that they should inhabit the whole earth; and
he marked out their appointed times in history and the boundaries of their lands. God did this
so that they would seek him and perhaps reach out for him and find him, though he is not far
from any one of us. 'For in him we live and move and have our being.' As some of your own
poets have said, 'We are his offspring.' Therefore since we are God's offspring, we should not
think that the divine being is like gold or silver or stone—an image made by human design and
skill" (Acts 17:26–29).

theological concepts that shatter atheistic spaces and invite nonbelievers to consider the existence of God. This song shares a dynamic expression of Christian experience interpreted in light of biblical truths via the medium of contextualized song, transmitted within a prison setting in a national context where Christians are still persecuted for their faith. *Songs of testimony*, such as Xiao Min's, naturally lead into *songs of faith* that seek to understand the nature of God and of living with him. The two types of songs are intertwined and overlapping. Songs of faith move deeper into a people's way of life as they reflect on God's intention for them. Providing arenas for processing life, songs of faith result in further witness to God's dynamic presence, which sustains and guides them. Active theologizing is taking place.

Thus, the arts are not static. Rather, they dynamically interact within lived human experiences, providing arenas of reflection for bringing God into a people's context. Engaging the arts in the creative process promotes active theologizing in the quest to know and relate to him. In this chapter I argue that contextualized arts promote active theologizing in relevant and meaningful ways. The process provides means for moving deeper into a people's worldview in ways that foster a growing understanding of God's dynamic presence among them. Earlier, chapter 3 presented "what" the arts contribute to cultural exegesis, showing how people *think* via the arts and their impact on cultural practices. In chapter 4, we considered the critical importance of translating the message holistically and symbolically by translating the Scriptures and the gospel message in tandem with expressive cultural texts. This furthered our understanding of what needs to take place in order to bring the message of the gospel into new contexts.

Translating the message, however, does not stop with the completion of a Bible translation. Nor does it stop with the development of culturally appropriate song forms that undergird and carry the gospel message further. Rather, translating the message launches and extends Christian witness into the question "Now what?" How do we take the next step and translate for lived praxis in following Jesus, for living Christianly in the midst of life's vagaries, and for dealing with the joys and sorrows of arising issues? This chapter addresses theologizing via the arts in ways that nurture new and maturing believers, while also serving to witness to the goodness of God. God's people have an ongoing need for dynamic expressions of Christian experience that guide them in and throughout life. We thus first consider the role of the arts in actively engaging with Scripture, followed by three vignettes by theologizing voices from the global church. We will conclude with key dynamics drawn from the theologizing processes in these vignettes.

Active Theologizing via the Arts

Active theologizing involves young and maturing communities of faith continually reflecting on God's revelation—the biblical Scriptures. They are meant to be read and understood within specific cultural and historical contexts. This means asking questions such as, What does the Scripture mean? and, What does it mean for *me*? Hiebert refers to this as "self-theologizing."[4] He argues that each community is a priesthood of believers (1 Pet. 2:9) who can read the Scriptures and understand them for themselves. This validates and respects each people group as they give voice to their understandings of God within their particular contexts. In a global world, each Christian community has contributions to make to the whole body of Christ. No one cultural group has developed a fully comprehensive systematic theology. Yet each one has important understandings about God that inform an overarching global theology, or metatheology, in a convergence that encompasses and draws from local theologies.[5]

Local theologies very often develop through art-creation processes. The arts take up the task of active theologizing as people respond to the question, What does it mean to be the recipient of God's Word in this present world?[6] or, What does it mean to live out the unchanging truth of the gospel in local settings? These questions are always contextually grounded—asked within unique historical, social, and cultural contexts, with the Scriptures at the center of the theologizing task. Visual artists in Africa and Asia, for example, paint scenes of Jesus and the gospel story into their own geographic locations, taking on the cultural signs and symbols of the local area. They bring the good news of Jesus Christ into the local picture.

The batik shown in figure 5.1 sets Jesus's instruction to cast the net on the right side of the boat, which results in an abundant catch of fish (John 21:6), in the artist's home context of Tanzania. The batik also reflects the great harvest and rapidly growing church on the African continent. Here an individual artist has not only brought the gospel story into his context, but has also symbolically indicated how God is at work among faith communities in Africa. The visual work offers opportunities for communities to gather around and discuss God's presence among them. Theological discussions in such communities inspire people to find more local stories of God's presence and work among them, and they give greater understanding of God's revelation within a people's particular context.

4. Hiebert, "Metatheology," 97.
5. For further discussion on doing global theology in relation to metatheological frames, see Hiebert, "Missionary as Mediator of Global Theologizing," 301–4.
6. Netland, introduction to *Globalizing Theology*, 17.

Daystar University student from Tanzania

Figure 5.1 The abundant catch of fish: a Tanzanian setting

It is paramount to reiterate that active theologizing via the arts centers on God's revelation through the Bible. The Bible story has set the agenda for active theologizing. The creative process begins with seeking scriptural understanding of life experiences. Artists bring their experiences into the creative arena of reflection, seeking to understand God and what is currently happening in their lives. Rather than beginning with an artistic product, the artist begins with God's Word and interweaves it with life's circumstances as people attempt to make sense of what is happening in life and learn of God's intent in the midst of it (see fig. 5.2). The arts, as life processors, facilitate active theologizing from local, insider perspectives.

Furthermore, the creative process fosters theological interpretations and explanations from the inside of culture rather than merely attaching rational explanations from the outside, as Western theologies typically do. Insider perspectives, which anthropologists call *emic*, bring to the Scriptures questions that are being asked from within their local beliefs, values, and assumptions, as well as from their sociocultural contexts. These questions differ from those of other cultural contexts. It is thus important to encourage

Figure 5.2
The centrality of God's Word in active theologizing

Illustration by Eric Tai

local peoples of a particular culture to create artistically. Preferably they will do so in relation to or within faith communities that function as hermeneutical communities.[7]

As Hiebert argues, "Theological reflections in different cultures must be done initially in the people's own conceptual categories and then evaluated in the light of global theologizing."[8] Global arts operate within these conceptual categories by interacting with the expressive languages of particular cultures; they facilitate working within insiders' worldviews and gaining insights about emic perspectives of a people. This use of the arts in bringing out worldviews is something new that needs to be more fully recognized, encouraged, and engaged. There is a great need to stimulate and encourage local theologizing via the arts. Academic studies of local theologies are fairly rare. That means that studying and learning from local theologies is in its initial stages, particularly when we consider that worldwide more than two thousand language groups practice Christian faith. As Lamin Sanneh notes, "More people pray and worship in more languages in Christianity than in any other religion in the world."[9] We have much to learn from one another as we seek to understand and grow in relationship with God. What follows are four initial studies

7. See King, "Bible: *Lex Canendi, Lex Credendi.*"
8. Hiebert, *Gospel in Human Contexts*, 180.
9. Sanneh, *Whose Religion Is Christianity?*, 69.

in local theologizing, ranging from the Harrist Church in Côte d'Ivoire, to the songs of Tesfaye Gabbiso in Ethiopia, to Xiao Min of China, and to the Senufo of northern Côte d'Ivoire.

Theologizing Voices from the Global Church

As noted above, the task of listening and learning from local faith communities as they interact with God in the theologizing process via the arts is still in its very early stages. As the global church grows numerically, faith communities are increasingly finding themselves more at home within their own contexts. As a result, we have a growing set of diverse cultural and linguistic theological expressions born out of the global church's confrontations with current life issues in the late twentieth and early twenty-first centuries. Individual case studies, when taken together as a whole, point to an emerging global theology. In many places, this appears to be taking place where the global church is experiencing rapid growth through revival and renewal movements, and in many cases where believers experience severe persecution and suffering. Expansive outreach appears to often be a hallmark of dynamic, interactive theologizing via the arts.[10]

Indeed, a growing consensus among theologians, especially non-Western theologians, seeks to listen to the global church through the expressive arts and the plethora of local theologies emanating from them. In the case of Africa, Henry Okullu explains:

> When we are looking for African theology, we should go to the fields, to the village Church, to Christian homes to listen to those spontaneously uttered prayers before people go to bed. We should go to the schools, to the frontiers where traditional religions meet with Christianity. We must listen to the throbbing drumbeats and the clapping of hands accompanying the impromptu singing in the independent churches. We must look at the way in which Christianity is being planted in Africa through music, drama, song, dances, art, paintings.[11]

Engaging the Scriptures at the point of current life issues forms the starting point of active theologizing in local cultural and historical contexts—often through the arts, as they are dynamic and interactive. We turn our attention here to two main arenas of theologizing that inform global theology: first,

10. See Balisky, "Theology in Song"; Hatcher, "Poetry, Singing, and Contextualization"; Krabill, *Hymnody of the Harrist Church*; and Walls, "Western Discovery of Non-Western Christian Art."
11. Okullu, *Church and Politics in East Africa*, 54.

emerging theologies resulting from initial encounter with divine revelation and, second, local theologies of suffering and persecution.

Emerging theologies. Emerging theologies explore and interact with a people's first encounters with the living God. Imagine an encounter in which you suddenly see everything you have been taught about a particular subject in a new light, such as when Nicodemus asks Jesus about what it means to be *born again* (John 3:1–8). As Nicodemus engages in honest dialogue with Jesus, he shows a desire to pursue the hidden meanings and new understandings Jesus is talking about. This same desire to understand more deeply is reflected in the emerging theologies of young believers engaging with God's Word. One of the most extraordinary examples of this comes from the Dida people of Côte d'Ivoire.

Vignette 5.1

The Harrist Church in Côte d'Ivoire: Putting Faith and History to Music

James R. Krabill
Adjunct Professor, Anabaptist Mennonite Biblical Seminary

William Wadé Harris (1860–1929) was a Liberian prophet-preacher who conducted one of the most remarkable evangelistic campaigns in the history of African Christianity. For eighteen months in the early 1900s, he trudged barefoot through the Ivory Coast and into the Gold Coast (Ghana), carrying a Bible and cross-staff, and accompanied by several women singers. He taught the rudiments of Christianity, instructed people to burn their fetishes, and baptized some 100,000 to 200,000 new believers.

Harris spent most of his early life in the Methodist and Episcopal churches of eastern Liberia and grew up loving hymns in the European and American tradition. During his prophetic journey, however, he encouraged early converts to compose songs and prayers in their own language. "God has no personal, favorite songs," he told them. "He hears and understands all that we say in whatever language." Harris discouraged the use of love songs and counseled believers instead to transform *dogbro* tunes—traditional "praise songs" sung to chiefs—into hymns of faith bringing glory to God.

One hymn dating from the 1920s defends Harrist practice from the criticism of newly arrived Protestant missionaries and catechists ("the Bible people"):

> We have Your Name, yes indeed!
> Yet the Bible people tell us

That with the work we are doing here,
We cannot come near to the Lord.
Why can't we come near to the Father? . . .
Each village has its own language;
Take this then to pray to the Father!

For over a century now, Harrist musicians have been putting their faith and history to music and passing it down in oral form to succeeding generations. This theological repository comprises thousands of original hymns and represents one of the truly remarkable achievements of the church on the African continent.

The lyrics of the above song serve as a defense for singing in one's own language. In the early 1900s this practice was frowned upon by Western missionaries and early local converts—"the Bible people"—who were being trained by the outsiders. Additionally, the lyrics reveal how songs communicate on multiple levels in the Dida cultural context. First, an issue is raised, thoughts are processed, and the text comments and speaks into the historical situation. Second, beyond addressing earthly issues, the lyrics hint at singing as praying. Spirituality is practiced via cultural songs. This is reminiscent of St. Augustine, the North African theologian of the fifth century, who stated, "He who sings once, prays twice." For nonliterate peoples, communicating orally via the arts was essential for functioning in life. It was embedded in their cultural practices and ripe for translating the gospel message.

The Dida and more than a dozen other ethnic groups evangelized by Harris were turning "from traditional religious beliefs and practices toward a new reality structured around certain rudimentary tenets of the Christian faith as prescribed by the Prophet."[12] Although Harris had made "the Book" available to the new believers, being nonliterate cut them off from accessing the written Scriptures.[13] The new believers developed an insatiable thirst for the Scriptures, which contained teachings about God and his Son, Jesus Christ. Without a translation of the Bible, they were forced to collect bits and pieces of the biblical message wherever possible, including Bible stories told to a Harrist preacher by a local shopkeeper from Sierra Leone. The preacher would immediately explain the stories to a choir assembled in his courtyard, after which the choir transformed them into song. The local custom of singing one's thoughts and faith resulted in early songs

12. Krabill, *Hymnody of the Harrist Church*, v.
13. Krabill, *Hymnody of the Harrist Church*, 365.

dealing with the creation of the world, the temptation of Job, the wisdom of Solomon, John the Baptist, Christ's coming to earth, Christ's healing ministry (Mark 5:25–34), Christ's teaching (Matt. 11:28), Christ's death and resurrection, Christ's reign on Mount Zion, the return of Christ, the last judgment, and heaven and hell.[14]

In the people's search for biblical truth, the Harrist hymns progressively became more informed by biblical tradition and fostered further active theologizing. Several theological themes came to the fore, among them a growing African Christology and perceptions about God. Christologically, they sang of learning to know a new "big brother," a common theme across the African continent, from Ghana to Kenya and Uganda.[15] Overall, the early Dida hymns answer the question "Who is Jesus?" by bestowing on him honorific titles, such as *king*, *lord*, *wise one*, and *handsome*. He is also acknowledged as a family member, as *father*, *son*, *offspring*, and *brother*. Jesus as a true healer provides another main emphasis; songs acknowledge Jesus as the "First Medicinal Grinding Stone," indicating local medicinal practices, and "Medicine for Our Troubled Deeds."[16]

African perceptions about God appear in hymns speaking about knowing that God existed before Harris came to evangelize them. When we create art, it can be a deeply spiritual endeavor. Encountering the truth of Scripture in the creative process can have a profound impact. They sang, for example, "We knew that God had made us, that He had placed us on this earth, . . . but we did not understand His affair."[17] Two major themes dominated as they grew in their understandings about the nature of God: that of "father" and "life-renewer." They also extolled the wonder of God drawing close to them. This stands in stark contrast to their pre-Christian beliefs that God is distant, faraway, and fairly inaccessible. They sang:

> We too, we have at last found our Father.
> We did not know that we were going to find our Father.
> But we have found our Father;
> Our Father is our King of Glory.[18]

A note of wonder and surprise likewise resounds in the following text describing God as Life-Renewer:

14. Krabill, *Hymnody of the Harrist Church*, 366.
15. See Stinton, *Jesus of Africa*, 146–52.
16. Krabill, *Hymnody of the Harrist Church*, 370–71.
17. Krabill, *Hymnody of the Harrist Church*, 372.
18. Krabill, *Hymnody of the Harrist Church*, 375.

Ayi wowo, the Lord gave birth to us, yoo![19]
The Life-Renewer, the Doer-of-Good gave birth to us!
We did not know
That the Lord was going to give birth to us two times![20]

The lyrics demonstrate the integrating of new information into the Dida worldview as they grew in their understanding of God. This is also true of the Cebaara Senufo, who live just north of the Dida. African concepts about God referenced in their songs include *Kolocoloo*, one of two Senufo deities referred to as the creator God, and the concept of God as father/ancestor (*touw*), "where any male who is older and also an adult is considered a father to the rest of the community."[21] They also refer to God as *Baba* (Daddy), indicating an intimate relationship, where *Baba* is one's actual father and the source of one's life. Concepts about God and Jesus are dense within the song texts. Notably, early Cebaara Senufo believers made no distinction between God the Father and Jesus the Son. An early popular song of 1987 speaks of "our father, Jesus," in the sense of being a father (*touw*) to the larger community. As more Scriptures were translated, song texts began to make a distinction between God the Father and Jesus, the Son of God. Similar to the Dida, through oral hermeneutic processes, an emerging theology among the Cebaara Senufo was moving toward more fully developed understandings of God.

Active Theologizing in the Midst of Suffering

In contrast to the above, theologies of suffering arise out of the trauma and dislocation of peoples as they confront political and ideological conflict and turmoil. This sets the point of theological exploration. Active theologizing in the midst of suffering takes place out of a need for stability and for making sense of what is happening, especially as a people's way of life and faith are being threatened from outside their faith community. The late twentieth and early twenty-first centuries are replete with the events of war and religious conflict. Christians, whose identities are *in* Christ, experience suffering and persecution. They find themselves turning to identify *with* Christ and his sufferings in the crucifixion. We consider here three contrasting examples in which theologies of suffering via song-making processes have emerged: Ethiopia, China, and a Sudanese refugee camp in Kenya.

19. *Ayi wowo*: a musical vocable, both a composition technique and a textual means of strengthening the element of surprise. Yoo: expressing agreement and gratitude.
20. Krabill, *Hymnody of the Harrist Church*, 375.
21. King, *Pathways in Christian Music Communication*, 140.

Ethiopia: Tesfaye Gabbiso in Prison

Following the Marxist revolution in 1974, Ethiopian Christians found themselves imprisoned for refusing to renounce their faith in Jesus Christ. Tesfaye, a gifted singer and minister imprisoned for refusing to recant his faith, composed songs during his imprisonment that first helped him and his fellow prison inmates endure and focus on God. His musical style is typical of Ethiopian singers, with the singing of embellished, modally developed melodies and performed with a strong nasal quality, a traditional characteristic. The songs are written in Amharic, the national language, and often accompanied by guitar, sometimes by the traditional Ethiopian harp, the *krar*. He says that his songs "usually come to him with words and tune at the same time. Often his inspirations would come in early morning walks when he was alone with God."[22]

Out of their immediate context, the songs came to ultimately nourish and sustain the Ethiopian church throughout a difficult national era. The story behind one of Tesfaye's most beloved songs, "When God Assists," demonstrates how songs are born in the midst of personal persecution and mocking as the composer seeks to maintain his allegiance to God and interacts with the Scriptures (see vignette 5.2).

Vignette 5.2

"When God Assists"
An Ethiopian Song Inspired by Suffering

Lila Balisky
Doctor of Missiology

Tesfaye Gabbiso, acclaimed Ethiopian gospel soloist for the past fifty years, relates how he and other Christian compatriots birthed an inspired, well-loved Ethiopian song while they were incarcerated for seven years during the Marxist revolution (1974–1991) in Ethiopia. He relates:

> While suffering from being stamped on, forced to lie in a muddy field or walk on our knees along a gravel road, the prison official would mock us, taunting: "Let's see if God can deliver you from all this." I was reminded of the words in Matthew 27:43, when Jesus's enemies said to him, "If you are the Christ, the Son of God, come down from the cross." But God was silent (Isa. 53:20) and Jesus said, "My God, my God, why have you forsaken me?" Even in the silence

---

22. Lila W. Balisky, "Songs of Ethiopia's Tesfaye Gabbiso: Singing with Understanding in Babylon, the Meantime and Zion" (DMiss diss., Fuller Theological Seminary, 2015), 71.

of God, we believed that he would honor us as we passed through yet another trial. During these continuing sufferings, the comment by that mocking official often came to our minds. A song was born, and soon our little group was singing a message we knew came from God and transformed our bitter experience into something beautiful. I now realize that this song "When God Assists" was given not only for us in prison but also for all the Christians suffering in Ethiopia.[a]

The following song text conveys Tesfaye's theological reflections drawn from this experience:

"When God Assists"
by Tesfaye Gabbiso

Chorus
When God assists, descending from the heavens,
When He wipes out all offences by His justice,
Haven't you seen the trap broken,
The captive freed and telling about His redemption?

Verse 1
Though there are many temptations on the pathway of life,
The righteous, calling upon the Lord, shall never perish.
God hears him cry, "Hold my hand."
He pulls him out of the swamp and leads him in victory.

Verse 2
When the enemy defies God and attempts to devour the poor and helpless
By terrifying words which he speaks in pride,
It is only God Who can reach down and save.
Trusting in man is vanity of vanities.

Verse 3
Stripped of all he has, deprived of everything,
Only the Lord stands by his side.
For one who is pushed aside in a foreign land,
The only foundation for his hope is his Lord.

Verse 4
The help of the saints will come from heaven.
After the ages are past, the Lord will return.
He will wipe away the tears from His children's eyes.
Glory and praise will be given to His name.[b]

[a] Interview with Tesfaye Gabbiso in *Birhan* magazine, issues 6 and 7, 1985 (Ethiopian calendar), 12.
[b] "When God Assists," song V-11 in Lila Balisky, compiler, *Songs of Tesfaye Gabbiso*, trans. Haile Jenai (Addis Ababa, Ethiopia: SIM Press, 2012), 85.

Notice here the deep dependence on God and awareness of his presence among the confined compatriots in prison, in the midst of their suffering. The song thoroughly interweaves biblical phrases and theological concepts with the reality of the singer's situation. The focus is on God at work in the midst of such cruelty and persecution. His presence is real and palpable. Themes of justice, setting the captive free, deliverance, and the righteous calling out to the Lord abound. The song not only speaks of God and his interaction with the righteous, but it also dialogues with believers and nonbelievers. It preaches by declaring that only God can save, that trust in people is vanity, and that ultimately God is the one who will make things right. Sounding very similar to the biblical psalms, it transforms the experience of one person into a song that reaches beyond prison walls and speaks to Christians throughout Ethiopia who are suffering. It also witnesses to the hope that is found in the Lord both now and in the future.

With severe times of tribulation and suffering comes a deep awareness of God's activity in the believer's life. The songs of Tesfaye relate how God is everything to him. Prayer and waiting on God are crucial; they are the mainstay of endurance. Deep intimacy, dependence, and faith in God are also real means for dealing with the enemy who taunts and jeers.

Lila Balisky, in her theological study of one hundred songs composed by Tesfaye, identifies a song that captures the heart of Tesfaye during his years of persecution.[23] Psalmic in nature, the song draws from Psalm 34:6; Psalm 61; Proverbs 18:10; and Psalm 116, reconfiguring them in expressive ways that are relevant to his prison experience. It boldly testifies to the activity of God in his life.

"I Will Call on God Who Deserves Praise"
by Tesfaye Gabbiso

Chorus
I will call on God who deserves praise.
And I will be saved from my enemies.
I will call on God who deserves praise.

Verse 1
When the flood of cruelty makes me scared,
And when the agony of hell encircles me,
When he asks me where my God is,
When my enemy scoffs at me,
When he scares me saying "Just wait,"

---

23. "I Will Call on God Who Deserves Praise," song I-10 in Balisky, *Songs of Tesfaye Gabbiso*, 22.

I will call on the name of the Lord.
And I will be saved from my enemy.

Verse 2
The name of the Lord Jesus for me is a strong tower.
Until this day whoever called on Him
Has not been embarrassed.
Because the One who lives in the cherubim
Gave me full hope.
I will in faith call upon His name,
And I will be saved from my enemy.

Verse 3
Whenever I am troubled I call upon God
Crying bitterly and brokenly in tears
I told Him the problems of my heart
Then he descended in vengeance;
He came thundering down from heaven
He disturbed them with His lightning
He dispersed them with His arrows.

Verse 4
He did not put me into the clamp of their teeth.
He always saved me from the trap which was set for me.
He protected me from Satan
Who would snatch away my freedom.
Praise be to His name, Hallelujah.
May I live in His bosom, the secret place.[24]

Tesfaye's transparency in admitting his own weakness and fear points to the depth of pathos and desperation in his experience. Yet he knows on whom to call. He testifies that his only hope is found in God. Balisky notes that the "just wait" taunt of the evil one is a threat, "but Tesfaye's secret place in God's heart is where he is kept through all the trauma of seven years when from one day to the next, he did not know what was going to happen. The word *guya* has been translated by Haile Jenai as 'in his bosom, the secret place,' a precious and holy closeness to God."[25] The intimate presence of God in his life is a reality that goes beyond words and sustains him throughout the ordeal.

These two songs only briefly introduce the corpus of lyrical theologizing found in the songs of Tesfaye from his years of imprisonment as well as from

24. "I Will Call on God Who Deserves Praise," song I-10 in Balisky, *Songs of Tesfaye Gabbiso*, 84.
25. Balisky, "Songs of Ethiopia's Tesfaye Gabbiso," 124.

the broader wellspring of thousands of indigenous songs that have emanated from a rich Ethiopian spirituality over a period of more than forty years.[26] We have seen a dependence on God in the midst of persecution during a brutal communist era, a theologizing in which the Scriptures play a central role for interpreting and making sense out of what was confronting the Ethiopian church during this historical period. Deliverance is a prominent theme that speaks to the activity of God in the midst of suffering.

China: Xiao Min and the Canaan Hymns

A second example of theologizing in the midst of suffering via the song-making process comes from China. During the Cultural Revolution (1966–76), local evangelists broke through the centuries of resistance to the gospel. The overflowing harvest of somewhere between thirty and seventy million Christians led to choosing between allegiance to the atheistic government and allegiance to Christ.[27] The Canaan Hymns, a collection of more than one thousand songs composed by Xiao Min, arose during this time. Imprisonment, as in the case of Ethiopian Christians, was part of the suffering imposed on members of the house church, including Xiao Min. While the Canaan Hymns can serve as a basis for the study of worship, they also express the gospel in Chinese culture. Rich in allegorical images drawn from nature, they not only bring about understanding but also arouse affections. For example, the image of a bamboo tree standing against the wind evokes ideas of loyalty and a sense of duty and endurance.[28]

Similar to the Ethiopian songs of Tesfaye, the Canaan Hymns are founded on the premise that the believer has a living, dynamic relationship with God, a radical redefinition of the concept of religion in China. "During the revolution, communism rejected religions as mere superstitions and 'belief in spirits.' The Canaan Hymns, in contrast, portray the divine as a relational Being, whose presence is real and who is near."[29] One popular hymn, "Beloved and I," draws from portions of the Song of Songs:

> My Beloved My Beloved leads me into his inner court.
> Words of understanding flow without end.
> Our love is as strong as death;
> Many waters cannot quench it.

26. Balisky, "Theology in Song," 447.
27. Sun, "Songs of Canaan," 8.
28. Sun, "Songs of Canaan," 2.
29. Sun, "Songs of Canaan," 3.

My Beloved is radiant—white beaming with red.
His beauty surpasses ten thousands.
My Beloved is mine and I am my Beloved's;
For eternity, we shall not part.

My Beloved leads me to the fields,
He leads me among the grape vines,
Among the lilies, he watches over his flock.
My Beloved and I shall walk together for all time.[30]

As Irene Ai-Ling Sun points out, in the Chinese context to hear a pentatonic melody sung in the language of ancient China and relating to the Christian God as "the Beloved" destroys the stereotypes of Christianity as a foreign, Western religion. For the nonbeliever it is a disturbing, jarring experience, yet for the faithful it "has the potential to grip one at one's innermost being."[31] What is worship for the faithful becomes a song of witness to the nonbeliever. This intimacy of relationship with God deepens further in songs of suffering that identify with Christ.

Emanating from the consequences of the Cultural Revolution, when religious activity was not allowed, refusal to join the government-sanctioned Three-Self Church[32] was considered an act of political rebellion. The house churches' ecclesiological belief in the headship of Christ over the church and their commitment to evangelism provoked persecution and imprisonment for many. One of the Canaan Hymns draws a picture of the pathways that would lead to imprisonment and hardship for those who refused to renounce their faith:

Although the *tao* road is hard to tread,
There is not a word of resentment.
Although tears cover the face,
My heart is sweetly satisfied.
Serving the Lord is not where,
Not under the leafy shade. . . .
Not in the midst of a warm room.
Must walk into the prison rooms.
Walking by the valley of tears
Must pass through Marah
So we could reach Elim.[33]

30. Canaan Hymn 85, "Beloved and I," in Sun, "Songs of Canaan," 4.
31. Canaan Hymn 85, "Beloved and I," in Sun, "Songs of Canaan," 4.
32. Otherwise known as the Three-Self Patriotic Movement.
33. Canaan Hymn (number unknown), "Because I Follow the Lord Ah," in Sun, "Songs of Canaan," 1–9.

In the midst of tears and persecution, the faithful find sweet satisfaction in identifying with their Lord and serving him. As in the exodus story, they expect bitter waters to come before they taste the sweet water of Elim (Exod. 15:22–27).

Nevertheless, a movement from lament to the sustaining promise of God's nearness also arises. The image of God's hands holding them throughout their ordeal sustains and comforts them.

> Tears of gratitude for His grace,
> Flowing without end.
> The heartfelt words spoken
> Do not seem to suffice.
> One pair of hands marked by nails.
> The sound of knocking upon a door long sealed.
> One gentle voice
> Leading our hearts away,
> Knowing this road
> Is the path of the cross.
> The wind, the rain is strong,
> Extremely difficult and very bitter.
> The Lord's kind and loving hands
> Holding my hands at all times.
> I don't have any reason,
> Why I should not tread the path beneath my feet?[34]

As in the biblical psalms, the Canaan Hymns express a movement from disorientation to orientation and the hope that is found in following Christ. Chinese believers often refer to Christianity as "the way of the cross." Suffering is viewed as a means of identifying *with* Christ in remembering him and following his example.[35] This theological theme is also taken up by Dinka Christians of South Sudan who find themselves forced to migrate to a refugee camp in Kenya.

Kakuma Refugee Camp: The Dinka of South Sudan

Finally, in Southern Sudan, Christians are being expelled into the Kakuma refugee camp in neighboring Kenya as a result of more than forty years of war with the Islamic Northern Sudan. Confinement in a refugee camp serves as a place of dislocation and forced immigration, a different kind of imprisonment.

34. Canaan Hymn 303, "Tears of Gratitude for His Grace," in Sun, "Songs of Canaan," 6.
35. Sun, "Songs of Canaan," 6.

Plate 1 Africa globe: how the world is viewed (Ghana, West Africa)

Molly O'Keeffe

Plate 2 The name of "Allah" as part of ship: written signal system (Turkey)

Molly O'Keeffe

Plate 3 Waltons Kilkenny Cross *bodhran* with Celtic Trinity knots (Ireland)

Molly O'Keeffe

Plate 4 Nativity with tulips: national flower and symbol of Turkey

Molly O'Keeffe

Plate 5 West African dancers: kinesic signal system (Côte d'Ivoire)

Plate 6 Redeemed Akongo with cross (Uganda)

Linnea Boese

Plate 7 Nyarafolo women singing and dancing new songs (Côte d'Ivoire)

Molly O'Keeffe

Plate 8 *Wayang gembol* puppets tell new story (Java, Indonesia)

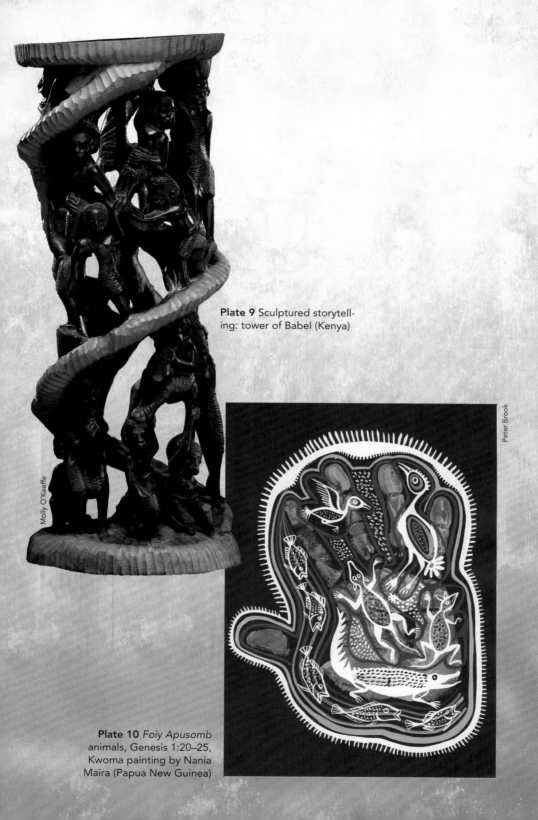

Plate 9 Sculptured storytelling: tower of Babel (Kenya)

Molly O'Keeffe

Peter Brook

Plate 10 *Foiy Apusomb* animals, Genesis 1:20–25, Kwoma painting by Nania Maira (Papua New Guinea)

Peter Brook

Plate 11 *Ap-gamba*
(The Lord's Supper),
Kwoma painting by
Nania Maira (Papua
New Guinea)

Molly O'Keeffe

Plate 12 The Lord's Supper (Argentina)

Plate 13 Roberta King introduces the Classical Arabic Music Ensemble: performance at "Songs of Divine Love" concert (Beirut, Lebanon)

Plate 14 Children singing and dancing for peace (Yogyakarta, Indonesia)

Roberta R. King

Plate 15 Wall mural at MUSA cultural center (Göttingen, Germany)

Roberta R. King

Plate 16 Music in the metro: performer's area (Istanbul, Turkey)

Instability and ambiguity about the future stare into the people's collective face. In the midst of this form of suffering, the church is once again experiencing rapid growth. In her illuminating study of Dinka Episcopal Christians, Karen Campbell shows how the Dinka revival of the 1990s got their worship right. A powerful wave of new songs emerged from the church that "struck at the very heart of what it means to be a Dinka Christian."[36] In an amazing paradox, the Episcopal Church of Sudan is recognized as one of the fastest-growing churches in the world in spite of contesting with major human challenges: war, famine, racial oppression, and displacement.

Finding and maintaining their identity in Christ as Dinka believers becomes an essential means of maintaining stability in the midst of all that is changing around them. The cross of Christ becomes a focal point for attaining stability and remembering who they are in Christ. They sing out:

> The cross on which Christ was nailed; the centre post,
> It stands between the evil Jok and believer,
> the person who has been marked with the sign of the cross on his
>   forehead.
> We Christians who have believed, the judgment will begin with us,
> And if there is no faith in us, how will we be able to escape?
> Pray to the Lord that he will give us strength so we will be able to live
>   with Him forever.[37]

Many aspects of this song do not make sense to many Christians around the world when they first read the text. What is a *Jok*? What is the significance of the person marked with the sign of the cross on his forehead? What is a center post? They are the deeply embedded cultural symbols and practices that bring to the surface firmly held convictions and values that inform their way of life. These very issues "act as a sieve, filtering this song from the universal language of Christianity into the very specific Dinka culture."[38] The song serves as a prime example of active theologizing that has gone through the process of critical contextualization, where biblical concepts have been considered in light of local cultural understandings. Campbell hypothesizes

36. Karen Campbell, "How Can We Sing Songs in a Strange Land? The Experience of Dinka Episcopal Christians in Kakuma Refugee Camp, Kenya," paper presented at the Global Consultation on Music and Mission, Fort Worth, Texas, 2003, 1.
37. Wheeler, *Land of Promise*, 96, cited in Campbell, "How Can We Sing Songs in a Strange Land?," 1. The text of this song is from Andrew C. Wheeler, *Land of Promise: Church Growth in a Sudan at War*, © Paulines Communications / Daughters of St. Paul, Paulines Publications Africa, P.O. Box 49026, 00100 Nairobi GPO, Kenya. Used with permission.
38. Campbell, "How Can We Sing Songs in a Strange Land?," 1.

that in such cases "contextualization occurs out of a need for stability and continuity in a culture where these elements are being threatened from the outside."[39] Dinka contextualized songs appear to arise out of the need to cling to something, in this case the cross of Christ expressed in cultural terms, as they seek to find security amid the chaos of displacement.

What lies behind the cultural symbols used in this song? First, it is important to know that the Dinka are nomadic cattle herders; their lives revolve around cattle. Cattle form their way of life. Their symbols reference their cognitive processing. The center post, for example, is the central place in the cattle camp, where traditionally all Dinka young men used to stay. Also, every home has a center post used as the supporting pillar of the house. Every cow in the cattle camp has its own center post, where it rests at the end of a day. Therefore, the center post represents the idea of support, location, and centrality. The cross becomes then the new center post that brings support and stability in a context of dislocation. The cross acquires meaning within Dinka culture while at the same time challenging traditional concepts of security.[40] Second, the sign of the cross on a person's forehead is a Dinka cultural way of blessing a person. The practice is to take the blood from the intestine of a cow that has been slaughtered for sacrifice and mark the forehead of the person to be blessed.

Additionally, a whole plethora of songs pick up the theme of blood and sacrifice in reference to Christ's shed blood and sacrifice. This is because blood, sacrifice, and covenant play major roles in the Dinka culture. Blood must be shed in order to make a covenant. Healing practices also require being covered with blood, while the shedding of blood also bonds the community together. The connection with Communion becomes obvious and relevant, and people readily understand the concept of atonement. The following song speaks to this issue:

> We are washed by the blood of Christ
> and yet we turn back to the wrong,
> past things that we have done.
> We reach to you, Lord save us,
> We have called upon you.
>   Peter Matiop Chol (1995)[41]

The song affirms the people's position in Christ and that one should not turn one's back on the covenant that has been made through Christ's shedding

39. Campbell, "How Can We Sing Songs in a Strange Land?," 2.
40. Campbell, "How Can We Sing Songs in a Strange Land?," 1.
41. Campbell, "How Can We Sing Songs in a Strange Land?," 7.

Photo by Jerome Starkey

Figure 5.3 Dinka cattle: a focal point of life

of blood. The Dinka culture takes covenant very seriously. One cannot take one's position and relationship with Christ lightly, especially due to the seal of the covenant made between them.

We can observe among the Dinka, then, a strong conscious need to present Christianity as first priority. During the active theologizing process, they unconsciously, and quite naturally, draw from the cultural mental models essential to their identity. The cross, blood, covenant, and sacrifice are themes common to both Christianity and their culture. This is the place where they are spiritually at home. God has come to them, is present in their midst, and empowers them to endure the harsh realities of daily living. The joining of Christian and cultural concepts unites Dinka believers with their past and affirms their identities. Continuity with the past, in light of God's presence, strengthens them to deal with the daily changes confronting them.

Key Dynamics of Active Theologizing

In each of these scenarios, suffering evokes deep dependence on God—indeed, desperate clinging to God that pulls them to engage with the Scriptures, often resulting in large corpora of lyric theology. In oral cultures, active theologizing

Figure 5.4 Dinka believers and the cross

naturally takes place in the midst of current life events via the song-making process. The songs function in two ways. They initially express believers' personal experiences in light of God's truth, and at the same time they witness to the existence and work of God among nonbelievers.

Interacting with and interpreting the Scriptures remains central to the theologizing task for local believers weaving together the gospel message, culture, and lived experience in songs that sustain, nourish, and form them spiritually. What can be noted from the studies above? Key dynamics of active theologizing include (1) the reorientation of cultural symbols and linguistic metaphors with the Christian message; (2) identifying with the suffering of Christ—the cross, his blood, and sacrifice; (3) relational aspects of knowing God in their presence; (4) calls to obedience and allegiance; and (5) the growth of "right worship." In these brief vignettes, we have observed common characteristics of God at work in the midst of suffering that are uniquely expressed via particular cultural contexts.

Transmission factors. Here it is also important to recognize the importance of transmission factors as indicators of theological relevance. The most widely used songs indicate a resonance of impact in the lives of the people. Widespread acceptance of particular songs, usage, and intense passion in song performance further indicate the significance of specific theological themes. For example, Balisky, in her study of Tesfaye's songs, asks, "Why do people weep, cluck, and respond so fervently to these songs?"[42] Singing the songs is deeply emotive and engaging for them. Likewise, among the Dinka, Campbell's research unearthed the strong social functions of music. Ezekiel Diing informed her that "music is not really music unless it is sung by a group of people. One person cannot make music on his own." He also noted that "a good song was one that was accepted by all people in the community and then sung by them."[43] Finally, one further example of measuring relevance of contextualized theology in art comes from the Nyarafolo Senufo's self-selection of key theological themes to be incorporated into regular weekly worship (see vignette 5.3).

Vignette 5.3

God's Word Published through Song

Linnea Boese
Bible Translator

One of the best outcomes of the Scripture song workshops that were held is the way that the idea of communicating important teaching through songs has taken hold. Several Nyarafolo believers now write songs after hearing a message at church that speaks to them. A man in the Tiepogovogo village church is noted for his talent in this regard. One such song has become unofficially part of the liturgy for each Sunday: "God knew that animal sacrifice could not take away sin, so Jesus gave himself to be that sacrifice." In their traditional culture, animal sacrifices are routinely offered for reparation of relationships with the spirit world any time there is an offense. So this foundational truth from God's Word is now underlined for all who come to church, believers as well as visitors, weekly. It has also been recorded and is being heard over the local radio. Other singers are also composing songs based on the Word. Many of them record the songs on their phones and bring them to the Ferke Nyarafolo Group (which began their song making), where the group still reserves one meeting per month to edit new songs together and practice them. They are thus putting together songs that teach about prayer, praise, Jesus's miracles, and the crucifixion and resurrection, as well as stories (Ruth, Noah, etc.). The Word continues to be published to this mostly preliterate people group through song!

42. Hatcher, "Poetry, Singing, and Contextualization," 451.
43. Campbell, "How Can We Sing Songs in a Strange Land?," 4.

Conclusion: Hermeneutical Communities and the Arts

In essence, we have observed examples of hermeneutical communities engaging the Scriptures as a means of interacting with God via local art and music-making. Local people have contemplated and processed the meaning and implications of following Christ and experiencing God-in-their-midst. Creating local arts for communicating Christ functions as a method of active theologizing. Such a method is experience based, set within historical contexts, and at the same time immediate, contemporary, and relevant.

Figure 5.5
Hermeneutical spiral and the arts

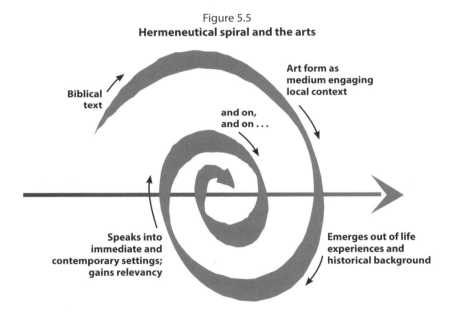

The church as a hermeneutical community plays an important role in theological reflection. As Hiebert emphasizes, "Understanding the Word of God must be an ongoing and living process that leads to discipleship under the lordship of Christ in every area of life."[44] The process forces interactive reflection that promotes transformation in the lives of people. What we see happening in each of the above examples is a spiraling interaction between text and context. Grant Osborne notes, "From its original meaning to its contextualization or significance for the church today, . . . it

44. Hiebert, *Anthropological Reflections*, 103.

is not a closed circle but rather an open-ended movement from the horizon of the text to the horizon of the reader."[45] As such, the arts address what Scripture meant historically, means personally, and means for the world. Such processes are not limited to Western contexts, but are happening worldwide, from local contexts to broader transnational settings. As the global church seeks to understand the good news that has come into the midst of particular worlds, the arts function as theologizing agents that allow people to draw closer and closer to God and his life-giving message. They witness to the presence of God in people's lives and draw others to move toward commitment to him.

Once music and the arts are allowed to engage both text and context, contextualizing the Christian faith for daily living becomes more viable. In chapter 6, we will dig into how the arts strengthen public witness in day-to-day life.

Questions for Discussion

1. What is the role of the art creation process in developing local theologies?
2. Why is it important to draw from local expressive culture and symbol systems as people engage with the Scriptures?
3. Find two examples of theologizing through the global arts in your local context that deeply affect you. What are the major themes emerging out of the written and cultural texts? What does this reveal about your context?

45. Osborne, *Hermeneutical Spiral*, 22.

Part 3

ENGAGING PEOPLES FOR CHRIST VIA GLOBAL ARTS

6

Contextualizing the Gospel in Daily Life via Global Arts

How do music and the arts foster living Christianly?

The arts are lived out in different ways across cultures and engage all of life. Most people worldwide do not think in self-contained boxes that separate religion from other dimensions of life. Many perceive only a very thin line between the sacred and the secular, if there is a line at all. Jesus asks us to move out into the "world," to go where the people are. He asks for faith communities to be people on the go—going, helping, and incarnating the gospel. Jesus demonstrated this throughout the Gospel of Luke, repeatedly reaching out to the poor and the sick. Not only did he speak of the goodness of God, but he also fleshed it out in real life. If, indeed, music and the arts engage all of life, how do we become involved with people in their local settings and influence them for the gospel? How do we get out beyond the walls of the church and engage people where they are?

People interested in following Jesus need to see what it means to follow him in daily life. This was driven home to me very strongly while visiting the Novosobirsk region of Siberia in 2001. Before we held our workshop on music and the arts in witness, I was asked to meet with local Yakutian believers to discuss living out the Christian life in ways that honored God. To begin, I asked each believer what brought him or her to faith in Jesus Christ, and one answer really caught my attention: "I was very interested in following Jesus Christ. I liked what I heard about him. However, I watched the missionary for more than two years before I was ready to make a commitment to Jesus Christ. I wanted to see if their message was real in their own lives." This Ya-kutian believer was looking to see whether knowing Jesus made a difference in daily living. How would it transform his life?

Such a response requires us to expand our equation for Christian witness via the arts. It begins with God's people, including musicians and artists, taking the initiative to reach out to others in whatever context they find themselves. Thus, it looks more as follows:

Figure 6.1
God's people, global arts, Christian witness

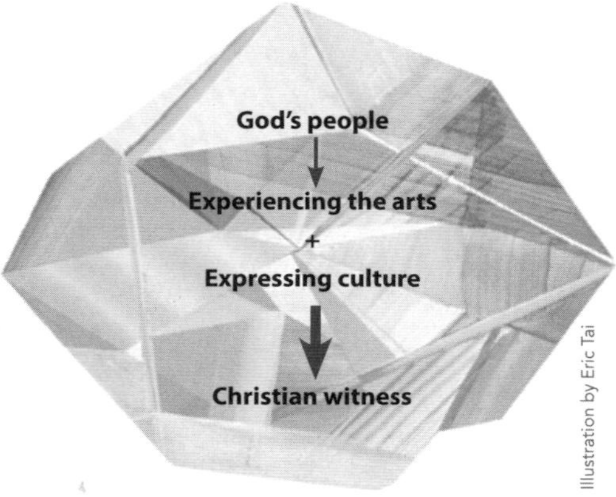

We see this process at work, for example, when the apostle Peter addresses the crowd in Jerusalem as they experience the coming of the Holy Spirit (Acts 2:14–37). Peter explains to the bewildered crowd how God is at work among them. In his address, he draws from three Scripture texts to make his case. Each text is in poetic, lyrical form and would have been well known among the people: Joel 2:28–32; Psalm 16:8–11; and Psalm 110:1. We see and hear Peter drawing from his own religious heritage, interweaving it into his argument and logic, but interpreting it and instilling it with new meaning. Peter translates and interprets poetic art forms—song lyrics—that help the people understand what God is doing in their midst on that day.

He refers to David's song lyrics in Psalm 16 as part of his explanation:

> I saw the Lord always before me.
>   Because he is at my right hand,
>   I will not be shaken.
> Therefore my heart is glad and my tongue rejoices;
>   my body also will rest in hope,

> because you will not abandon me to the realm of the dead,
>   you will not let your holy one see decay.
> You have made known to me the paths of life;
>   you will fill me with joy in your presence.
>   (Acts 2:25–28; cf. Ps. 16:8–11)

The crowd reacts with a dramatically positive response. When the people hear Peter's explanation, "they [are] cut to the heart" (Acts 2:32) and want to know what they should do. This prompts Peter to further explain how they, too, can receive the promise of salvation and the Holy Spirit. As a result, three thousand people are baptized and added to the number of followers of Jesus. The Holy Spirit uses a *song* to help provoke this amazing response to the gospel!

It is important to note that Peter weaves lyric theology into his address in ways that speak deeply to the people surrounding him. He uses a practice called intertextuality—integrating older texts together and interpreting them in light of the new reality of the resurrected Christ and the coming of the Holy Spirit. The poetic art forms are not compartmentalized separately from everyday life. Rather, they are intuitively and quite naturally infused into Peter's communication style. The gospel, as told by Peter, draws from the people's cultural and religious heritage in ways that help them understand how the message is relevant to them, initiates further dialogue, and moves the people toward becoming new creations in Christ (2 Cor. 5:17). Going forward, the people still live within their contexts and continue to speak the same languages, yet live in ways that reflect a shift in allegiance toward Jesus Christ.

Thus, Peter models for us a form of contextualization of the gospel that employs the arts in naturally affecting the audience. Knowing the religious heritage and Scriptures of the audience, he draws from them and the deeper levels of culture to persuasively communicate the heart of his message. And this is just one powerful example—deep-level communication does not stop there. Ultimately, contextualization of the gospel requires being intentionally comprehensive in all of life. Effective contextualization becomes holistic transformation of the individual and the dynamic living out of the Scriptures within a particular context. Craig Ott and Stephen Strauss explain, "Scripture should penetrate every aspect of society and transform every part of culture. All church life and Christian living should reflect scriptural truth in clear and compelling ways. Contextualization must be comprehensive."[1] The arts have important roles to contribute to living Christianly in all of life, within peoples'

---

1. Ott and Strauss, *Encountering Theology of Mission*, 284–85.

social and cultural contexts. Just as Peter freshly interpreted what God was doing with the coming of the Holy Spirit to the throngs in Jerusalem, God's people need to work with the arts to make a difference.

This chapter discusses how contextualized arts move Christian witness and the gospel message into daily life, beyond church walls and written texts into society, both for individuals and groups of people. How do believers, as bearers of the gospel, extend compassion and care into societies where sickness, violence, and disaster have created great need? How do the arts shape and form believers for faithfully following Jesus within their own contexts, both personally and in ways that affect their local communities and societies? How do believers develop meaningful events and rituals that address life cycles in ways unique to their cultural contexts and that lead to transformed lives? The number of possibilities is overwhelming. We focus here on two essential arenas that critically affect Christian witness: (1) the arts as public witness and (2) the arts in daily life.

The Arts as Public Witness

The news on television and social media is overwhelming, discouraging, and depressing—full of hauntingly sad images of HIV/AIDS orphans, deadly diseases, poverty, and traumatized victims of war and natural disasters. Where is God in the midst of desperation, illness, injustice, devastation, and life-threatening crises? What is the role of music and the arts in these scenarios? The good news comes from an emerging recognition that music and the arts can make a difference in affecting society. Medical ethnomusicology, for example, is a newly emerging discipline that comprises integrative research in "the study of music, medicine, and culture."[2] Likewise, others are employing drawing and theater in ways that foster psychological healing in diverse cultural contexts.

Songs of Life: Music, Witness, and Medicine

While mission work has always included the healing of diseases through hospitals and community health programs, there is a growing realization that the arts as expressive culture can contribute to health education, instilling comfort and hope to languishing medical patients while also communicating the good news. Traditionally, mission medical work has brought physical healing while also bearing witness to the healing power found in Jesus Christ. Not only are healing and faith interlinked, but many cultures across Africa view

2. Roseman, "Fourfold Framework for Cross-Cultural, Integrative Research," 19.

religion, healing, and music as intimately linked. Music often plays an integral role in healing rituals, including in communities that still practice witchcraft. Seeking to counteract and speak into the situation, ethnodoxologist[3] Megan Meyers works with young people in Songs of Life workshops that play into the dynamic of Christian faith. The workshop has two goals: "(1) to create songs based on health topics that could be used in ongoing health teaching and educational campaigns in the surrounding community, and (2) to develop composers who could continue to use the songwriting method to create songs that edify and grow the local church."[4] The newly trained composers sing out:

> We want to see people free of malaria,
> Because malaria is a harmful sickness
> We believe that together we can win,
>   Yes, we can win![5]

Songs of Life workshops have been integrated into health education projects in Mozambique. Meyers summarizes medical teaching content and also serves as musical midwife in helping these principles come to life through culturally appropriate musical forms. She explains:

> Their shining faces said it all. The young participants were proud of the song they had created, and were glad to be able to share it with other participants. All their hard work in learning about diseases, some of which had killed friends and relatives, was now being transformed into songs that would be repeated—in schools, in homes, and on the road.[6]

With the help of a guitar, the wordsmithing of the song was entirely the work of the young men. Although the people were too shy to dance, the song began with a catchy chorus that the audience immediately picked up, followed by rhyming, almost rap-like verses, and local spontaneous vocalized "whoas" soaring above the melody—a bit like a young Michael Jackson when he sang with his brothers.

The workshops have multidimensional benefits. First, they educate the young people themselves about how to prevent and treat disease. They also

3. An ethnodoxologist encourages contextualized art forms in Christian communities around the world based on a blend of concepts from ethnomusicology, missiology, worship, and the arts.
4. Meyers, "Songs of Life," 41.
5. The text above is an English translation of a song composed and sung in Portuguese: *Queremos ver pessoas livre de malaria, Porque a malaria e uma doenca prejudicial. Acreditamos que juntos venceremos, sim venceremos!* Meyers, "Songs of Life," 41.
6. Meyers, "Songs of Life," 44.

teach them how to compose songs in groups—a skill for continued health education and church development programs. "Songs of life" are composed and made available to the local community to play an important role in a country that has only one doctor per 44,000 people,[7] in which HIV/AIDS ranges from 11 to 25 percent of the population, and where fatal diseases include tuberculosis, typhoid, and malaria—each preventable and treatable. Such efforts form a holistic witness that goes beyond merely preaching about eternal life to living the abundant life Jesus promised in John 10:10. The weaving together of good works and the gospel bears witness to the reign of God and offers "a transformative process for the in-breaking of the Kingdom of God in the public health arena."[8]

Trauma and the Healing of Psychological Pain: Visual Arts and Ethnodramatology

Around the world, people encounter horrific events in their lives. Trauma results when people are overcome by intense fear, helplessness, and horror in the face of threatened death. How can one cope with such pain that is often internalized, ignored, and left to fester? For healing to take place, people need to express their pain in safe places where they feel heard and understood. The arts provide arenas for dealing with feelings of anger, doubt, and abandonment in nonthreatening and secure environments. The church often denies these feelings in light of the call to praise the Lord at all times. As the various psalms teach, though, there are times for lament and crying out to God.[9] Two interactive arenas that provide safe spaces for expressing one's emotional and psychological pain in healthy lament are drawing and drama.

Vignette 6.1

Healing Trauma through an Art Exercise

Harriet Hill
American Bible Society

We had already started the two-week Trauma Healing Workshop in Aboukobe, Ghana. The six participants from Côte d'Ivoire were delayed due to civil unrest

7. Meyers, "Songs of Life," 42.
8. Meyers, "Songs of Life," 47.
9. Laments appear throughout the Scriptures and make up the largest category of song genre in the book of Psalms. Lamentations, an entire book, is a lamentation making a complaint that God listens to. Hill, "Arts and Trauma Healing."

in Abidjan that closed down the airport. When they arrived, I arranged to lead them through some of the materials on the Sunday afternoon. This included the art exercise to express their pain.

I gave them a big sheet of paper and markers and told them to get quiet and ask God to show them the pain in their heart, and then to start drawing without thinking about it too much. "Just let the pain come out through your fingers," I said.

We had twenty minutes of silence as they all drew. Then I invited them to share their drawings and talk about them with the group. They all were eager to do so.

Figure 6.2 Koya's art exercise from a trauma healing workshop

This is Koya's drawing (see fig. 6.2). When he stopped drawing and looked at it, he said, "Oh! I didn't realize I was hurting so much!" He explained that the grave marker on the bottom left was the grave of his father, who had been a leading pastor in the area. Since his death, oversight of the churches fell to Koya. To his surprise, he portrayed these churches as a chain choking him.

The five crosses on the bottom right are people who died in the conflict. The three figures above the crosses are their children. Koya explained that the hardest day in the life of the church was when they had to send their children south to the demilitarized zone so that they could continue their education. There would be no phone contact, post, or possibility of visits. They had to trust God to watch over them. It was a tearful send-off.

As Koya explained the drawing, he noticed he had only one leg. "I feel stuck, unable to move," he said. One of the others in the group said, "Look, your heart is on the wrong side!" Koya said, "I hoped you wouldn't notice that. The person next to me is my wife, and her heart is still large. But my heart is small and hard, and I'm moving away from her."

This exercise allowed Koya to come to grips with what was going on inside him. Later, he expressed his pain to God in a verbal lament and brought his pain to the cross of Christ. "By his wounds we are healed" (Isa. 53:5). Koya went back to Côte d'Ivoire with new strength.

Notice that two art forms were integrated into trauma healing for Koya—drawing and poetry (most likely as song). Drawing therapeutically helped this victim of violence to bring his internal pain to the surface, to process his story, and then to tell his story in a lament.

Playback Theatre offers yet another approach.[10] In vignette 6.2, we see how it can help someone not only to deal with inner tensions but also to feel heard and understood in a community.

Vignette 6.2

Playing Back Healing

Julisa Rowe
Artists in Christian Testimony International

"We know you're in there, pastor! Open the door, or we will kill this girl!" Pastor Bitok peered out his window at the gang of youth beating on his door and holding down a screaming girl. It was his landlord's daughter. He recognized some of the youth. To save the girl he unlocked his door; the gang rushed in, smashing his furniture, grabbing all they could carry, savagely whipping and beating him, breaking his spine, and leaving him paralyzed. "This is a warning, pastor, for sheltering the enemy and for marrying outside our tribe. We're watching you!"

The Playback Theatre actors listened intently as Pastor Bitok shared his story. When he finished speaking, they would immediately play his story back to the audience. The event was a trauma healing forum following Kenya's 2007–2008 postelection violence, and the pastor was one who was savagely beaten for sheltering members of the targeted tribe in the area.

10. See http://www.playbacktheatre.org.

As the drama team emotionally and artistically played back the story, all eyes were riveted to the stage as the audience listened and cried. As the actors finished, they turned to Pastor Bitok. His head was buried in his hands as he wept. People were amazed—Kalenjin men don't cry![a]

Afterward, he said:

> When I shared, it was still personal. When the drama team began to act—especially the guy who took my place and acted on behalf of me—I felt it's no longer me, it's someone else feeling it. And when people responded, when people began to express their emotions with me, I felt the burden is no longer on me alone, I have people who feel with me, people who identify with me, people who have taken over the burden. So right now, I feel so free. It brings a lot of healing.

[a] The Kalenjin people consist of a group of related peoples—Kipsikis, Nandi, Pokot—and others who live in west-central Kenya, northern Tanzania, and Uganda, and who speak southern Nilotic languages of the Nilo-Saharan language family. "Kalenjin People," *Britannica*, September 24, 2010, https://www.britannica.com/topic/Kalenjin.

We have seen that the arts are flexible enough that they can be powerfully engaged in situations of life stress. They function as life processors, as means to reflect and work through the experience of pain and disease. In such situations of dire need and immediacy, the arts can be adapted to the context and bring comfort and consolation. Notice that in each case God's people have sought to bring the hope of the kingdom of God by employing the arts in particular contexts and situations. God's people engaging with the arts become important elements of the message. His people are following Christ's teaching in incarnational ways and representing Christ among peoples who have been victimized and need relief from overwhelming stress.

But how might we avoid such situations of horrendous violence and injustice in the first place? How can we help people to follow Christ in ways that foster living Christianly with one another in ways that speak more deeply into cultural values and beliefs? Witness and worship that slavishly follow what others bring from the outside does not engage many of the deep-level questions confronting local peoples who are living within their local contexts. During my years in Africa, I often overheard African leaders bemoan, "Christianity in Africa is five miles wide and only an inch deep." With the African church among the fastest-growing churches in the world, evangelism has been and continues to be a main focus, most often with little or no time to adequately attend to living as Christians within African contexts. The churches lack intentional focus on deep-level cultural issues. Such nominalism is not unique to Africa, however. It is found worldwide and takes on different forms and expressions.[11]

African Christianity (and that of other parts of the world) needs, then, to look at witness via contextualized arts extended into all areas of life. Contextualizing the gospel via the arts requires addressing all of life. A lot of living takes place between the bookends of Christian witness and worship. From contexts where the Christian faith is newly accepted to those where the Christian faith has been long established, issues of the gospel and culture in daily life need to be continually addressed. Next, we consider critical life scenarios where contextualized arts have contributed to maintaining allegiance to Jesus on a daily basis. Christian witness includes fostering a maturing of faith for living Christianly. Such maturing becomes the grounding foundation of "Christ in you, the hope of glory" (Col. 1:27)—a key to believers' ability to move out into society and bear incarnational witness to Christ.

The Arts in Daily Life: Living between the Bookends of Christian Witness and Worship

In the Great Commission, Jesus identifies a series of practices for going into all the world: (1) make disciples of all nations; (2) baptize in the name of the Father, Son, and Holy Spirit; *and* (3) teach them to obey everything that the Lord has commanded (Matt. 28:19–20). In other words, living Christianly is composed of becoming a faithful follower (disciple) of Christ, being baptized in the name of the Triune God, and obediently following the teachings of Christ—all within one's cultural context. While worship and witness are the two main purposes for the existence of the church, a lot of living takes place in between. The process of making disciples and teaching them to obey all that Christ taught is fleshed out in everyday encounters between Christians and surrounding nonbelieving neighbors. We will consider practices of employing the arts as part of this daily living, yet in expanded roles—roles that extend the arts out from proclamation and witness into storytelling, discipling, celebrating life events, and linking back to worshiping. We intend to focus on what takes place—or should take place—in between the witness-worship dialectic.

---

11. "The situation in Africa and the West is very different. I would say that the West is nominal because it has seen Christendom as the religion of Jesus and it is unacceptable (nationalism, tribalism, violence and war are wrapped up with Christendom). Africa is more like Europe in the fourth or fifth centuries. Its people and cultures are still being evangelized. The conversion of a culture takes centuries, not decades. African discipleship and the conversion of its cultures (mores, laws, etc.) is still in the early stages." Scott Sunquist, email correspondence with author, May 22, 2017.

Figure 6.3
The arts: from witness to worship and life-in-between

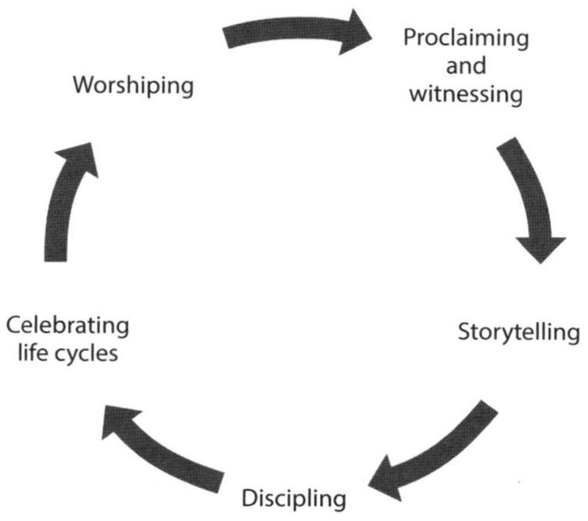

It's important to note that witness, like worship, is intended to be a lifestyle rather than merely compartmentalized moments of activity. Figure 6.3 shows each of these dimensions, which are embedded in culture and interlinked. We need to critically contextualize each dimension in ways that bring the relevancy of the gospel to a people in their daily lives, within their unique contexts.[12] In two formative places believers interact with the arts in their daily lives: discipleship (spiritual formation) and celebrating life cycles. These make up the main topic of this section.[13]

Discipling: Songs and Paintings That Transform Lives

Discipling through the arts, which nourish people at a deep level, is most effective when appropriate to local contexts. Contextualization of the gospel takes on unique, distinctive forms and symbols that speak into a people's everyday lives within their own milieu. Although many connections form between peoples as they are constantly moving back and forth between village and city life in Africa and elsewhere, each context maintains distinctive elements from its location, especially in relation to language and worldview.

12. In practice, research, and the literature, mission studies have focused mainly on contextualized arts for and in worship and witness. As this is a fairly young area of investigation, much is still to be done, and many major areas require further in-depth research studies. Interrelated and highly critical for living Christianly, these two arenas of contextualized arts in discipleship and celebrating life cycles have yet to be adequately addressed on a comprehensive basis.

13. "Preaching," declaring God's Word in the assembly, will be addressed in the following chapter in relation to oral communication.

Songs in rural African life. Ceewaa, the market lady, was walking home to her village with other women after a long day of bargaining and selling her produce at the local market in northern Côte d'Ivoire. Just as the village women were doing, she joined in the custom of swearing at and derogatorily criticizing one another. She was just doing what she and the others had always done. Yet this particular Cebaara Senufo market lady claimed to be a Christian who "walked the Jesus road." That evening, she went to the village prayer meeting and heard a new song based on Matthew 7:3–5 for the first time. It advised, "You hypocrite, first take the plank out of your own eye, and then you will see clearly to remove the speck from your brother's eye." Since experiencing that song, she has changed how she interacts with the market women as they walk home. The song transformed the way she lives out her daily life walking the Jesus road. In her setting, the song communicated so persuasively that she matured in her faith and holistic transformation took place.[14]

Furthermore, Ceewaa naturally expected the song to speak to her on a spiritual, religious level, as is common in African worldview and practice. As a nonliterate person, music serves as a major expressive language that plays a dominant part of both religion and daily life.[15] John Mbiti, a noted scholar on African religion, summarizes the prominent role of religion in African life:

> Religion . . . is by far the richest part of the African heritage. . . . [It] is found in all areas of human life . . . [and] has dominated the thinking of African peoples to such an extent that it has shaped their cultures, their social life, their political organization and economic activities. We can say, therefore, that religion is closely bound up with the traditional way of African life, while at the same time, this way of life has shaped religion.[16]

Expressive culture in Africa, such as songs, dance, visual arts, and even architecture, plays a dominant role in shaping religious and daily life. As Jean Kidula argues, the "invocation of the spiritual into the natural is evidenced in the practices and arts of daily life."[17] An awareness of the supernatural always pervades African daily life. For example, non-Christian traditional sacrifices of rice, chickens, or goats are offered throughout the day to guarantee good harvests or protection from the spirits as a baby is being bathed or as one begins one's journey to market. Songs, proverbs, and other art forms are integrated into these practices. This means that the arts are highly

14. King, *Pathways in Christian Music Communication*, 176–92.
15. Kidula, "Music Culture: African Life," 46.
16. Mbiti, *Introduction to African Religion*, 10.
17. Kidula, "Music Culture: African Life," 46.

Figure 6.4 Daily life: women at the well (Republic of Congo)

formative as well as expressive. It is essential to include them as part of the discipling process; then they can contribute to maintaining allegiance to following Jesus on a daily basis.

Songs in contemporary African life. We need not limit discipling via the arts to traditional Africa. Cultural practices continue and move into city and urban life in updated forms. With the rise of gospel music in Kenya, where Kenyan singer-songwriters are composing their own contemporary, contextualized forms of gospel music, songs continue to advise and influence daily life. Christian television programs, such as *Joy Bringers*, make a practice of interjecting music into discussions about living Christianly in contemporary society. Faustin Munishi serves as one example. A Tanzanian superstar gospel singer and pastor, Munishi became well known in Kenya during the 1980s. He specializes in writing Christian lyrics in Swahili, a national language of Tanzania and Kenya. His songs address issues in daily Christian living. For example, in his song "I Am under the Rock," Munishi addresses and personifies negative behaviors such as drunkenness and adultery that he sees as "sore spots in social and spiritual relationships, and how these are resolved when Christian standards of living are followed, both to safeguard against false accusations and to provide accountability."[18] Munishi admonishes his audience, in a way similar to the psalms, to tell these enemies that "Jesus hides me, I am under the rock." In other words, protection and strength from temptation come from Jesus.

Munishi's song that addresses sin, *Mwana wangu una nini* (My child, what is it?),[19] provides a fascinating example of the use of metaphors and allegories that intrigue his East African audiences. Written as a dialogue, yet sung as a solo, the song speaks into deep levels of cultural concerns in light of biblical teaching. The metaphor of an uncle personifies sin, reminding them of the familiar cultural practice of addressing their parents through a middle person. He warns that the "uncle" could misrepresent them or even harass

18. Kidula, "Polishing the Luster of the Stars," 418.
19. Example 2: Munishi, tape 4, side B, track 3 in Kidula, "Polishing the Luster of the Stars," 419.

them. He encourages the children to speak directly to their parents, not to fear talking with them. Ultimately, he relates the metaphor to one's relationship with God and to the way "the devil pretends to be an advocate (uncle) when his true intentions are to suppress the rights of God's children."[20] He sings:

My child, what is it?
Why are you depressed?
What has befallen you?
Do not hide it
I see that you have changed
Your countenance is different

Listen Father
Uncle tortures me
Everything you give me
Uncle takes it away
Or else, he threatens
To tell on me to you

For many years now
Uncle has been torturing me
When you give him work
I am the one who does it
Or else, he threatens
To tell on me to you

Uncle gives me
All his loads to bear
Until I am so tired
I can't be a slave anymore
I confess my error now
Judge me as my father

Listen my child
I have heard
All that you have done
I have forgiven you
Don't hide your errors again
If you confess you will be forgiven

Stand up for your rights
Like a child of God
Your religious habits/traditions

20. For the full song text in both Kiswahili and English, see Kidula, "Polishing the Luster of the Stars," 419.

Can become like an uncle.
If you don't confess, he will tell
Your errors to father God

Father is God the Father
Satan is the uncle
You are the child
You know your own faults
Your faults as of today
Jesus has forgiven
He has saved you, and Satan
Will not control your rights again[21]

Popular culture in the form of an African gospel song, then, serves as a life processor for shaping and forming people in living out their Christian faith in ways that honor God and move them toward greater righteousness into their lives.

Munishi also directly addresses issues that arise in the misappropriation of "Christian" rituals and ceremonies. While many choral works, known as *makwaya*, convey the biblical narrative, Munishi starts by addressing contemporary behavior during the Christmas season and from there develops the true reason for Christmas.[22] He advises his church flock as follows:

I am not saying that there is anything wrong with making merry, jumping around, celebrating, having new clothes, shoes, special food, etc. Let us celebrate Christmas because God's child is born. He was born in Bethlehem to save us.

But I am saying that drunkenness, prostitution and adultery, greed, stealing and thievery, vexation, disputes at Christmas are totally wrong because Christmas is not any of those things. So let the celebration be appropriate, that is, be done in a holy manner.

The one born at Christmas was neither a drunkard nor greedy. He was not deceitful nor cunning. He is the Savior of the world. So don't mess up the meaning of Christmas with the way you celebrate it. Celebrate it in a worthy fashion.[23]

In such texts, Munishi is doing artistic critical contextualization that considers cultural practices in light of the Scriptures. Thus, we need to look for

21. English translation by Jean Ngoya Kidula in Kidula, "Polishing the Luster of the Stars," 419–20. Used with permission from the Society for Ethnomusicology.
22. Jean Ngoya Kidula, "'Sing and Shine': Religious Popular Music in Kenya" (PhD diss., University of California Los Angeles, 1998), 177.
23. Translation by Jean Ngoya Kidula, not in poetic form, but the general gist of each verse, in Kidula, "'Sing and Shine,'" 177.

what is going on in popular and folk culture, indeed in all forms of expressive culture, including those we do not normally consider using in Christian practice. More is taking place in such musical genres than outsiders are aware of. This also holds true in Western popular culture, including hip hop culture and forms of music not usually found in the church. Daniel White Hodge speaks of the paradigm shift that has taken place in the Western world. He suggests and convincingly argues that folk culture and popular culture have greater impact worldwide today than high culture, which has traditionally been the forte of Christian worship practices.[24] This sobering statement needs to be taken seriously.

It is important here not to argue that one or the other is better. Rather, we need to investigate and pursue employing the best expressive languages suited for each cultural context. We often limit the uses of song to the purposes appropriate in our own cultures, and therefore we fail to discover the significant and different ways that songs are used within different peoples' cultural contexts. We miss opportunities inherent to the situation by assuming that we understand the culture. We inadvertently choose to remain ignorant of differing cultural practices. Rather than building bridges, we often create barriers to affecting believers at the deeper levels of culture and allegiance to Christ.

Vignette 6.3

Discipling Youth in Beira, Mozambique

Megan Meyers
Bible Institute of Sofala; Baptist Bible Institute, Beira, Mozambique

On a humid night in Beira, Mozambique, hundreds of Christian youth gathered for an open-mic concert. The room became uncharacteristically quiet as Ibraimo shared about his broken past and challenged his peers to greater maturity. "I'm an artist and a Christian. What is my responsibility? To be a light, to show people what God's done in my life through my music—to shine the values, the transformation, the liberty from sin, and to show God's love to my neighbors."

How did Ibraimo, who left home at age thirteen, come to this level of Christian maturity? He found a church that embraced him as he was, a rap artist. Rather than insisting that he abandon the art form he loves, the church

24. Hodge, *Soul of Hip Hop*, 68–70.

recognized his hunger for spiritual instruction and encouraged him to join a small group. Soon he started leading a small group and participating on the worship team.

But that wasn't enough for Ibraimo, who knew there were many youth who would never darken the doors of the church. So he created a rap group, Sementes de Abrão (Seeds of Abraham), whose express purpose was to "preach" (through rap) in the community outside the four walls of the church. Ibraimo also recognized the need to encourage fellow Christian artists, and three years ago he launched a monthly open-mic concert. This ongoing event has empowered Christian artists in their craft and their faith, as well as launched numerous creative ministries in the broader community—raising artists and reaching people through the creative arts.

As you can see from the preceding vignettes in this chapter, effective mission in the twenty-first century requires a different kind of mission group, one in which both artists and ministers honor one another and collaborate together. Participatory arts easily accessed by the whole community are essential. At the same time, we also call for naturally gifted and highly trained artists within any context to participate in both witness and worship. We need artists who are passionate and discerning disciples of Christ. They need to be able to "think Christianly about . . . what values they defend and promote in their workplaces and in their art, architecture, film, and music."[25]

Beyond this, musicians and artists need to function as cultural mediators, what Paul Hiebert calls "inbetweeners." As cultural mediators who can move between the cultural arts, musicians and artists can help participants understand one another and mediate in the face of disagreements. They must know the cultural art forms of both cultures well, not just their own. In doing so, they demonstrate love for both groups of people as they identify with them in their common humanity. This form of incarnational witness fosters "bold witness to the gospel without arrogance or control"[26] and functions at profound levels of authenticity and trust. As inbetweeners, musicians and artists ultimately seek to build bridges of understanding, mediate relationships, and negotiate partnerships in ministry. They minister out of a place of sincere love for the people before and among whom they are living out their lives in love with Jesus Christ. Musicians and artists are increasingly vital to global witness and the global church.

25. Myers, *Engaging Globalization*, 247.
26. Hiebert, *Gospel in Human Contexts*, 186.

But Who's Discipling the Artists?

A word about God's people is appropriate at this point. God's people, who interact with and employ the arts in Christian witness, worship, and life in between, include a range of Christian believers seeking to witness to the gospel. Musicians and artists who provide opportunities and create the resources for the work of the kingdom are included in this group. We often look to the arts for resources or products that can be integrated into communicating the gospel and leave behind the musicians and artists. However, in order to do effective discipling and celebrating-of-life events in public arenas, the artists themselves are in need of discipleship. They need a growing, dynamic, vital, and maturing relationship with the Lord Jesus Christ.

Artists who can shape and form others through their art need shaping and forming themselves. They cannot sing about what they do not know. Incarnational Christian witness requires growing, maturing Christians, including artists, to represent and model Christ. As in the case of Ibraimo, artists have much to offer in terms of ministry in church services, and they are also aware of enhanced ways of reaching out to the local community, among peoples that the church might not otherwise know how to engage and help to grow. Including musicians and artists as a regular part of ministry and mission teams needs to be the norm for Christian organizations and churches—not the exception. And, as is often the case, many also become pastors and missionaries. Vignette 6.4 offers a means of developing and discipling artists in the process of making art.

Celebrating Life Cycles

Anthropologists such as Victor Turner and Mary Douglas have long argued that it is difficult to create and maintain deep sacred beliefs unless they are related to sacred communities and sacred rites. Christian rites in evangelical churches usually include baptism, the Lord's Supper, life-cycle rites such as baby dedications, marriages, and funerals, each one giving corporate expression to the Christian faith. Hiebert encourages those of us from the West to learn how to incorporate and express our faith "using living sacred symbols and rites that renew and transform us both individually and corporately." He does so with the hope of raising our awareness to the critical role of rituals in religion. These play an especially important role in Christian witness worldwide, particularly in non-Western cultures, in which rituals are central in the lives of the people. If we ignore ritual, Hiebert argues, we stand in danger of "bringing a gospel that is purely information to be believed rather than a *way of life to be lived.*[27] Culturally appropriate Christian rituals hold great potential for getting the gospel message off the printed page and processed into the lives of local believers.

The effort to include ritual in Christian living requires fostering and encouraging rites of passage. These rites of passage address the need to deal with life transitions in ways that nurture transformational living as followers of Jesus. This became a pressing reality as one pastor-musician on a short-term visit to southern China offered to help Bible translators. What did the local people want to learn from him? They asked for help in creating Christian rites of passage and celebrations of major life events. In vignette 6.4, he takes us with him to experience the significance of these Christian rituals in China.

Vignette 6.4
What Is a Christian Ritual?

Nathan Watkins
Adjunct Professor of World Music, Azusa Pacific University

The waters of baptism were pleasantly warm for the newest Christ followers of the D Minority (name withheld for protection). Of course, this is not too surprising given [that] their baptism was furtively conducted in the bathroom tub of a hotel room, . . . away from the wary eyes of family, . . . away from the prying eyes of neighbors, . . . away from the suspicious eyes of the Chinese government. But truly, the water temperature was the least of their concerns.

Hugs all around were followed by taking the Lord's Supper together for the first time, rice cakes and rice wine serving as the elements. Then they created a worship circle, and the new believers were taught a few simple choruses to sing. The total event took two hours from start to finish and marked the beginning of their new life in Christ.

Figuring out how to mark that salvation moment was not difficult. The elements of water, bread and cup, and music were not hard to imagine, create, or adapt in the context. The New Testament is clear about salvation and how Christians worldwide can mark this special moment. Far more challenging for those young believers are the other non-Christian events that typically mark life in the D Minority: weddings, childbirth, the shift from childhood to adulthood, funerals, the honoring of ancestors, even celebrating the new year.

27. Hiebert, *Gospel in Human Contexts*, 99 (emphasis added).

Since the New Testament has virtually no examples or guidelines about those kinds of life-stage events, Christ followers in the D Minority legitimately question how rituals might be created that are both God honoring and culturally meaningful.

- What format should they follow?
- What symbols ought to be involved?
- Who should officiate at the ceremony?[a]
- What music should be created and/or performed?
- What kind of art would be appropriate for the event?
- What traditional elements, if any, can be included that would give the ceremony validity in the cultural context without ushering in overtones of non-Christian faith practices?

These questions, and more, ask what "working out your salvation with fear and trembling" (Phil. 2:12) looks like in southern China today.

[a] As of this writing, there is no established local church, church polity, or leadership among the D Minority to wrestle with these issues.

Creating rites of passage among the D people in China was one of their first questions, not to be ignored until a later date. The process requires deep levels of cultural understanding and needs to be done mostly by cultural insiders. Often, music and the arts play integral roles in marking life transitions and establishing identity. In most African Christian communities, celebrations of life include birth, naming ceremonies, baptism, puberty rites (i.e., circumcision), confirmation, marriage, and death. However, not all indigenous rites of passage are appropriate for living out the Christian faith. Some need to be withdrawn or changed. Historically, for example, Logooli ritual life in western Kenya initially accommodated the coming of Christian ideas in the last century. The affected rituals include (a) the abandonment of *liswakila*, sacrifices usually made on behalf of a child two to three months old; (b) the adjustment of the circumcision rite; (c) the adjustment of the wedding; and (d) the cessation of annual communal sacrifices.[28] Yet many rites are essential in addressing major life transitions such as births, weddings, and funerals in light of the Scriptures. Holistic transformation requires discernment as to which need to be retained and infused with the Christian message. At this point local voices need to lead in critical contextualization of these rituals in light of the Scriptures.

28. See Kidula, *Music in Kenyan Christianity*, 65–66.

Places where the Christian faith has taken root over the last 125 years, as in western Kenya among the Maragoli, can serve as models for showing how such rites can be adapted, often in ways that contrast greatly from Western practices. Funerals in Africa, for example, are major rituals that can last over a period of days, with music and the arts playing significant roles in expressing grief and serving as integral markers of the rite. Jean Kidula, in her "Diary of a Christian Funeral—A Long Expression of Grief through Music,"[29] recounts how her father's funeral proceeded over a period of three days that led up to the funeral service and the burial. The death was announced in the village with a great amount of wailing and with the singing of Christian hymns and choruses. This did not happen just at one time but continued throughout the days and evenings whenever guests arrived at the home to show their respects. Guests often announced their arrival with wailing as well. Driving the body from the mortuary to the church and then to the home was accompanied by singing and dancing. Later in the evening, the Kidula sisters, who had grown up performing Christian songs together, sang their father's favorite songs in English, Swahili, Logooli, and any other language they could sing in. They sang children's songs, church songs, folk songs, and some of their favorite songs. This was just the first day. Music and singing became a part of the local environment throughout the event as people took part in various dynamics of expressing grief and honoring Kidula's father, the departed Christian statesman, pastor, and pioneer missionary.

This ritual commemorating this Kenyan pastor presents just one example among many different rites that mark life-cycle events throughout the world. The long list of varying rituals that play significant roles in the lives of people worldwide reveals major contrasts in life cycles. Among the Navajo, for example, the first laugh of a Navajo child is of major significance and marks the child's moving from the spirit world into the physical world. This means that the child is now fully human and present among the people. It is usually celebrated with a laughing party closely associated with Navajo culture— something that was condemned by earlier gospel messengers. The question for believing Navajos then becomes "How should Christian Navajos celebrate this grand event?" A laughing party contextualized for Navajo Christians included meeting in a *hogan* (the place considered to be religious), proclaiming the name of Jesus in the languages of people attending the event, worshiping with contextualized songs that reflected traditional Navajo ceremonial singing,

---

29. King, Kidula, Krabill, and Oduro, *Music in the Life of the African Church*, 81.

prayer in multiple languages, and the celebration of the gift of laughter that Navajos recognize as coming from the Creator.[30]

It is important to note how the life-cycle rituals are adjusted to meet the expectations and needs of local believers in maintaining allegiance to Christ. These rituals reinforce ideas, values, and teaching through audio, kinesic, visual, artifactual, and physical spaces. Ritual involves a layering of knowledge that is not only heard but also felt, seen, experienced, and expressed. Such knowledge acquisition reinforces individual and collective memory.[31] Multivocal use of living symbols combined with ritual reenactments communicate at profound levels that affect living Christianly on a daily basis. The ultimate goal is that Christianity and the arts become not just functional but, as in the case of Logooli believers, also vibrant aspects of a people's daily life.[32] Integrating the arts in life rituals leads to the kind of transformational living that declares God's saving glory among the nations.

Conclusion

In between the bookends of witness and worship, communities foster life that is infused with maintaining allegiance to Christ by employing contextualized arts for witnessing in public arenas, discipling, and celebrating life events. The arts, as culturally embedded expressive languages, speak first into arenas of public witness, such as health education that teaches communities about methods for avoiding rampant diseases. The arts become therapeutic when addressing the pain of trauma and contribute to the healing of psychological pain from persecution or postconflict settings. Second, integrated into daily living, the arts become natural partners in the work of the church, from witness to worship and life in between. Discipleship and celebration of life cycles comprise two oft-overlooked arenas. Yet, as we have seen, when thoughtfully and appropriately engaged, they potentially have a deeply transformative impact. As life processors, the arts are not limited to or compartmentalized within the church building. Rather, they move out and facilitate life.

This truth is a blessing when we consider that millions of people around the world prefer or are confined to nonliterary communications. Music and the arts, as expressive languages, are interwoven into all of life, including religious life. Thus, we need to intentionally pursue a comprehensive contextualization of the gospel in oral modalities.

30. Charles, "Laughing Party."
31. Kidula, "Music Culture: African Life."
32. Kidula, *Music in Kenyan Christianity*, 70.

Preaching the gospel story by employing culturally informed artistic oral modes is an essential part of witnessing in the public arena. We turn to this art of storytelling in our next chapter.

Questions for Discussion

1. How do the arts foster contextualizing the gospel into all of life?
2. Reflect on the ways that Christian musicians and artists are forming followers of Jesus through their music and/or their artistic media.
3. In what ways can the church and mission agencies intentionally disciple artists?

7

Telling God's Story among Oral and Postliterate Peoples

How can we share the gospel story among peoples who do not read?

Throughout its history, Western missions has placed great stress on literacy—both reading and writing. This is certainly understandable since the Word of God is foundational to our Christian faith. And the intentions of sharing the most important message in the world are indeed honorable. "Making disciples" often meant teaching people to read the Scriptures and to write. In some places, becoming literate was a requirement for baptism or church membership. However, such practices created outreach voids where many nonbelieving peoples were never reached. It also built up communication barriers between peoples. Nonliterate peoples believed that the Christian faith was foreign, or that God was just another god who could not speak to them in their own language. He seemed irrelevant—they did not need to deal with him. However, this misunderstanding can be avoided: literacy is not the only way by which to communicate. People have always communicated through sight and sound. They have never stopped and continue today in both actual and digital forms.

My Story: The Maasai Reject the Story of the Prodigal Son

I'll never forget the day when Moses, a Christian Maasai from Kenya, came into my office at Fuller Theological Seminary in Pasadena after I had just moved back to the States. He had been pursuing a master of divinity in the States for the past six years and had recently moved to Fuller for the PhD program. Moses had just returned from a trip to visit family in Kenya. One of his goals had been to share the story of God's love. He found himself in a quandary and was now asking for help in processing what he had experienced.

One evening as he sat with his family in Kenya, he was asked to tell the children what he had been learning in that foreign land where he had been studying. Moses chose to tell the story of the prodigal son. Surprisingly, as the story continued, the adults started leaving the group in disgust. Moses emphasized that God the Father not only forgave the son, but he also welcomed him home with a big party, rather than with punishment. This was highly offensive to the Maasai family. The uncle responded by yelling at the children that they dare not remember such a despicable story. The story ran against Maasai cultural values. The adults had no respect for a God who did not know how to punish his son.

The next day, though, the young boys from the group not only talked about the story they were not to remember; they also made songs about it. Among the Maasai, song is a common way of remembering, discussing, and communicating. Moses's brother was a greatly admired singer-songwriter who composed an interactive song based on the "despicable" story he had heard from his brother. The song served both as a means of retelling the story *and* as a means of initiating further discussions with the uncle and the elders of the village. The selected genre, known as *eoko*, goes beyond merely singing information. It also functions as a socioeducational tool. The song form is grounded in a question-answer pattern that allows for improvisation wherein people sing their current thoughts as a form of group dialogue. Its purpose is to get people of different ages to interact with one another on the spot. The *eoko* genre is especially adept as a means for processing new or controversial thoughts, such as those told in the story of the prodigal son. The following Sunday, the newly composed storytelling song based on the prodigal son was sung and received well. Processing of new information had taken place in a culturally informed manner.

Moses was stunned at the contrast in dynamics: same story, yet a different method of communication. While he had studied well and was theologically knowledgeable, the linear, propositional method of presentation as practiced in the United States did not connect well with his people. Back in his home

Skyler Russell Photography

Figure 7.1 Maasai singers and dancers

area, Moses encountered the dynamics of oral communication. Oral communication is based on a way of thinking that processes, is memorable, and communicates through a combination of signal systems that are not print oriented. To convey something close to the intended message of the story requires a different sociocultural format. In this case, the *eoko* not only facilitated telling the cognitive information of the story, but also functioned as a means of processing and persuading via social connections and relational interaction. When telling the story of the prodigal son in Kenya, Moses encountered what missiologists and secular scholars have been discovering since the last half of the twentieth century: the large majority of peoples around the world function as oral communicators.

The arts play essential roles in oral communication and gospel witness. Storytelling, drama, songs, proverbs, dance, and visual arts communicate powerfully as they combine together for fully integrated, multisensory experiences that "speak the Word" in holistic and profound ways. The arts bring to the surface deeply embedded cultural and life issues. As expressive languages, they carry significant means for affecting and transforming people's ways of thinking and for increasing allegiance to God. This chapter aims to break the myth that one must be an astute, fully literate reader before confessing faith in Jesus Christ. We take a look at orality and relevant communication methods for witnessing among the majority of the world's nonliterate peoples. We also hint at how twenty-first-century postliterates, mainly in the West, also prefer oral formats. With the ever-increasing rise of digital technology worldwide, the impact of the arts and orality are not diminishing. Rather, they are taking on new emphases and functions. Increasing in significance worldwide, arts—from classical to folk to popular—are providing the content and major substance for film, radio, audio, digital, and social media. Sight and sound are on the rise.

Orality in the Twenty-First Century

In our fast-paced world, we find ourselves connecting through oral, visual, and digital media. While we highly value print literacy, millions of people around the world communicate through oral methods of communication.[1] Many have never had the opportunity to learn to read, or if they can read, they choose not to. As the late Avery Willis, former director of the International Orality Network (ION), is known to have claimed, "Seventy percent of the world's people today can't, don't or won't read."[2] While such statistics may seem inflated, the sad reality is that nonliteracy[3] is rampant throughout the world, including in the United States. Some 32 million adults in the US cannot read beyond a fifth-grade level, 70 percent of prison inmates cannot read beyond a fourth-grade level, and 19 percent of high school graduates cannot read at all.[4] UNESCO's Institute for Statistics reports that more than one-half of children and adolescents are not learning worldwide.[5] Other statistics point to 774 million adults worldwide who are not able to read.[6]

What does this mean for effectively telling the gospel story and interacting with the Scriptures in daily life among oral, semi-oral, or digital-preference

1. "Despite the steady rise in literacy rates over the past 50 years, there are still 750 million illiterate adults around the world, most of whom are women." "Literacy," UNESCO Institute for Statistics, accessed October 25, 2018, http://uis.unesco.org/en/topic/literacy.
2. Jewell, "Winning the Oral Majority," 56.
3. I find "nonliterate" a more appropriate term than "illiterate." I will use these terms interchangeably.
4. "About Us," Literacy Inc., accessed October 25, 2018, http://literacyinc.com/about-us.
5. "More Than One-Half of Children and Adolescents Are Not Learning Worldwide," UNESCO Institute for Statistics, September 2017, http://uis.unesco.org/sites/default/files/documents/fs46-more-than-half-children-not-learning-en-2017.pdf.
6. Tom Steffen notes that "according to a study by the US Department of Education, National Institute of Literacy released April 4, 2013, some 774 million people around the globe cannot read. Females hold the highest illiteracy rate at 66 percent." Steffen, *Worldview-Based Storying*, 1.

peoples? The implications are staggering. Erik Aasland reports below on the case in Kazakhstan.

Vignette 7.1

Translated Evangelism Materials or "Teaching Tales" in Kazakhstan

Erik Aasland
Adjunct Assistant Professor of Anthropology,
Fuller Theological Seminary

When Kazakhstan opened up after independence in the early 1990s, missionaries and their agencies reached for *Operation World* to locate data needed for strategy. According to the overview, literacy in Kazakhstan was 99 percent. There was great excitement at the thought of being able to translate evangelism and training material from Russian and English to effectively reach the Kazakhs. Unfortunately, the Soviet literacy statistics led them astray. Soviet officials had generated the following syllogism: 1. Our educational system works. 2. Ninety-nine percent of school-age children and youth are in school. 3. Therefore we have 99 percent literacy. Years later there were storerooms full of books and booklets that just did not sell and were not used in the classroom. The agencies had not worked with a valid literacy statistic and had also failed to consider other contextual matters related to the effectiveness of a literature-translation approach. Factors to be considered besides the literacy rate include whether people remain readers into adulthood and the role and possible preference for orality-based resources, plus the issues of similarities in worldview between the source documents and the ministry context.

Meanwhile, in the course of teaching in a Kazakhstani Bible school, I realized the importance of working with storytelling and proverbs in effectively teaching and training Kazakhs. I began focusing on teaching through stories. Kazakhs have a wealth of stories and proverbs that are told together in a rhetorical and pedagogical approach. My wife and I began to write short stories and parables that incorporated Kazakh as well as biblical proverbs. The response to these "Teaching Tales" was so positive that we eventually wrote a book with Kazakh stories and accompanying proverbs addressing moral issues. We developed stories that spoke to current issues in Kazakhstani society. Once we had field-tested the stories, we only included the ones that Kazakhs found most significant. We understood that we were modeling for Kazakhs an

effective way to reach their people. We made a point to tell Kazakh believers
that their own similar stories could outshine ours.

Walter Ong, an early orality scholar in the late twentieth century, discussed
the modern discovery of primary oral cultures. He verified the longevity of
oral traditions by citing examples from the Old Testament, such as the book
of Ecclesiastes.[7] Ong identified three main types of oral learners: (1) primary,
(2) residual, and (3) secondary oral learners. Primary oral communicators
consist of people who live in contexts where literacy is not known, practiced,
or desired. They think of words as sounds, not as ink on paper. They often
can move easily between languages since they do not need to think of the
words in print first. Residual oral communicators are people who have been
exposed to literacy in learning to read and write. Yet they maintain a strong
preference for oral learning over literacy. Secondary oral communicators, according to Ong, are people who depend on electronic audio and visual communications.[8] We see this group expanding worldwide with the ever-growing
explosion of digital and multimedia communications. While people are highly
literate, they prefer to acquire information and entertainment from electronic
media. Significantly, digital platforms now also make it possible for primary
and secondary oral communicators to directly interact through oral forms of
communication, such as storytelling, song, and proverbs on platforms such
as YouTube and Facebook.

Thus, all the world is telling their story—just in different ways. Orality
and literacy coexist side by side. While orality among humans has persisted
from time immemorial, written forms of communication are also valid. Oral
and literate communicators interact with one another on a daily basis. In
today's world, the boundaries between them are often fuzzy and blurred.
For instance, we can find "illiterate masses living in the midst of literate
groups" and "semi-literate folks who are functionally illiterate."[9] Influxes of
immigrants and refugees, who encompass all levels of orality, are influencing
the warp and woof of nations. They are creating a complex of intercultural
communication dynamics as they draw from such a wide array of literacy
levels and learning preferences, from oral to semi-oral to digital. This reality
opens vast opportunities for witness, especially when we grab hold of orality
as it is practiced in the midst of varying degrees of literacy. What all of these

---

7. Ong, *Orality and Literacy*, 16.
8. Ong, *Orality and Literacy*, 135.
9. A. Smith, "Communication and Continuity through Oral Transmission," 3.

peoples have in common is communication through oral means, especially through stories. Music and the arts lie at the core of orality, taking on unprecedented significance in missions.

Storytelling and Orality

Over the last forty years, evangelical missionaries have been experiencing an emerging revelation. Surprising "aha" moments are affecting their quest to effectively communicate the gospel. Missionaries and cross-cultural workers are discovering that reliance on propositional theology has missed the mark when making Christ known among the nations. They have been looking everywhere for critical keys to witness and come up short. A story makes this point.

Searching for the hippo. A young girl once longed to see a hippopotamus in the river near her house. One day, her parents informed her that a hippo was in the river and that she should hurry to see it. Excited, she ran to the riverbank looking for the hippo. Her enthusiasm quickly turned to disappointment: she could not find it. She searched up and down the bank, but the hippo was nowhere to be seen. Finally, she scrambled on top of a big rock in order to get a good vantage point from which to view the entire river. Still, she could not see the hippo. Disappointed, she went home and told her parents how hard she looked but could not find the hippo. "You didn't know it," explained her parents, "but the very rock that you climbed on was the hippo. It was under your feet and you didn't know it!"[10]

Often beneath our feet lie the very things we search for: the cultural resources to make Christ known. From the Ifugao people in the Philippines to the Kazakhs, from the Builsa in Ghana to the Madia hill peoples in India, missionaries and Bible translators are discovering that foundational communication resources pervade the cultures where they are working. Tom Steffen, an early adopter and leader in the orality movement, explains:

> As I began to work systematically through the New Tribes Mission evangelism model—Word, God, Satan, Humanity, Sin, Judgment, Jesus Christ—I soon discovered that the Ifugao of the Philippines were totally unimpressed with such a propositional presentation. They had difficulty understanding it, much less telling others the "good news." So much for a church planting movement! Shocked and surprised, it was back to the drawing board.[11]

10. Moon, *African Proverbs Reveal Christianity in Culture*, 1, retold in Clapp, *Peculiar People*, 251.
11. Steffen, *Worldview-Based Storying*, 139.

Steffen confesses that he had somehow missed the fact that "the gospel was a good tale to be told, not just taught propositionally through some systematic plan."[12] Alternative pedagogical possibilities and preferences had always been available yet remain unacknowledged, unidentified, undervalued, and untouched. N. T. Wright explains one of the complications: "Stories are often wrongly regarded as a poor person's substitute for the 'real thing,' which is to be discovered either in some abstract truth or in statements about 'bare facts.'"[13]

For Steffen and many well-intended gospel witnesses, the realities of first-century Christianity seem to have remained hidden within the pages of the Bible, God's storybook. In the Gospels, for example, Jesus not only gives us content but also models a method.[14] He is a storyteller par excellence. The three parables of the lost sheep, the lost coin, and the lost son comprise the whole chapter of Luke 15. Then, Luke 16 takes up yet another parable. Note that each story warranted inclusion in the sacred Scriptures that we seek to teach. Indeed, each story *is* Scripture. Jesus, whom Kenneth Bailey identifies as a "metaphorical theologian,"[15] modeled and validated doing theology through storytelling. His example influenced the early church and Christian witness.

A plethora of oral communication forms drive the study and practice of orality. They include storytelling, proverbs, drama, riddles, puns, tongue twisters, recitations, pithy sayings, and songs. Orality is often referred to as oral literature, where literary forms are delivered in the spoken communication.[16] Ruth Finnegan expands the range of forms by including poems, dance, myths, and drum language,[17] pushing the limits of the meaning of "literature" beyond the printed text. Orality also needs to be pushed beyond being logocentric, beyond the limits of reproducing words only. Language is only one of the twelve signal systems of communication. Comprehensive communication is composed of both the verbal and the nonverbal, and it embraces the full gamut of signal systems, as found in painting, sculpture, mime, and a full range of visual arts.

The critical characteristic of orality is that it designates a preference for learning and gaining information through ways other than print, such as through media that is *not* printed. Steffen provides a helpful definition: "Orality denotes pedagogical preferences designed to process, remember, and communicate verbally and pictorially through social connections, rather than through

12. Steffen, *Worldview-Based Storying*, 139.
13. Wright, *New Testament and the People of God*, 38.
14. Kraft, *Communication Theory for Christian Witness*, 11–23.
15. Bailey, *Finding the Lost*, 28.
16. See Okwepo, *African Oral Literature*, 3–4.
17. Finnegan, *Oral Literature in Africa*.

literate forms."[18] To Steffen's verbal and pictorial communication, it is also important to add aural (audio) communication in order to round out the full range of verbal and nonverbal genres. God is not limited to making himself known in words only: he makes himself known in multiple ways.

Storytelling and Worldview

Storytelling, broadly defined, lies at the foundations of orality and is highly significant in revealing a people's belief system and values. Indeed, all genres of oral arts are embedded within the worldviews of a people. They play pivotal roles in shaping, countering, and evoking holistic transformation of a people's life scripts. In his latest work, *Worldview-Based Storying* (see vignette 7.2), Steffen argues that we must recognize the essential role of worldview in shaping the way we see and interpret the world on three levels: symbol, story, and ritual.

Vignette 7.2

Transforming Worldview through Storytelling

Tom Steffen
Emeritus Professor of Intercultural Studies, Biola University

Worldview defines one's identity, communal and national values, and social roles. Digging below the surface, worldview is composed of symbols, stories, and ritual. This trilogy plays a pivotal role in the construction, deconstruction, and reconstruction of one's worldview. Let's consider them individually before considering the specific role of storytelling.

Symbol seeks to summarize and synthesize complex issues through images that project meaning through silent speech, thereby creating one's individual and corporate identity. Symbol serves as an economical means to magnify and multiply meaning that determines one's worldview. But symbol demands more than silent speech. Symbol requires spoken speech; symbol screams out for something more—story.

Story is much more than an art form, diversion, entertainment, illustration, or literary genre; it is a way to structure thought. It is a way of knowing. Story helps conceptualize experience, interpret reality, provide identity, and offer a community of insiders. It forms one's worldview. Story is not just what one

18. Steffen, *Worldview-Based Storying*, 12.

hears or sees; it is also what one hears and sees through. Worldview construction finds one of its massive roots buried deep in story.

Ritual paints a micropicture of reality. It institutionalizes and legitimizes meaning and identity (from individual to international), and it summarizes and synthesizes specific aspects of worldview. Designed to outlive the moment, ritual recalls, reenacts, reexamines, reactivates, reinvigorates, repulses, reinvents, redirects, renews, relives, reevaluates, renovates, replaces, and rejuvenates cultural values, behavior, and relationships. Reality and relationships are assigned symbols, defined through stories, and reviewed through ritual.

Stories read, heard, or seen magically transport individuals beyond the familiar to the unfamiliar. Sometimes exposure to the unfamiliar proposes attractive lifeworld alternatives that beg for exploration. These tantalizing rival stories do this in part by offering alternative symbols, values, identities, and rituals. They offer an alternative worldview through lived precedent.

This triad continually constructs and cements our worldview. In relation to Scripture's story, the interlinking of symbol, story, and ritual has the power to deconstruct worldview and transform it in ways that honor the Eternal One. For one's worldview to be transformed, there must be re-symbolization, re-storiation, and re-ritualization. Offering rival stories is one of the strongest ways to bring about such transformation.

Steffen argues that worldview and storytelling are inextricably interwoven, shaping and influencing the ways people think and interpret life experiences. We must be aware of how worldview affects reception and interpretation of a message. As we have seen throughout this book, the arts engage all three culturally embedded elements of worldview: symbol, story, and ritual.[19] This worldview trilogy offers a road map for doing Christian witness through music and the arts, including oral communication and the telling of the grand gospel narrative.

Of the multitudes of oral genres found in various cultures, we turn to three foundational ones: storytelling, proverbs, and song. We consider them in relation to their unique cultural contexts. It's important to remember that each genre is deeply embedded in culture, functioning beneath the surface. Therein lies their power to communicate at profound levels. The arts construct worldview by combining story, symbol, and ritual in ways that facilitate powerful storying, including storying of the gospel message. As such, the creative arts carry great potential for fostering a lived Christianity *in* culture that bears witness to God's story, generating paradigm shifts and transformed lives.

19. Steffen's work further addresses worldview storytelling, taking into account shaping the story for honor/shame, pollution/purity, and other worldview life scripts.

Figure 7.2
Global arts and storying

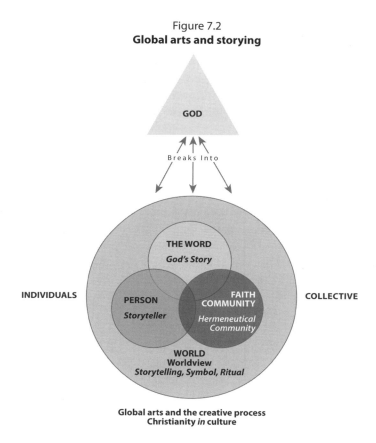

Global arts and the creative process
Christianity *in* culture

Storytelling

The intention of storytelling is to create interaction between people, to raise questions about the essential conditions of what it means to be human and to elicit a response. Storytelling seeks to produce a full-bodied experience that captures the mind, the imagination, the emotions, and the will. Story, whether experienced around the evening campfire or at the cinema, serves to captivate people so much that they enter into the world of the storyteller. They find themselves identifying with the characters and emotionally responding to the characters' struggles, battles, victories, and temptations. Stories are composed of four main elements: characters, a story line, conflict, and resolution. The parables of Jesus, such as the prodigal son (Luke 15), intend to teach a lesson that draws the listener into identifying with the characters in such a way that they find themselves grappling with the issues and the intended meaning, bringing new understandings about the nature of God. In the midst of storytelling, an interactive transaction is taking place in the minds of the story participants as they apply the story to their own life experiences or struggles. If received through print or other media, storytelling is dialogical, whether in person or in a mental dialogue. Since storytelling fosters identification with the characters, it promotes a sense of connection. As Steffen emphasizes, "Stories are exchanged experiences."[20]

Good storytelling is based on metaphor, the symbolic dynamic that promotes relating with the characters and their dilemmas. Screenwriters concur that metaphor propels story as it engenders and represents the human condition. Christopher Vogler reveals that "every good story reflects the total human story, the universal human condition of being born into this world, growing, learning, struggling to become an individual and dying."[21] Thus, stories do not convince through logical persuasion, but "they surprise by identification."[22] They are accessible to all people, whether literate, semiliterate, or nonliterate.

Without story as a means of identification, next to no means exists for connecting with the God of salvation and understanding the significance of Jesus's sacrifice on the cross. The incarnational aspect of the gospel is lost. Ruth Christopher Vaz, Bible translator in central India, tells of witnessing to her nonliterate mother for more than fifteen years. After patiently listening to Ruth's explanation, her mother would always decline to follow Christ, saying, "It is good, but it will not be suitable for me." Her mother explained further: "How could I? Your faith has so much to do with books. You sing from a book, read the Bible and write a journal to be a Christian. But I'm not literate!" Speechless, Ruth realized she had never thought about that.

As a Hindu, Ruth's mother was well informed about her religion through a multiplex of art forms, each relating and explaining the stories of Hinduism. Ruth explains that her high-caste mother did not need books to know her gods. She regularly attended all community events at their village: the recitals, the *bhajans*,[23] the *kathkalashepa* (storytelling), concerts, traditional dances, and the annual enacting of the *Mahabharatha* and *Ramayana*;[24] all of these oral

---

20. Steffen, *Worldview-Based Storying*, 140.
21. Vogler, *Writer's Journey*, 24.
22. Shaw, *Storytelling in Religious Education*, 61.
23. Religious devotional songs widely employed in the Hindu religion, although Jesus (*Yeshu?*) *bhajans* are on the rise.
24. *Mahabharatha* and *Ramayana* are two epic poems of ancient India. Written in Sanskrit, they consist of stories based on mythological characters. The *Mahabharatha* contains foundational teachings on the development of Hinduism between 400 BCE and 200 BCE, which are regarded by Hindus as texts about Hindu morality and history. The *Ramayana*, beloved in many countries where Hinduism is practiced, recounts the story of Rama's life. See "*Mahabharatha*,"

events had taught her about her religion. Her mother sat through entire nights listening to these live performances. Also, their village has ancient temples with stories of Hindu religion artistically painted on the inside walls. Her mother can "read" the sequences of stories painted in rows (just like today's comic books, but with no text). To her, becoming a Christian means not only a new God but also a new method—that is, the *book method*! That was why she had decided that Christianity was *unsuitable* for her![25]

Numerous multisensory ways of telling the stories of the Hindu religion had shaped and formed Ruth's mother. The oral stories tell about characters with whom she can relate. Oral storytelling was her means of relating to the "gods" in her world. She had no means of relating or connecting with the stories in a book, the printed word.

What implications then follow for telling the gospel story? If, indeed, "biblical narrative is theology seen in living relationships and enacted in story form,"[26] as Grant Osborne argues, then methods that generate connection with the gospel message are critical for making Christ known worldwide. We need culturally shaped methods of engaging God's story that challenge deeply entrenched, non–gospel-oriented allegiances. We need culturally appropriate genres that foster relating with and connecting with the God of the universe.

Biblical narrative, telling God's story—foundational to Christian witness—is occurring throughout the world in multiple genres, as most suitable to a particular culture. A suite of local paintings from Genesis 1 to the Lord's Supper in Papua New Guinea represents such witness taking place in Papua New Guinea.

Vignette 7.3

The Creation and the Lord's Supper in Papua New Guinea

Peter Brook
MA in Intercultural Studies, Theology and the Arts
Wycliffe Australia EthnoArts Consultant

I first met Nanias, a local artist, when he came to sell his paintings at the compound where I was living with my wife and children in the town of Wewak, on the northwest coast of Papua New Guinea. As fellow artists, we quickly became close

Encyclopaedia Britannica, published November 29, 2017, www.britannica.com/topic/Mahab harata; "*Ramayana*," *Encyclopaedia Britannica*, published October 5, 2018, www.britannica .com/topic/Ramayana-Indian-epic.

25. Ruth Christopher Vaz, "My Journey towards Orality: Reflection and Report" (term paper, ME515 Global Storytelling and Song, Fuller Theological Seminary, Fall 2004).

26. Osborne, *Hermeneutical Spiral*, 220.

friends. Looking through his portfolio of work one day, I noticed he had another style of painting very different from the "tourist art" I had seen. This turned out to be his clan's traditional painting style, which adorned men's meetinghouses, a very important part of the Kwoma people's culture.[a] After spending some time in his rural village, we embarked on an ambitious project of documenting some of the Kwoma traditional iconography. Learning the significant cultural importance of this traditional art form, I asked Nanias to consider painting some stories from the Bible in this style. After thinking this through, he asked for a Bible, saying he wanted to get these new paintings "right."

Nanias returned a couple of months later with a suite of paintings that used traditional and new iconography depicting Genesis 1–2, and four paintings communicating the life of Christ. As Nanias read the Scriptures and painted in his traditional style, he formed a biblically shaped theology, and he was transformed. When we took the paintings out to his community and he talked about them with his fellow elders and artists, they exclaimed, "These are ours, we understand these stories."

Nanias's painting "*Ap-gamba* (The Lord's Supper)" (plate 11 in color photographs herein) generally follows the traditional design elements of Kwoma sago bark painting created for adorning the upper half of the ceilings of the men's ceremonial meetinghouses of the Kwoma-speaking people of Papua New Guinea. Kwoma bark paintings are predominantly "nonfigurative," with clan totems as the main subject. Very few traditional Kwoma paintings bear "a direct visual resemblance to the entities they depict."[b] Although considered nonfigurative and abstract, they are, however, representational. For this painting, Nanias has made some significant changes when compared to the traditional Kwoma bark paintings, yet it remains distinctly Kwoma with its visual. For the twelve disciples, he employed facial imagery usually reserved for spirits or mythological figures. In his depiction of the Last Supper, Nanias inverted the mouth for the face associated with Judas in order to distinguish him from among the Twelve. The shooting star with an anthropomorphic face, in the center of the painting, is an important Kwoma motif. Traditionally a shooting star was thought to be the soul (*mayi*) of an important man who had recently died and was on his way from the village in which he lived to the underworld beneath the black lagoons in the Kwoma area.[c] Nanias modified this traditional motif to represent Jesus at the Last Supper.

[a] Ross Bowden, *Creative Spirits: Bark Painting in the Washkuk Hills of North New Guinea* (Melbourne: Oceanic Art Pty Ltd, 2006), 1–6, 11–23.
[b] Bowden, *Creative Spirits*, 11.
[c] Bowden, *Creative Spirits*, 17.

Notice how story and symbol converge in Nanias's paintings. The culturally informed symbols take up the weight of the story and are recognizable to local believers—the hermeneutical community—as *their* stories. This is the ultimate goal. While these symbols may need translation for outsiders, the hard work of translating for local peoples has been completed. The story now belongs to them. Notice, too, how in the process of creation, the artist developed a biblically shaped theology that led to his own personal transformation. Additionally, Nanias has created a work that engages the deeper levels of culture appropriate for village leadership at the men's meetinghouse. Not only does the painting witness as it hangs on the walls of a men's meetinghouse, but it also initiates opportunities for relational dialogue with his fellow village elders and artists. Nanias and Peter established an innovative method for storytelling based on artistic painting.

Proverbs

Proverbs are pithy sayings that point us to profound insights. They abound in cultures worldwide and play essential roles in oral communication. Researching and taking a closer look at proverbs as cultural symbols deepens communicating in contextually significant ways. Indigenous symbols, such as proverbs, also open pathways to discovering deeper aspects of culture hidden beneath the surface. Jay Moon argues that "proverbs . . . may serve as open windows into the worldview of the culture, thereby providing a good place to start in understanding the deeper aspects of culture."[27] They function as powerful vehicles for communicating commonly held truth and wisdom in memorable and persuasive ways. For example, this East African proverb from the Sukuma people of Tanzania offers a profound insight:

> I pointed out to you the stars and
> all you saw was the tip of my finger.[28]

It shows the listener that vast treasure (the stars) surrounds us, and yet very little of it is accessed (all you saw was the tip of my finger).[29] According to one interpretation, the richness of available wisdom is often overlooked, and sometimes people focus on the wrong part of a particular topic. Proverbs'

27. Moon, *African Proverbs Reveal Christianity in Culture*, 2.

28. Sukuma (Tanzania) proverb, quoted in Healey and Sybertz, *African Narrative Theology*, 17. An alternative version is "I pointed out to you the moon, and all you saw was my fingertip."

29. A scriptural parallel may be drawn to grasping "how wide and long and high and deep is the love of Christ" (Eph. 3:18).

ability to teach truth can also be used religiously: African theologians acknowledge that proverbs form a cultural "bridge between traditional African religiosity and biblical teaching."[30]

Proverbs specialize in revealing cultural values and wisdom. Significantly, they are also defined by their context,[31] and the way proverbs are used within a particular context determines their meaning. One of the most commonly used proverbs in Eastern Africa exclaims, "When two elephants fight, it's the grass that suffers." On a continent plagued by violence, war, poverty, and injustice, the proverb generates multiple applications and meanings. The "grass" often references the plight of "women and children." However, depending on the story and its intent, the proverb could be used to comment on economic, political, or any other social injustice. Thus, proverbs provide flexible resources for making a point. From Lebanon comes a proverb speaking into the dynamics of peacemaking: "As long as your neighbor is in peace, you're in peace. So, wish the best for your neighbor." Highly apropos in a land that experienced a fifteen-year civil war in the last half of the twentieth century, the proverb speaks into the need to "love one's neighbor" as a part of peacebuilding. Yet it also conveys a universal truth and resonates with biblical teaching.

Aasland notes that collections of proverbs are context-specific. He says that collections with "no accompanying description, as is the case with numerous books of proverbs, are of little help in clarifying the meaning of these same proverbs." Thus, inserting summary proverbs enhances and brings clarity to stories; proverbs can bring a conclusion to the story. He further shows how studies in cognitive science have concluded that summary proverbs and story are interrelated. Story and proverbs interface in a way that increases the understandability of both the story and the proverb.[32]

From Tanzania, the Sukuma proverb, "The poor man without work went to the chief's palace with his dog," leads the culturally informed listener to a specific lesson, if one knows the related Sukuma story. This serves as an example of how both story and proverb bring clarity to the intended message. The associated Sukuma story goes like this:

> Once upon a time there was a poor man who did not have a job or a place to stay. Finally, he went with his dog to the palace of the Sukuma chief. The chief warmly received the man with his dog. The poor man was accepted as part of the royal family, and both he and his dog were fed by the chief. Later on,

30. Mbiti, "Children Confer Glory on a Home," ii.
31. Aasland, "Two Heads Are Better Than One."
32. Aasland, "Two Heads Are Better Than One," 3.

enemies came to kill the chief. The dog barked, the alarm was sounded, the chief escaped, and his life was saved.[33]

The story is intended to teach about hospitality. Without the proverb, the story can be interpreted in general, nonspecific ways. The proverb, like the story, needs further clarification. When set together, however, both the story and the proverb take on associative meanings that become memorable and persuasive for practicing hospitality, a deeply embedded worldview value among the Sukuma people.

Thus, proverbs are supportive genres that can be inserted into storytelling to supplement, underscore, and bring conclusion to a chosen topic. Viewed as a minor genre, they are typically included with other genres such as folktales, legends, toasts, rhetorical addresses, and song texts. Proverbs have the potential to persuade and the power to forge a path (way of thinking) alternative to what is normative. Proverbs serve as rhetorical tools intended to "present possibilities, rather than to be evaluated for truth values as in the case of propositions."[34]

Song

In songs, the verbal and nonverbal communication systems meet. They further foster a convergence of art forms that aggregate a multiplicity of symbols. Song takes up story, proverb, and sound, which undergirds and heightens the story. Song, like storytelling and proverbs, is culturally embedded and context-specific. The increased numbers of signal systems in song intensify the significance and social impact of the story as it engages the full range of oral learners: nonliterates, semiliterates, literates, and postliterates. Songs take on different cultural configurations and forms, as defined by the people of a culture. For example, song in sub-Saharan Africa expands the basic Western definition of song as text and tune (melody) to incorporating verbal, artifactual, audio, kinesic, and spatial signal systems. Joyce Scott, a missionary specialist in the musics of Kenya, defines African music thus: "Every Kenyan knows that music is something that goes in the ears, comes out the mouth, and you do it with your body."[35] Text always lies at the foundation of music in Africa: a message is expected; song is oral communication.

In other words, musical sound is inextricably linked with the totality of a story's message. Yet, to be honest, it is not the music itself that attracts Africans the most. Ultimately, it is the story being told. The music opens up

---

33. Healey and Sybertz, *African Narrative Theology*, 170.
34. Aasland, "Two Heads Are Better Than One," 7.
35. Scott, *Moving into African Music*, 29.

the story to the listener-participant as it tells its persuasive message set on an audio-with-movement foundation. This was demonstrated in a powerful way one Sunday in Côte d'Ivoire when one of the most beloved singer-songwriters was visiting Korhogo, the capital town of the Cebaara Senufo region. The highly gifted storyteller-singer Nɔnyimɛ had composed a new testimony song about Kafana, a man from the village of Torogo. Kafana had endured and suffered increasingly difficult attacks from Satan over a fairly long period of time. The story line reveals and digs into deep-level worldview issues concerning the spirit world that enslaves people in their daily lives. It addresses the nitty-gritty of what confronts and controls all of life for Senufo nonbelievers. Nɔnyimɛ's song lasted between twenty and forty-five minutes. She was asked to sing it at all three services that Sunday: the morning worship service, the afternoon prayer meeting, and the Sunday evening service. Organized in a complex pattern of call-and-response, Nɔnyimɛ sang out the opening statement as she "preached in song" and told the story about Kafana's arduous journey of coming to faith in Jesus, the one who gives freedom. Here is what she sang. Watch how she develops her story for the purpose of witnessing to the freedom found in Jesus:

The Man from Torogo[36]
by Nɔnyimɛ Silué

Thematic Statement:

> Jesus said to come, and he will lift your burdens.
> If Satan has burdened you too much,
> Come, Father (*baba*) will lift your burdens (2×)

Development/Exegesis:

1. Brothers, if you are too burdened, it is still the burdens of Satan.

   Response (after each line): Jesus said to come, and he will lift your burdens.

2. Brothers, if the *sandogi*[37] tires you, it's the burden of Satan. Come to Jesus.

---

36. This is a shortened version of the song. For the full song text and written documentation of Kafana's conversion, see King, *Pathways in Christian Music Communication*, appendix D (243–55). Original text is Cebaara translated into French by Josef Ngana, translated into English by Roberta R. King. Used by permission of Wipf and Stock Publishers. www.wipfandstock.com.

37. *Sandogo* is the "women's divination society constituting the core female leadership in the village; Sondogo elders work closely with male authorities in the *Poro* (men's divination) society." Glaze, *Art and Death in a Senufo Village*, 259.

3. Brothers, if traveling on the path and the *foofiiyi*[38] of Satan wears you out,

4. Behold, if the demons are tiring you, Jesus says to come to him.

5. Sacrifices fatigue you. They are definitely the work of Satan.

6. Behold, if the fetishes are tiring you, Jesus says to come (to him), he'll save you.

7. If the troubles of Satan are tiring you, come to Jesus.

9. Jesus says to come; he'll free you from all these bad (heavy) burdens.

10. He'll free you from these burdens of Satan and give you his.

Nɔnyimɛ continued singing out the story, and the people responded after each line, "Jesus said to come, and he will lift your burdens." In a shortened form, here is how the story proceeded:

Brothers, I'm going to tell you a story of a brother. Our brother Kafana, the one who grew up in Torogo; Do you know him? Do you know Kafana of Torogo, whom Satan caused to suffer? Brothers, the devil made Kafana tired. He suffered a lot; At night, when he laid down to sleep, he saw . . . ; Brothers, the demons were close to him with cars. . . . And Satan said, "If you accept my work and work for me; If you put up with all sorts of bad things and do my work; The prohibitions that I say, if you accept them; Afterward, I will give you wealth and lots of riches; If you see these beautiful cars and they run, can you refuse them? In this world, everyone wants riches. If you see a great treasure, can you refuse it? That is why Kafana accepted the prohibitions of the devil. It was in order to have riches."

After that the demon told Kafana not to drink water that the people have drawn from the well; The water that is in the cesspool, he drank this water; After that, the demon told Kafana to not eat any of the food that his wife prepared for him; After that, the demon told Kafana not to talk with his mother anymore; After that, the demon told Kafana not to talk with his wife anymore; Brothers, a man and his wife, not talk anymore? Brothers, with whom are we supposed to talk in order to have joy? After that, the demon told Kafana to not drink any more water at all; He should drink the liquid from grass; After that, the demon told Kafana to eat leaves; Brothers, a man of this century, he ate leaves? Has the man become an antelope in order to graze on grass?

Jesus has really saved Kafana from such enslavement. One day the devil told Kafana, "Nothing in this world has power over me." "Only God, the eternal

38. "*Foofiiyi* is a 'thing' (example: a python) that a person worships, and that is the 'god' of that person, said to protect the person from harm and evil and to which they offer worship once a year at a given time. All orchestrated by Satan." Jane Vandenberg, email correspondence with author, June 13, 2017.

one on high, has power over me—only him." Brothers, you who worship Satan, he knows that God has power over him; That is why Kafana thought of Jesus; Brothers, Jesus saved Kafana and delivered him from the demon; Jesus has power over the demon; He chased the demon far from Kafana; Jesus rescued Kafana from this slavery and gave him peace; Today, Kafana eats food, drinks water, and farms. Alleluia!

You, who do not yet believe, and hear the word of Jesus; You say to us. "But do I suffer like Kafana?" You say, "The devil does not give me the same kind of burden as Kafana." Do you know that tomorrow there is an eternal suffering? For the eternal fire is much worse than that of Kafana. Think about heaven; Don't stop to look at the world; Jesus has come in order to give us eternal life; First of all, he has given us "rest" of the heart; Jesus has delivered us from the sandogi and chased the evil demon far from us. You, whom the devil is making tired, won't you believe? Brothers, you who have a heavy burden, come to Jesus; You, whom Satan is making suffer a lot, come to Jesus; You, when the devil is making you tired, won't you believe?

Thematic Restatement:

> Brothers, Jesus says to come, he will lift your burdens.
> If the burden of Satan is tiring you,
> Father (*baba*) says to come, he will lift your burdens.

At the end of the song on Sunday evening, Pastor Dossogmon, with sweat streaming down his face and gleaming eyes, turned to me and exclaimed, "Who says that songs do not communicate!" It had profoundly touched all who had participated in singing and clapping. The song had directly addressed the worldview of spirits that control their daily lives, which required people to sacrifice to the spirits continually. This particular Senufo storytelling form allows for a high text load, can be shortened or lengthened as needed, and requires a great deal of participation. Anticipation builds as the group sings the response and waits to hear the next part of the story. There is a great amount of repetition, a critical feature in oral cultures, which do not document the words on paper. The form is also improvisational; new content or a person's name can be inserted, bringing the message home to unique individuals or the group. Finally, Nɔnyimɛ not only tells the story; she also advises and reasons with the people and concludes with a salvation call. She turns an indigenous storytelling song style into an evangelistic song form, adapting it for the purposes of God's kingdom. There is much to learn from this former sorceress and oral learner who has changed her allegiance to the Lord Jesus and now witnesses through the gifts given to her.

Key Factors in Telling God's Story

Having considered three main genres of orality, what implications can we draw for effectively telling God's story via the arts? Drawing from orality, the practices of oral communication play essential roles among all peoples, yet audiences reveal vast distinctions. Since 70 percent of the world's people cannot, do not, or will not read, we should not allow ourselves the luxury of assuming that everyone is literate.[39] Neither should we assume that everyone communicates just as we do. Rather, Christ's commission calls us to move into people's oral worlds for telling God's story. We do well to take into account several key factors.

Identify and know your audience's preferred learning style. Are the people with whom and among whom you are communicating primary oral learners, residual oral learners, or secondary oral learners? Are they fully nonliterate, semiliterate, or postliterate? All three types of learners participate in storytelling, just in different formats. Primary oral learners will depend heavily on storytelling, proverbs, and other related forms such as drama. They will learn predominantly through face-to-face interactions and ritual events that reenact the story visually, aurally, and spatially. Residual oral learners are able to read, yet prefer oral means of interacting, while secondary oral learners move into the digital worlds of film, audiobooks, platforms such as YouTube and Facebook, and smartphone apps.

Research and investigate cultural characteristics. Seek to learn about a people's worldview and how they construct thought. Observe, identify, and learn symbols and stories from the people. Learn how ritual has been shaped and how it forms people now. Initiate discussions with the people that help you learn about cultural art forms. Seek to learn (1) those forms with which a particular group of people has greatest affinity and (2) which ones are best suited for telling high-content narrative. Storytelling and proverbs may be preferred in one region of the world, while working with visual arts takes priority among other peoples.[40]

Explore which medium best communicates the gospel among a people. There is no hard-and-fast template for telling the story of Jesus orally. The story can be told in multiple ways. Therefore, integrate the various oral media that are appropriate to a particular people and context. For example, a group of Indonesian young people who follow Jesus are adapting the *wayang gembol*, a narrative storytelling form that employs highly ornate puppets based on oral

39. Jewell, "Winning the Oral Majority," 56.
40. For more ideas on how to work with oral cultures, see Schrag, *Creating Local Arts Together*.

traditions practiced for centuries. They are telling the stories of Jesus in new ways as they fuse this ancient tradition with electronic keyboards and guitars that reflect their identity as professional, urban people. Bringing these two oral forms together, they are creating narratives that tell the gospel story in a way that brings its message home in their context.

Photo by Molly O'Keeffe

Figure 7.3 Storyteller (Côte d'Ivoire)

Conclusion

Telling God's story and sharing the Scriptures are foundational in making Jesus Christ known and worshiped worldwide. The gift of salvation comes wrapped in different art forms. Working beneath the surface, the arts reveal and shape worldview through symbol, story, and ritual. In Christ-centered witness, the arts function as expressive languages that wed verbal and nonverbal signal systems together in creative, multisensory, fully embodied experiences. They join together in testifying to God's glory and salvation. The possibilities have no limit as the arts story the gospel in ways that are relational, interactive, and incarnational. We need to capture them for Christ-centered witness, for just as the apostle John wrote, "The whole world would not have room for the books that would be written" (John 21:25), so too the world cannot contain all the stories that could be sung or told about Jesus.

Storytelling through the global arts, however, is not limited to daily living in peaceful times. While peoples still desperately need to hear the gospel story in the twenty-first century, we see also a dire need to work toward overcoming the barriers and pain of conflict and violence. Storytelling through the global arts provides spaces for building relationships among peoples that foster overcoming misunderstandings and moving people toward one another. Calls for peace resound throughout the multitude of wars worldwide. Many solutions for conflict transformation seek to respond to that call. Is there a place for music and the arts? We consider next the contribution of the global arts to sustainable peacebuilding, with a particular focus on peoples of different faiths.

Questions for Discussion

1. Why is storytelling so prevalent and important in the twenty-first century?
2. Discuss the significance of orality for Christian witness.
3. What are the most helpful and meaningful oral art forms for your unique context? How can you employ them more effectively?

8

Global Arts in Peacebuilding and Interfaith Dialogue

How do the creative arts foster loving our religious neighbors?

At a time when sounds of violence and war are deafening, something unusual is happening. Musicians and performing artists are joining in pursuing peacebuilding and interfaith dialogue among religious peoples. They are joining in the growing impetus to make a difference in the lives of people who are living in conflict and fractured relationships. Hawai'ian young people perform together on the ukulele in Israel with Muslim and Jewish young people as a means of bringing peoples of different faiths together. A Western classical pianist initiates the building of relationships with local musicians in Tripoli, Libya, that result in a national media event. A Christian rock band from the United States joins with a Muslim rock band in Indonesia as a means of educating a generation of peacemakers. Large transnational festivals share their religious and devotional music performances in Fez, Morocco. Meanwhile, a Muslim sheikh and a Christian pastor in Pakistan share in performing the psalms, while in Beirut, Lebanon, a classical Arab music ensemble shares from their common religious scriptures and ancient poetry based on the Middle Eastern practice of *cantillation*, a reciting of the scriptures. The groundswell continues unabated.

Singing about war and peace among religious peoples is not new to the twenty-first century. Rather, it reaches back to ancient biblical times. The psalms abound with the desire to overcome one's foes, imploring God to defend against enemies and praising him as it comes to pass.[1] When Psalm 133:1 first declared, "How good and pleasant it is when God's people live together in unity," it was speaking into a world experiencing strife, including sibling rivalries, tensions between extended families and village communities, competition among clans, and religious tensions between the Judean and Samarian communities.[2] It seems people have always had longings for peace. A traditional proverb from Lebanon underscores this reality well: "As long as your neighbor is in peace, you're in peace. So, wish the best for your neighbor."

Jesus takes living together peacefully to a whole new level. When asked for the greatest commandment, he points to a Hebrew prayer, the Shema: "The most important one . . . is this: 'Hear, O Israel: The Lord our God, the Lord is one. Love the Lord your God with all your heart and with all your soul and with all your mind and with all your strength.' The second is this: 'Love your neighbor as yourself.' There is no commandment greater than these" (Mark 12:29–31). He linked the two commandments, referencing them as one unit. Loving our neighbor is integral to loving the Lord with all of who we are. Mark Labberton refers to loving our neighbor as a dangerous act, one that pushes us beyond our comfort levels: "If we say we love God and don't love our neighbor, it turns out we don't love God. In other words, our faith is only fiction."[3] What does this imply for musicians and artists? Not only are they to worship God with all of who they are, but they must also reach out to their religious neighbors. As they seek peaceful relations among their religious neighbors through music-making, they are testifying to God's salvation and glory.

Loving one's neighbor naturally implies building relational bridges to peace. Indeed, scholars and practitioners of peacebuilding are searching for nonviolent approaches that lead to sustainable peaceful relations. John Paul Lederach identifies the major question: "How do we transcend the cycles of violence that bewitch our human community while still living in them?"[4] What methods and approaches will transform broken and fractured relationships on local, national, and global levels? Lederach suggests that peacebuilding requires a vast array of processes, approaches, and stages to transform various situations of tension and conflict toward more sustainable, peaceful relationships.[5] This

1. The NIV translation of Psalms references "foes" 33 times and "enemies" 68 times.
2. See Goldingay, *Psalms 90–150*, 564–65.
3. Labberton, *Dangerous Act of Loving Your Neighbor*, 30.
4. Lederach, *Moral Imagination*, 5.
5. See Lederach, *Little Book of Conflict Transformation*.

opens the door to music-making as a key player in peacebuilding. Based on more than three decades of working in the field of peacebuilding, Lederach observes with stunning clarity:

> The artistic five minutes, I have found rather consistently, when it is given space and acknowledged as something far beyond entertainment, accomplishes what most of politics has been unable to attain: It helps us return to our humanity, a transcendent journey that, like the moral imagination, can build a sense that we *are*, after all, a human community.[6]

Peacebuilding in and of itself is a complex, vast topic beyond the scope of this chapter. A number of convergences, however, allow us to consider Lederach's "artistic five minutes" as a crucial means of recognizing the common humanity between peoples in conflict, including people of different religions. Peacebuilding seeks to build bridges of relationship; music-making is a means of bonding peoples together in transformed relationships. Peacebuilding addresses differences between peoples of different faiths; music-making is practiced by peoples of all religions. Peacebuilding pursues opportunities for dialogue between peoples. Indeed, dialogue is a required avenue and outcome in the peacebuilding process. We thus find interfaith dialogue to be inherent in the peacebuilding process among those of different faiths. Joined with music-making, peacebuilding and interfaith dialogue form avenues for witness as the arts excel in expressive dialogue, forging relational bonding in profound and persuasive ways.

The purpose of this chapter, then, is to explore the contribution of music and the creative arts to peacebuilding and interfaith dialogue among religious peoples. While our global village includes Hindus, Buddhists, and peoples of other world faiths, we focus here on Muslim-Christian relations. I maintain that there are points of connection that serve as bridges for building sustainable relationships, such as exchanging and learning one another's art forms or performing together. The question before us is clear: How do we show and extend neighborliness to peoples of different faiths via the arts? Based on my research on songs of peace and reconciliation—*(un)Common Sounds*—we will consider how music-making can be a constitutive part of peacebuilding and interfaith dialogue as it engages musicians, artists, and God's people with their religious neighbors in ways that foster sustainable relationships. We do so by reflecting on what is happening on the ground worldwide through a series of current vignettes and accompanying analyses of the key dynamics at play.

6. Lederach, *Moral Imagination*, 153.

Engaging in Interfaith Dialogue via Music-Making

Interfaith dialogue, like peacebuilding, seeks to establish relationships among and between people that result in harmonious living together. Music-making is a form of dialogue between people. It provides spaces where peoples are free to relate with one another, coming together in ways that do not naturally occur in daily life. A number of key dynamics emanate from such musical interactions. We begin our pursuit of peaceful relationships by turning to an evening of music-making that resulted in interfaith dialogue. Join me in going back to this warm, balmy Southern California evening in the fall of 2016.

My Story: A Benefit Concert for Syrian Refugees

Having just enjoyed a delightful Middle Eastern meal beforehand, my Palestinian-Jordanian friend and I head over to the local Presbyterian church to enjoy the music concert in aid of Syrian refugees. As we enter the church reception area, I am amazed at the flurry of activity. The buzz of excitement and animated joy fills the air. But then I become confused. Standing before us are three lovely, Arabic-speaking young women, beautifully adorned in their *hijab* (Muslim head coverings), meeting and greeting us. Encountering Muslims inside a Christian church is strikingly different, if not a bit jarring. I try to take in the enormity of what is happening. They smile and direct us into the sanctuary-turned-concert hall for the evening. It holds a mixed crowd of Christian and Muslim families of about two hundred people. People converse amicably with one another as a sense of welcome, delight, and anticipation permeates the setting. It somehow has a local community feel to it. Something good is happening.

One of the local pastors walks onto the platform with the pulpit pushed aside and welcomes us. With very little introduction, he invites a West African Senegalese *griot* to come and perform on his twenty-one-string kora (fig. 8.1). I am delighted to hear an authentic kora performance. What a priceless opportunity, in Southern California no less! The *griot* explains that his twenty-one-string harp-lute with its ornately decorated calabash resonator is inscribed in gold with the name of Allah in Arabic script on it. As a Muslim, he says he is on a mission, called to serve God and to help others: hence, his participation in the event on behalf of Syrian refugees. He plays and sings a number of songs. One of his songs tells about mothers and how their wombs are the laboratory of God. As the song is full of religious and cultural symbolism from a different worldview perspective, it is difficult to follow all that he is explaining. The audience, however, displays an attitude of openness and willingness to listen. And the music itself is of the highest performance level.

During the intermission, the pastor shows slides and explains how he and a group of churches first connected with Syrian refugees in the local school. They saw needs and have been attempting to meet some of the most immediate ones. These churches represent a local Christian community building bridges with people forced to flee their homes, many of whom follow a different faith. An offering is taken.

Next, a Jordanian immigrant of Palestinian descent who is a Christian is invited to perform on the oud, "a short-necked plucked lute of the Arab world" (fig. 8.2).[7] He explains more of the Arabic music

Figure 8.1 The kora of West Africa: twenty-one-string harp-lute

tradition, including the intricate scale system, called the *maqams*, and launches into singing a Christian song, *Salaam, salaam, yarabi salaam* (Peace, peace, O my Lord, peace). He also includes folk songs. Then he breaks into "How Great Thou Art," in Arabic for the verses and English for the chorus, so that everyone in the audience can participate at some point. He offers it as a prayer on behalf of Syrian refugees.

Finally, the Jordanian Christian closes off the evening with a well-known Arabic folk song. As he begins to play, the dynamics of the concert immediately shift. The focus of the music slips off the stage and into the auditorium. Faces in the audience light up with delight as they recognize a beloved folk song. Slowly and with growing momentum, some of the Muslim immigrants come forward and start to line dance, men clasping hands and holding them high in the air. Amazingly, they are dancing in front of what is usually the altar area. Now the local church members and attendees hesitantly begin to come forward and join in while young Muslim women in their *hijabs* come to the front to capture photos on their smartphones. Smiles and excitement

---

7. Sadie, *New Grove Dictionary*, 25:25.

Photo by Molly O'Keeffe

Figure 8.2 The oud, a Middle Eastern musical instrument

abound. The young Arabic-speaking men participate and dance with skill. There is something for everyone to be involved in. A spontaneous mix of people are enjoying being together. Multiple barriers are breaking down as people relate with one another on new levels, bonding and feeling united in community, participating in the music and dances. Smiles shine everywhere. Joy and delight abound. The grimness of a difficult past is left behind as people join together in living in the moment. But wait: as the music is coming to a close, we hear someone crying. A lovely Syrian woman wearing a silk scarf and her husband both reach downward, trying to console their three-year-old daughter. The music has stopped, and she wants more: the child is asking in tears, "Why can't the music go on?"

I have never experienced such a multifaith gathering in the United States, a nation that struggles with Islamophobia. An Arab folk dance had migrated with the refugees into the house of the Lord, and there was joy. The space in front of the altar was filled with joyful dancing, reminiscent of David dancing "before the LORD" (2 Sam. 6:14). Amazingly, it was all taking place within a local Presbyterian church in Southern California, not far from San Bernardino, where a notorious terrorist attack by a man claiming Islamic faith had recently taken place. It is obvious that connections and friendships had been building before this event as one Christian community had been reaching out to help their new neighbors. Music-making served as a catalyst for forging relational bonds as the Christian and Muslim communities then came together to reach out to their new religious neighbors. It added a new dimension to the psalmist's words: "How good and pleasant it is when God's people live together in unity" (Ps. 133:1).[8]

Key Dynamics of Music-Making as Interfaith Dialogue

What was going on in the midst of the benefit concert? The event displayed key dynamics and processes inherent to music-making. An evening of musical performance generated new possibilities for experiencing what we have in common as human beings. Three major elements of music-making were occurring: (1) creating musical spaces of relating; (2) *musicking*, a new concept to be explained; and (3) encountering contrasting music-cultures.

Creating Musical Spaces of Relating

Coming together around a common cause through music-making opened up a social space for relating with one another. Contrasting groups of people, each negotiating cross-cultural and interfaith differences, entered into a declared safe space for building affinity and creating new bonds between them. They experienced an interface between musical sound and society that generated "a set of recognizable behaviors that link music to various broadening social and expressive spheres"[9] that can be transformative, especially in the emotional domain.[10] Musical spaces foster the negotiation of relationships, toward or away from one another. Ethnomusicologists maintain, "Music's primary meanings are not individual at all, but social."[11] When groups encounter and engage with one another, the interaction initiates shifts toward an openness to attachment with one another. These shifts take place on varying levels according to people's perceptions, attitudes, and previous involvement with one another as they enter into the music event arena.

The range of moving toward one another encompasses a continuum of relational attitudes and behaviors at five different stages: (1) enmity and exclusion toward people who are different, (2) encounter with "others," (3) engagement, (4) embrace, and (5) relating as neighbors (see fig. 8.3).

---

8. See also Lev. 19:34: "Any immigrant who lives with you must be treated as if they were one of your citizens. You must love them as yourself, because you were immigrants in the land of Egypt; I am the LORD your God" (CEB).

9. King and Tan, *(un)Common Sounds*, 270.

10. Racy, *Making Music in the Arab World*, 11.

11. Small, *Musicking*, 8.

Figure 8.3
Musical spaces of relating

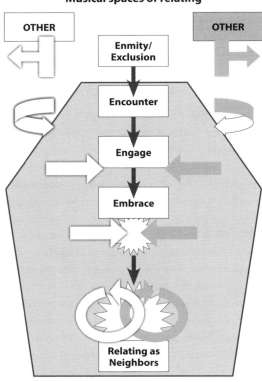

MUSIC EVENT ARENA

Roberta R. King and Sooi Ling Tan, eds., *(un)Common Sounds: Songs of Peace and Reconciliation among Muslims and Christians* (Eugene, OR: Cascade, 2014), fig. 19. Used by permission of Wipf and Stock Publishers.

Note that individuals within each group represented had to make a conscious decision to come and be present. Some may have come and encountered people of different faiths for the first time but were drawn to the event due to their interest in world music. In contrast, others had already been engaging in interfaith relationships; they entered into the occasion with an openness to move further into knowing and understanding one another that could lead to embracing and showing neighborliness to those now living among them. As participants experienced a music representative of each group, the recognition of a shared humanity grew, even when a music may have been foreign to them. Such new perspectives toward one another's common humanity laid the groundwork for affording dignity, respect, and growing trust. Major transformative components of peacebuilding through public and expressive cultural practices generate "collective identities that are fundamental to forming and sustaining social groups, which are, in turn, basic to survival."[12]

Participants and audience at the benefit concert described above experienced an immense amount of joy as peoples who had been involved with one another came into a third space of music performance. Such musical spaces of relating foster further bonding and growing neighborliness that crosses bridges of difference into sustained and harmonious living with each other.

Musicking

What was taking place within the music event arena has come to be called *musicking*.[13] Musicking pushes the concept of music beyond that of a noun or just another commodity. Music is not a product to merely be plugged into an event. There is more to music than meets the ear as it engages people within their social settings. Christopher Small argues that music can be a verb and thus terms it *musicking*. He argues that "the fundamental nature and meaning of music lies not in objects, not in musical works at all, but in action, in what people do. It is only by understanding what people do as they take part in a musical act that we can hope to understand its nature and the function it fulfills."[14] Musicking, according to Small, serves as an action verb: "to music is to take part, in any capacity, in a musical performance."[15] This opens up music events to investigating a full range of activities, including performance, listening, rehearsing or practicing, composing, dancing, ushering, taking tickets, and offering refreshments.

Meaning, impact, and significance arise out of what people are doing as they participate in music events. This means that when young Muslim women greeted me at the door of the church, they were playing significant roles in musicking. Not only were the performers significant for the evening, but also the people who joined in the folk dance at the end of the concert and the young Muslim women who took photos on their smartphones, plus the small child who cried when the music stopped. Each activity and person involved contributed to the totality of meaning for the evening. Musicking is a significant form of human encounter, indeed dialogue, "in which everyone who is present is taking part, and for whose success or failure as an event everybody

---

12. Turino, *Music as Social Life*, 2.
13. For a full discussion of the *musicking* concept, see Small, *Musicking*.
14. Small, *Musicking*, 8.
15. Small, *Musicking*, 9.

who is present has some responsibility."[16] Everyone who participates in the music-making event contributes to it. Such an event lends itself to being fully multisensory and one of heightened experience. Not only do the participants contribute to the event, but the occasion also affects them. Such occasions function as a form of human encounter and dialogue. The musicking that took place at the benefit concert fostered interaction and made a profound impact as the evening proceeded. People experienced musical dialogue as they learned about and experienced one another in profound ways. An enhanced sense of community emerged.

Encountering Contrasting Music-Cultures

Each of the performers represented their community as they sang and played indigenous instruments unique to their social group. Each performance established identity for differing segments of the audience. In addition to being sung in vernacular languages that established identity, the music also voiced both cultural and religious identity. The encounter between contrasting music-cultures served as a metaphor for a welcoming encounter between differing cultural and religious groups. In a country where rock music and hip hop dominate the airwaves, it was striking to hear indigenous and popular music from West Africa and the Middle East. It was striking to look up at the pipes of the church organ hanging on the sanctuary wall while hearing music from different parts of the world. A metaphorical "unmute button" was pressed that gave voice and recognition to the participating social groups through the performance of their representative music. Then worldview symbols and beliefs surfaced, such as the inscription of the word "Allah" on the outside of the calabash resonator of the kora, and the theological statement concerning the womb of the woman as the laboratory of God. Although not fully understood at the time, they each built into a sense of recognition of and openness toward one another.

At the end of the concert, a major shift in dynamics occurred due to the switch in cultural performance styles, a moving into a different set of rules and purpose defined by a contrasting music-culture. A "concert" setting quite typically sets up what Thomas Turino identifies as "presentational" music, in which a performer or group of artists "prepare and provide music for another group, the audience, who do not participate in making the music or dancing." Functioning within this realm, as expected in most Western settings, requires intense listening and an expectation of professional excellence on the part of the performer. It assumes spaces of meditation and contemplation

16. Small, *Musicking*, x.

for individual listeners. Participatory music, on the other hand, is "a special type of artistic practice in which there are no artist-audience distinctions, only participants and potential participants performing different roles, and the primary goal is to involve the maximum number of people in some performance role."[17] This is what took place with the line dance, when members of the culture inherently knew what was expected, stood, and joined hands to participate. Musicking through music and the line dance brought a social cohesion and bonding to the whole group that evening. Life as usual was suspended, and people were released to be themselves within whatever group they identified with. Some from one group chose to identify with another group as they joined in a dance that was foreign to them. The event carried out musical hospitality in a wonderful way that recognized and validated a people as a socioreligious group through sharing in performed music.

Identity formation was taking place as sonic and muscular bonding generated a sense of unified community. Turino summarizes this concept with great insight:

> Music and dance are key to identity formation because they are often public presentations of the deepest feelings and qualities that make a group unique.... Through moving and sounding together in synchrony, people can experience a feeling of oneness with others. The signs of this social intimacy are experienced directly—body to body—and thus in the moment are felt to be true.[18]

Ultimately, interacting through expressive cultural practices such as music and dance from different societies helps "us achieve a balance between understanding cultural difference and recognizing our common humanity."[19] In the midst of musicking at a benefit concert, each group was able to express and maintain its unique identity while at the same time recognize and enter into cultural and religious differences present among them. No one was forced to give up their uniqueness. In giving voice and affording respect through musicking, a oneness—people sharing in a common humanity—was momentarily achieved. This step in the peacebuilding process bonded and moved the group forward toward sustainable, harmonious relationships. The event substantiated sociologist Tia DeNora's claim that "music is a resource . . . for world building."[20]

17. Turino, *Music as Social Life*, 26.
18. Turino, *Music as Social Life*, 2–3. Turino acknowledges William H. McNeil's 1995 work that suggests the term "muscular bonding" for the feeling of oneness derived from moving and dancing together in close synchrony and adds the term "sonic bonding" when the same happens through music-making.
19. Turino, *Music as Social Life*, 3.
20. DeNora, *Music in Everyday Life*, 44.

Interfaith Dialogues of Beauty and Art

As we have seen above, interfaith dialogue takes place through a multiplex of relational interactions via musicking. The desire to help new religious neighbors thrive and feel more at home in the new local community knit them together as they discovered one another through musicking. In the midst of the event, dialogical interaction was taking place. Theologians and missiologists identify dialogue as a constitutive element in mission and witness, foundational to building relationships.[21] Interfaith dialogue includes several ways of engaging in interactions between peoples of contrasting faith traditions. These ways include dialogues of (1) daily life, (2) social action, (3) spiritual experience, (4) theological exchange, and (5) musical collaboration (see fig. 8.4). In the research study *(un)Common Sounds: Songs of Peace and Reconciliation*,[22] Sooi Ling Tan and I explored the contribution of music and the arts in fostering sustainable peacebuilding among Muslims and Christians. Researching and holding consultations in Lebanon and Indonesia, we discovered that musicians were indeed engaging in interfaith dialogue and building toward sustainable peace. Musical collaboration emerged as an additional dialogue, where artists either take the initiative or play major roles in designing and engaging in interfaith dialogue through the processes of musicking. We turn here to a number of vignettes that address and contribute to each of the five areas of dialogue. Our goal is to show the multiple pathways that can be pursued as well as to gain a deeper understanding of how music and the arts function as interfaith dialogue. Taken as a whole, the global arts in peacebuilding and interfaith dialogue form a dialogue of beauty and art.[23] As women and men come together and share what is precious, deeply meaningful, and emotionally profound in their visual arts, literature, dance, and music, it initiates an experiential appreciation of each other, igniting the imagination with the possibilities of living together.

Dialogue of Musical Collaboration

Artists and musicians play key roles in initiating interfaith dialogues of beauty and art. They are often the ones who envision and willingly begin the journey of reaching out to and discovering their religious neighbors. They can do this both internationally and in local cross-cultural witness. For example,

21. Bevans and Schroeder, *Constants in Context*, 383–85.
22. See King and Tan, *(un)Common Sounds*. See also songsforpeaceproject.org.
23. I am grateful to Steve Bevans for his enthusiastic encouragement and review of the *(un)Common Sounds* documentary film screened at the American Society for Missiology meetings in 2014, where he suggested a "dialogue of beauty or art."

Figure 8.4
Dialogues of beauty and art

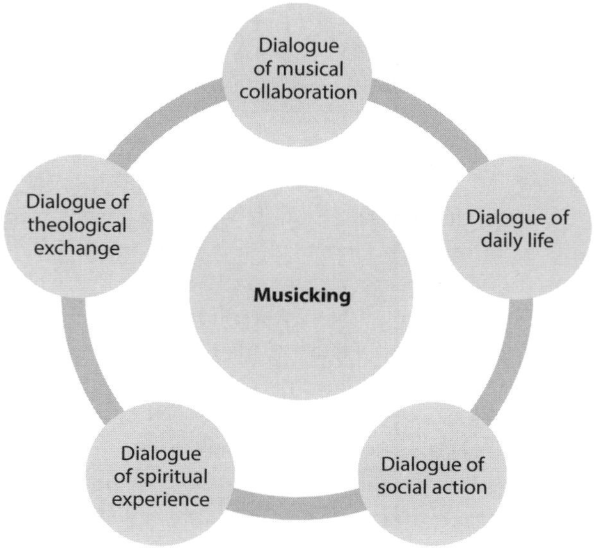

the ukulele, originating in Hawai'i and also a transnational instrument played worldwide, provided a means of musicking by Hawai'ian young people along with Muslim and Christian youth in Israel.

Vignette 8.1

"Ukuleles for Peace"
Peacebuilding and Ongoing Relationships

Guy Higashi
Doctor of Missiology; Former President of Pacific Rim Christian
College (Hawai'i) and New Hope Christian College (Oregon)

The ukulele is a part of my Hawai'ian cultural heritage. One of my fondest memories is from when I was ten years old, sitting on the living room floor around a ukulele songbook, where my brother, sister, mom, dad, and I played the ukulele, singing Hawai'ian, Japanese, Filipino, and Christian songs together. It was the way we learned about the Hawai'ian Islands, our ethnicity, and our neighbors. Today, the ukulele has become a transnational instrument. Ukulele virtuoso Jake Shimabukuro calls the ukulele the "Facebook of musical instruments" since the ukulele links and connects people from all around the world together, most often through "ukulele circles."

It was through the ukulele that my students and faculty from Pacific Rim Christian College in Hawai'i were invited to visit the group Ukuleles for Peace in Israel. Ukuleles for Peace (http://www.apikai.com/ufp) promotes bringing together schoolchildren from both Jewish and Muslim faiths on a regular basis. It began as an antiwar statement developing cultural exchange between child soldiers and a love for ukulele music, out of which friendships could be birthed. They sing in Arabic, Hebrew, and English. When we arrived, our Hawai'ian group found ourselves joining in a ukulele circle in the lobby of a Tel Aviv hotel. Ukuleles for Peace shared Hebrew and Arabic songs, while we shared Hawai'ian and Christian songs. They even sang a Beatles number with us. In the end, we all sang "This Little Light of Mine" together in English. We left a dozen ukuleles with them so that they could continue to invite more and more children to build friendships. We kept in touch over the next five years. To my surprise, nearly six years later, I received an email and video from the children of Ukuleles for Peace. In their desire for ongoing friendship with us, they had chosen to learn and perform "This Little Light of Mine" in English, Hebrew, and Arabic. They introduced the video with "to our friends from Hawai'i, we'll sing 'This Little Light of Mine'" (see in the webography under United States). In the broadest sense, the ukulele was an amazing way to be a witness of Christ to the children and families in Israel.

International travel in a global world makes coming into contact with the far ends of the earth an everyday possibility. A shared love for the ukulele, often played in ukulele circles, provided an opportunity to reach out in witness on a visit conceived as a onetime, short-term venture. An easily learned, accessible instrument brought people together around a perceived "neutral" instrument and initiated international relationships. The Israeli children chose to translate a song into their languages as a sign of friendship. Their collaboration on a common task enhanced friendships among themselves, plus provided a means of offering musical hospitality from afar and maintaining contact with their friends in Hawai'i.

Intentional collaborative exchange carries potential for breaking stereotypes and deepening friendships within local and across global communities. These ukulele players show us just one example of musical collaboration. Other possibilities include going deeper into cultural exchange where musicians not only learn about and from each other by performing each other's music, but also learn with one another by creating and composing together.

Musical collaboration, in any of its multiple forms, develops through interactive processes that are participatory and dialogical. The next section presents a model for taking interactive engagement further in forging relational bonds that promote peacebuilding.

Dialogue of Daily Life

In the dialogue of daily life, women and men of different faiths get to know one another as people. Through the daily rubbing of shoulders, a shift in perceptions occurs: from seeing abstract faiths such as Christianity, Islam, or Buddhism to seeing concrete, named persons as new friends. Musicians and artists have unique opportunities for gaining entry into a society and building friendship through sustained periods of interaction. In Libya, for example, a Christian musician and academic practitioner took the relational dynamics inherent in musical practices and the possibilities of peacebuilding to another level. Realizing the psychological misperceptions of ethnicity (as an American) and religion (as a Christian) living in the Libyan Muslim environment, he sought to change the paradigm with the hope of transforming perceptions into ones of mutuality, trust, and generosity.[24]

Starting small and interacting as musician to musician, an American Western pianist and a local Libyan oud player began by listening to each other's preferred musics, establishing identity in the context of relationship, and bonding into deeper connections of relationality. The American's Muslim hosts would often show musical hospitality by turning the radio to a full range of Western art forms, from Mozart's *Eine kleine Nachtmusik* to Bryan Adams's "All for Love." Conversations revolving around various musics created moments of mutualism, recognition of one another. The American likewise showed interest in the music of his hosts, both recorded and live. Over a period of three years, he continually showed a special interest in the musics that were a regular part of daily life in Libyan society. One of his relationships was "built solely from cruising Tripoli's streets for hours listening to Arabic popular music and discussing the improvisation of Andalusian Flamenco jazz guitarist Paco de Lucia."[25] Wherever music was taking place in the local society in places that he could access, he regularly attended, participated, and learned to sing the songs that were a part of the culture. He attended music festivals and local weddings, where music plays a prominent role, seeing each of them as opportunities for dialogues in daily life. Ultimately, through the building of trust and friendship, the American pianist and the Libyan violinist

24. See King and Tan, *(un)Common Sounds*, 158–77.
25. Holton, "Performing toward Peace," 165.

discovered themselves performing together in a fusion of Middle Eastern and Western musical elements, such as the *īqī* (rhythmic mode) on the piano, with an interweaving repetitive violin melody, in a concert of largely Western classical music at a top concert hall in Tripoli. They later realized that the metaphorical import of the event was more significant than the music at the concert. It was "the first time within living memory that an American and a Libyan had performed music together publicly."[26] It took place in a context where their two countries had more than four decades of sordid history between them. Continued sharing and performing together had generated webs of interaction that could be further sustained. The musicking did not stop with one concert; long after the event, the American musician was recognized as one who demonstrated a love for the peoples where he lived.

Dialogue of Social Action

Dialogues of social action find peoples of various faiths uniting around a basic human right or against a particular dehumanizing injustice. The benefit concert for Syrian refugees (above) fits into this category. Another collaborative musical effort seeking to educate young people in living peacefully is taking place in Indonesia.

Vignette 8.2

PeaceGeneration in Bandung, Indonesia

Sooi Ling Tan
Academic Dean and Program Director of the DMin in Leadership,
Asia Graduate Schools of Theology (AGST) Alliance

Imagine! It is often assumed that diversity polarizes. However, this was not the case in Bandung, Indonesia. On two special occasions, hundreds of ethnically and religiously diverse young people, from different parts of Indonesia and from as far as the United States and Canada, joined hearts and hands to play and to experience music for peace. Organized by PeaceGeneration, Bandung, Indonesia, it began in 2010 with Rock the Peace, a concert that featured, among other bands, The Mahad, a group of Muslim high school students in Bandung, and North of Here, an American band consisting of Christian musicians. This mushroomed into the PeaceTival and Rock the Peace 2 in 2015, a daylong affair that saw increased band participation anchored by The Mahad and Air

26. Holton, "Performing toward Peace," 158.

Marshall, a Canadian Christian duo from Canada. At the same time, peace-building conversations were taking place through workshops and information booths set up by twenty organizations that shared the same vision for peace.

Skeptics may say that the impact of these events is only temporary. I argue, however, that these are necessary initiating points that foster bridge building. First, organizations and individuals with a shared passion for peace working together in these events provide a strong model of peacebuilding and offer a viable alternative response to conflict. Second, PeaceGeneration's strong combination of peace education with peace activities shapes a new generation that understands the fragilities of differences and is able to respond positively in peace. Finally, as one participant points out, "music brings us together. No matter what race or culture, a lot of people find connections in music." By acting on and living out these commonalities, we provide stepping-stones for building bridges to peace.

No more fitting picture of collaboration could be found than the performance of the concluding song of Rock the Peace 2, titled "Looking for Peace." Sung in English and Indonesian and performed by all the members of Air Marshall (Christian) and The Mahad (Muslim), this freshly collaboratively composed song aptly expressed the hope of a new generation. The song starts off with a wistful quest:

> Traveled the world through the seven seas,
> Looking for the answer, looking for . . . peace.

And it ends on a note of hope:

> I found it, when we love, there is no fear.
> I found it, and it starts right here.

A number of essential dynamics are taking place in the work of Peace-Generation. With a goal to educate the next generation, they have employed musicking as a means to initiate points of connection. Collaboration is taking place on multiple levels, with rock groups from two diverse nations sharing and performing their musics for one another and collaborating in the composing process. Music events offer initial points of interaction that foster bridge building.

Dialogue of Spiritual Experience

The arts are intimately linked to forms of worship and spiritual experience. Sharing in activities such as worship and prayer promotes understanding of how people engage in their faith. This particular dialogue most often is limited to observation and presence. Observing and being present while people are at worship offers recognition and fuller understanding of deeper levels of spirituality. It triggers an internal processing of attitudes toward one another and deepens discussions that may follow. Dialogues of spiritual experience can take place at local, national, and global levels. They can range from sharing a meal at the breaking of Ramadan, the holy month of fasting, to attending Christmas music programs together, as well as transnational festivals that bring together Muslims and Christians performing their musical practices of worship onstage. Such engagement fosters the important work of building bridges toward friendship, as Cliff Cullen suggests in vignette 8.3.

Vignette 8.3

Art, Friendship, and Peacebuilding

Cliff Cullen
MA in Intercultural Studies, Islamic Studies
Peacebuilding Practitioner

I believe that the most essential step in the peacebuilding process is for people to first become friends. Until we become friends, we cannot hope to bring about peace in the world.

However, making friends can be difficult, especially across cultural/religious boundaries. For the last few years I have been working with a group of people whose goal is to help Christians and Muslims become friends. Whenever we bring a group of Muslims and Christians together, we encourage them to communicate about their respective faiths to each other. Often we see an artistic element when people express their faith because art can communicate so much.

I vividly remember the first interfaith dinner I attended. A Muslim family had invited a group of Christians to attend an *iftar* dinner in their home during the month of Ramadan. Before the Muslim family broke their fast at sundown to serve dinner, they performed the evening prayer. One of the family members with a beautiful voice performed the *azan* (the Muslim call to prayer practiced throughout the day) to call everyone together. Then the family lined up and performed the prayer, with its recitations and bowing. It was a very moving experience. One of the things I began appreciating was the artistic expression embedded in the prayer. The artistic way that my new Muslim friends expressed their worship to God displayed great beauty. Observing this communicated to me much about my friends' faith.

This experience helped set the foundation for a friendship that has continued to grow and deepen.

On the global level, the dialogue of spiritual experience through large-scale events, such as the Fez Festival of World Sacred Music, moves spiritual practices out of sanctuaries and religious centers onto the world stage. Spiritual practices become accessible and appreciated for their artistic beauty and the expertise of those on stage in an atmosphere that allows both Muslims and Christians to experience their diverse art forms together. The Fez Festival takes place in Morocco, a nation reportedly 99 percent Muslim and less than 1 percent Christian and Jewish.[27] The context of the event creates an open environment of musical hospitality that lends itself to the enjoyment of multiple concerts that take place over a period of ten days. The musical offerings include ones that place Christian and Muslim performance groups together on the same stage. African American gospel singers find themselves performing with Pakistani Qawwali singers,[28] and looking on while Greek Byzantine monks from Athens share their religious music on the same stage as the Al Kindi Ensemble with the Munshidins (whirling dervishes) of the Damascus Mosque.

Such festivals and events generate imagined worlds of spirituality that speak into profound longings and desires for global communities of peace. The festival, founded on "a universal mission of peace and establishment of cordial relations between people,"[29] provides spaces of encounter focused on cultural poetry, song, and dance that foster mutual respect and dialogue in a type of imagined and "contemporaneous community."[30] Although one another's music traditions are not fully understood—indeed, many are viewed as exotic—a sense of imagined community forms among peoples wholly unknown to one another. Many people come with longing for those around them to understand who they are through their music. It is a profoundly moving experience to hear your own sacred music performed with peoples of differing faiths also intently listening. I'll never forget the moment in the 2008

---

27. "The World Factbook: Africa: Morocco," Central Intelligence Agency, last updated May 1, 2018, https://www.cia.gov/library/publications/the-world-factbook/geos/mo.html.

28. Qawwali is a devotional song genre associated with Islam, most commonly practiced among Pakistani Sufis.

29. Fatima Sadiqi, "Paths to Creation: Message from the General Director," in *Programme du Festival de Fès des Musiques Sacrés du Monde* (Morocco: Fondation Esprit de Fès, 2008), 9.

30. Anderson, *Imagined Communities*, 6.

Photo by Roberta King

Figure 8.5 Whirling dervishes of Damascus and Byzantine priests at the Fez Festival

Fez Festival when I found myself weeping as the words "that saved a wretch like me" from "Amazing Grace" were sung. Nor will I forget responding to a question about the beautifully performed Arabic song on peace from the Muslim couple seated next to me. They quickly turned to me and excitedly asked, "Did you understand what the song meant?" Though I could relate at an emotional level, I had to sadly admit that I did not understand the text. Yet it was an initial beginning of recognizing each other's spiritual desires to know God. Mealtimes and concerts over the course of ten days provided opportunities to meet many of the same people who had attended an earlier concert. The length of the festival allows people to dialogue beyond just initial introductions to one another.

Dialogue of Theological Exchange

Often people think of the dialogue of theological exchange as taking place among scholars and theologians. Seldom does it reach out into the local populace. The arena of musicking, however, offers the direct voicing of Holy Scriptures and sacred poetry, which can ignite the processing of deeply held beliefs and life experiences in public settings. Taking place in contexts rife with centuries of historical animosity, the impact can be especially profound when singing divine revelation shared in common such as the psalms. In Pakistan, various psalms played in the styles of the Muslims' and Christians' shared music-culture helped to promote peace.

Vignette 8.4

Psalms and Sufis in Pakistan

Rev. Eric Sarwar
PhD Candidate, Fuller Theological Seminary
Pastor, Artesia City Indo-Pak Christian Reformed Church

The much-loved book of Psalms was the first hymnbook in Pakistan. Our mission had a "Psalms and Sufis" project, in which we shared and distributed a book of Psalms and the Gospels in the Sindhi language at a Muslim Sufi shrine. As director of the Tehillim School of Church Music and Worship, I was invited by the famous Sindhi Sufi shrine *Bhit Shah* to visit and bring our music team to the shrine and sing the psalms.

My father had given our psalms album (produced with Heart Sounds International, 2005) to a Sindhi Sufi music promoter. He was so inspired by listening to the psalms that he asked to meet me. For security reasons, I initially refused, but a year later I finally agreed to meet him at our recording studio in Karachi. During our conversation, I expressed my interest in visiting the famous Sufi shrine of Shah Abdul Latif Bhittai, the great poet laureate of Sindh. His collection of poetry, *Shah Jo Risalo*, comprises nearly thirty *surs*, or musical compositions, with hundreds of verses. A few days after my conversation with him, I was given permission to visit the shrine.

The chief spiritual leader happily welcomed us, saying that we were the first Christians to ever visit the shrine. The room was full of devotees, as well as journalists who were there to report on this meeting. After we shared our thoughts and purpose—promoting religious tolerance, love, and peace—our host invited us to return for the birthday of Shah Latif, on May 22, 2012, and perform psalm settings at an all-night event, along with Sufi singers. During this meeting, as a token of love, peace, and harmony, I presented him with a gift: a picture of Christ on the cross, and also a copy of the New Testament and Psalms in the Sindhi language. The leader's love and openness amazed us, removing our fears. Onlookers understood that this was a very special event indeed. At the end of our brief meeting, our host asked his son to lead us into the shrine and visit the tomb. A procession escorted us to the shrine, accompanied by special red-colored linen sheets, and opened the inner door of the grave for us. This door is usually opened only for high officials. I saw this as God opening the door for us to engage with Sufis.

Rev. Sarwar's initiative took major steps toward peace by building bridges of commonality through sharing sacred texts and performing in a common musico-religious practice of singing the psalms. Notice how the relationship developed and progressed over a period of time. Rev. Sarwar had taken an early initiative with the Psalms and Sufis project by developing materials that could lead to initial and ongoing relationships through a locally recorded CD made in association with Heart Sounds International from the United States. He entered the shrine by a circuitous route, based on a web of various relationships, involving his father, a Sufi music producer, and Rev. Sarwar's request to be invited to the shrine. The book of Psalms, with its sacred texts for both Muslims and Christians, had triggered the journey toward performing psalms together all night at a Muslim shrine, a first-of-its-kind event in creating a lived tradition that demonstrated possibilities for God's people living together in harmony (Ps. 133:1). The gifts given to the Muslim leader represented the love and peace of Christ and did not compromise who the Christians were representing. The process had torn down walls, broken through barriers, built bridges to harmonious relationships, and even crossed bridges into shared musicking, resulting in further possibilities of moving toward sustained peacebuilding.

Navigating Cultural and Religious Distinctives

One caveat must be clearly noted. Pursuing interfaith dialogue via the arts in multifaith contexts requires additional considerations of religious traditions and music-cultural practices. Unique to the world of Islam is the ambivalent place of music in the Middle East, indeed anywhere the Muslim faith is practiced. Since the days of Muhammad, arguments have circled around the permissibility of music. It is widely believed that music is *harām*, "forbidden" or "unlawful," in Islam. Countless Arab philosophers—for example, Abu Hamid al'Ghazali (1058–1111) and a number of modern Western scholars (Farmer, Nelson, Shiloah, al-Faruqi, and others)—have engaged the issue over the centuries.[31] The arguments are numerous and complex. The Qur'an does not directly address the admissibility of music, nor does it even mention music. The hadith, the sayings and actions of Muhammad that offer guidelines for religious thought and behavior, prove contradictory in relation to music. Muhammad's statement "Allah has not sent a prophet except with a beautiful voice"[32] is used to support music. Muhammad is also known to

31. See Marcus, *Music in Egypt*, 89–95.
32. Shiloah, *Music in the World of Islam*, 33.

have requested a frame drum to be played at a wedding. On the other hand, clear condemnation of music in another hadith reports Muhammad saying, "Allah sent me as a blessing and guidance to all creatures. He sent me to annihilate the string instruments and the *mazāmīr* [plural of *mizmār*]."[33] There is a continuum, then, from music as *harām* to music as admissible.[34] As outsiders, we need to be careful about how we approach music and rely on informed musicians and academics who know local cultural practices in relation to religious perspectives. Although Muslim peoples disagree about the place of music, it certainly is highly prized and practiced throughout the Muslim world. In many places, musicians and nonmusicians in Muslim contexts are admissible, such as we have observed in Libya and Indonesia.

When pursuing interfaith dialogue among religious peoples via the arts as an outsider, it is also important to research the intersection between religion and cultural practices of the arts. Beginning as a listener and then as participant-observer in dialogue with local musicians lays a foundation for crossing bridges into ongoing relationships and sustainable peacebuilding. As some Muslim spiritual leaders have shared, their ultimate concern is that music should not detract from honoring God. Rather, it should honor and reverence him, something that I find true for Christians as well.

Conclusion: Interfaith Dialoguing toward Peace via the Arts

In conclusion, we have observed how musicking, as a major dialogue of beauty and art, fosters multiple ways of loving our religious neighbors. Coming together through sharing and experiencing one another's music provides spaces for relating with one another by initiating points that foster bridge building, with potential for drawing people toward one another. Four major themes have arisen from each of the musicking examples of interfaith dialogue presented here. First, musicians and artists serve as initiators of musical collaboration for the sake of building bridges of love, peace, and harmony. They play important roles in the peacebuilding process. Second, musicking often plays an integral part in projects such as fundraising and educating for peace. Even at festivals, though billed as the main event, musicking facilitates coming together and connecting in addition to other activities such as lecture

33. Nelson, *Art of Reciting the Qur'an*, 41–42, quoted in Marcus, *Music in Egypt*, 89–90.
34. We have touched on only one aspect of the complexity of "music" in Middle Eastern settings in relation to Islam. Other aspects touch on, for example, how the *azan*, the call to prayer, is not considered music but recited text, in spite of the highly intricate and artistically developed ways of performing the *azan*. For a fuller discussion of the relationship between Islam and music, see Marcus, *Music in Egypt*, chap. 6, "Islam and Music: Is Music *Harām?*"

discussions, eating together, and experiencing a different part of the world. Third, a key feature of high value in interfaith dialogue through musicking is that of musical hospitality, in which one listens to and chooses another's music as a means of honoring, respecting, and touching the deeper levels of identity. Fourth, interfaith dialogues via the arts spark new relational dynamics and connections. This forges bonds of interfaith friendships with potential for continuing in sustainable ways. Thus, musicking and collaborative art-making contribute a vast array of opportunities for tearing down walls, breaking through barriers, building bridges of hope, and even crossing those bridges into sustained living in harmony.

The arts in peacebuilding and interfaith dialogue are only one facet of dynamic witness to Christ in the twenty-first century. With people constantly on the move, building and maintaining relationships takes on new forms. The internet is creating new opportunities for staying connected worldwide. The character of cities and outlying areas is shifting dramatically, leading to a predominant hypermulticulturalism. The shifting dynamics and processes of globalization are generating additional and innovative practices for engaging all peoples worldwide. What are the implications in our contemporary globalizing contexts for the global arts and Christian witness? We turn to these dynamics next.

Questions for Discussion

1. How do the global arts serve as bridges to our religious neighbors?
2. Discuss the concept of musicking and the five dialogues of beauty and art (fig. 8.4) in relation to peacebuilding and interfaith dialogue among peoples of different faiths.
3. Drawing from one of the dialogues in figure 8.4, design an interfaith event that brings together peoples of different faiths.

9

Appropriating Global Arts in Multicultural Settings

What happens when global arts are employed in highly multicultural contexts?

In 1999, as I started packing up to move from Daystar University in Nairobi, Kenya, to Fuller Theological Seminary in Pasadena, California, the world seemed to be spinning away at an unprecedented rate. As Western media dominated both television and radio, Africa felt increasing pressure to westernize. TV evangelists and Christian contemporary worship songs seemed to overpower most aspects of daily living, including the background music at my local bank and in the hallways of the Nairobi airport! Anything great and wonderful was described as "tech." The cultural dynamics were shifting: "What's from the West is best!" dictated the practice of the day. Yet I knew the people also experienced an unaddressed longing to develop a Kenyan Christian identity. When I raised the issue in classes, students responded deeply. Simply singing and sharing cultural songs in class provided opportunities to work through worldview values and contribute to the spiritual and theological formation of students. As I left for the States, I knew I would miss Daystar students and the opportunities to grow personally from our interactions.

Yet, when I arrived at Fuller Theological Seminary in Pasadena, California, I was pleasantly surprised to find a large group of Africans, former colleagues and students, working on higher degrees. I was delighted to be able to continue the fellowship and, most importantly, to worship in African ways. But I also found a plethora of other cultural groups of people at Fuller. As I taught about the music-cultures of the world in class, we did not have to go far to experience people's music firsthand. Students who wanted to learn about the musics[1] of India only had to drive twenty-six miles to the University of California at Los Angeles (UCLA) for a student performance. Many of the UCLA students performing were of Indian heritage, and their families were all in attendance. Surprisingly, the very next week, there was a South Asian concert at the church right next door to Fuller Theological Seminary. If my students had only waited one week to do their music observations, they could have just walked across the street. I also discovered Kan Zaman,[2] a Middle Eastern music ensemble composed of Arabic-speaking immigrants living in Southern California rehearsing weekly just two blocks away from Fuller's Pasadena campus. They welcomed me as I began the journey of learning to sing in Arabic and helped me connect and grow in friendship with peoples of the Middle East and their cultural traditions. The nations are living among us, everywhere. Often, we only need to walk across the street!

What is it, then, to bear witness to Christ in the burgeoning cities of the twenty-first century, in hypermulticultural contexts? In short, it's complicated! No one seems to be able to keep up with the changes and dynamics. Just getting a handle on the processes of our constantly shifting global world challenges everyone. Secular academics in globalization, missiologists, and ethnomusicologists regularly lament and commiserate with one another about the speed of change. It's incredibly difficult to keep up with the vast amount and pace of information in an era of intensified technology and media, from print and audio to social and digital. Globalization is multiplying exponentially with the continually "widening, deepening and speeding up of worldwide interconnectedness in all aspects of contemporary social life, from the cultural to the criminal, the financial to the spiritual."[3]

Culture and the arts are directly linked into the processes of globalization, and they actively function right alongside the major globalization dynamics of economics, finance, and technology.[4] Amazon, YouTube, and Facebook

---

1. I intentionally use the word "musics" in the plural in this chapter to indicate distinct music cultures that arise within language, ethnic, and cultural groups.

2. With a change in directors, Kan Zaman has since changed its name to Layali Zaman. They now rehearse even closer to Fuller. I am grateful to them for their continued warm welcome and for allowing me to learn and perform in concert with them. Several have become good friends.

3. Held, McGrew, Goldblatt, and Perraton, *Global Transformations*, 2.

4. In addressing the enormously complex and multidimensional topic of globalization, Myers suggests the metaphor of a gemstone with many facets wherein each facet contributes

operate globally and digitally out of the reach of national governance. They facilitate experiencing cultural diversity in ways previously limited to world travelers and missionaries. Each culture appears to be treated on an equal basis; digital access is open to all, depending on internet and computer availability. Here is the point. Our increasing interconnectedness is stretching, expanding, intensifying, and accelerating our social relations.[5] We can now interact with people online with whom we would not have otherwise come into contact; musicians and artists are finding each other across continental divides to collaborate on projects. Many of us turn to the internet first to find the latest music or the music of our homelands and to connect with longtime friends, colleagues, and relatives who have moved to different parts of the world. We are no longer so isolated from one another, as "the local and global intermingle."[6]

Beyond musicians and artists connecting online, refugees and immigrants similarly maintain connections with friends and families back home or in other cities. Peoples are on the move worldwide, and they are staying connected in new ways. Globalization is not only a technological phenomenon but, more importantly, a relational phenomenon.[7] Relational dynamics lie at the heart of witnessing to Christ, and, as we've already seen, music and the arts are key players facilitating relationships across cultural borders. This holds true digitally as well.

Global interconnectivity mandates new dimensions in witnessing to Christ's sacrificial love through the arts. Cities, with their urban and transnational contexts, bring together peoples in unlikely convergences and gatherings. As more local art forms go global through the media (i.e., hip hop, ukulele playing, and whirling dervishes), a wider divergence of aesthetics and taste is evolving that gives voice, place, and identity to hidden or marginalized peoples. In this chapter, we look at artistic encounters taking place through the global arts worldwide. We first identify the shifting dynamics, processes, and ways people are connecting and interacting with one another. We then turn our focus to what is happening worldwide in hypermulticultural contexts, specifically cities. Finally, we consider arenas of engagement where creative innovation in the arts in Christian witness is taking place.

---

to the beauty and integrity of the whole gem in distinct ways. Tucked away among those interactive multiple facets—comprising economics, finance, politics and governance, religion, crime, disease, and technology—is that of culture. Myers, *Engaging Globalization*, 35.

5. For a fuller discussion of his suggested major processes of globalization, see Steger, *Globalization*.

6. Steger, *Globalization*, 15.

7. Myers, *Embracing Globalization*, 38.

Encounters in the City

Worlds of diversity meet up in the city. More than 800 languages are spoken in New York City, with the densest number of spoken languages located in Queens.[8] Los Angeles claims people from over 140 countries who speak 224 languages. Each city is unique in its makeup, often organized geographically by ethnic groupings, such as Koreatown, Chinatown, Thai Town, Little Ethiopia, and Little Tokyo, all found within the perimeters of Los Angeles.[9] The range of ethnic restaurants and world musics extends without limits.[10] As city dwellers, individuals have greater freedom to move about in public spaces, choosing with whom they want to affiliate. Street musicians and concerts in the park, for example, offer individuals opportunities for new aesthetic encounters.

Thriving musical and artistic diversity. Rather than the expected global gray-out of language and culture, postmodern cities thrive on greater musical diversity than ever before. As ethnomusicologist Philip Bohlman notes:

> It is clear that the old models of immigrant culture, with the traces of the "old country" disappearing after three generations, were overly simplified. The city offers many opportunities for acculturation and the formation of musical hybrids. It also offers many more opportunities for celebrating diversity.[11]

Celebrating diversity becomes the platform for encounter and for building social relations. Peoples on the move bring with them their languages, culture, and music. Their encounters push the boundaries of the arts as traditionally defined. "High" culture encounters "low" culture. The lines become blurred as they move to more of a horizontal relationship. At the same time, each people's music functions as a valid world of music.

Shifting concepts of music and the arts. Ruth Finnegan alludes to what happens when all musics are acknowledged and valued in *The Hidden Musicians: Music-Making in an English Town.* She argues:

> Once one starts thinking not about "the best" but about what people actually do, . . . then it becomes evident that there are in fact several musics, not just one, and that no one of them is self-evidently superior to the others. In Milton Keynes [the British village studied], . . . there are several different musical

8. According to the Endangered Language Alliance (ELA). See Gus Lubin, "Queens Has More Languages Than Anywhere in the World—Here's Where They're Found," *Business Insider*, February 15, 2017, http://www.businessinsider.com/queens-languages-map-2017-2.

9. "Los Angeles, California, Population 2018," World Population Review, accessed May 17, 2018, http://worldpopulationreview.com/us-cities/los-angeles-population.

10. Bohlman, *World Music*, 134.

11. Bohlman, *World Music*, 136.

worlds, often little understood by each other yet each having its own contrasting conventions about the proper modes of learning, transmission, composition or performance.[12]

Finnegan's statement is seminal to communicating Christ via the global arts. Not only does she break down the long-held ethnocentric barriers of contrasting high and low art cultures, but her seemingly passing comment about the differing musical worlds as often little understood points to a core element in making Jesus Christ known and followed. Just as exposure to various spoken languages surrounding us does not itself imply creating understanding between peoples,[13] neither do neighboring worlds of music guarantee the development of similar understandings. Though music can be appreciated on a surface level, the more deeply held meanings of the music require deeper connections with the people making the music. Cultural musics and their arts, as well as the cities of the world, constitute integral, core elements of a people's identity. Of ultimate importance are the opportunities for relating with one another through a people's music and art cultures. What then is going on? How are people connecting in a hypermulticultural, globalizing world?

Discovering Diverse Worlds of Music and Art in the City and Beyond

We can map the hyperconnected encounters between people through the music and arts taking place in cities worldwide. When peoples move around the world, they carry with them their lived religious traditions and cultural practices. People's musical practices are portable, and their messages are transposable, available for shaping and reshaping new cultural encounters within the city.[14] Thus emerges world music, the "music that we encounter everywhere throughout the world, limitless, and without boundaries."[15] Often classified as popular music in contrast to classical music, world music incorporates traditional, ethnic musics that have often been popularized through the addition of electronic instruments and/or adapted contemporary rhythms. The musics of numerous peoples (diasporas) find their place on the world stage. This results in a vast array of fusions and hybrids that map out relational

12. Finnegan, *Hidden Musicians*, 6.
13. Hollinger, *Postethnic America*, 3.
14. Portable practices and transposable messages arise through the mobility of individuals and are two key characteristics of a global, hyperconnected world on the move. As portable practices move into new contexts, their messages are transposed into new keys as they interact within the new contexts. See Csordas, "Introduction: Modalities of Transnational Transcendence," 261–62.
15. Bohlman, *World Music*, i.

dynamics, both the positive and the contentious. Diaspora, festivals, and emerging networks form three core components lying at the heart of city life and its thriving intercultural dynamics.

Diaspora

The term "diaspora" refers here to a group of people who have found themselves displaced from their original homeland.[16] Placelessness and putting down roots in new contexts are conditions of diaspora, a life situation heavily articulated by world music.[17] The music of diaspora addresses the conditions of being displaced from one's homeland and resonates with the history and geography that connects the displaced back with their homeland. For the refugee and immigrant alike, the musics of diaspora help to reestablish a sense of place and identity as they are negotiating their new life settings. For example, Arabic speakers who have migrated, whether voluntarily or under duress, share common musical traditions. Pan-regional musics popularized through the media—such as the songs of singer Umm Kulthum, the "lady" of Cairo, Egypt, and of singer Fairuz (Lebanon), renowned stars of the Middle East—become focal points of commonality embraced across national boundaries. Maintaining their home roots, Middle Eastern peoples continue to enjoy and relate with one another through music events in local clubs, church events, and concert performances throughout Los Angeles. YouTube serves as a means for learning the songs of their heritage. Artists travel regularly between the Middle East and the United States, maintaining connections and replenishing repertoires. Negotiating the nuances of different aesthetic tastes and traditions shapes new configurations of regional diasporic community in the midst of diversity. A cross-mix of genres strives to find balance and commonality in the arts that foster people's feeling at home in their new settings.

Cities are made up of multiple diasporas. South Asian and African immigrants and refugees all seek to create their own arenas of being at home in new contexts. Musical instruments, as portable artifacts that easily travel with a people, link them to their lived traditions. The *njembe* (drum) from West Africa, the *sitar* (a classical string instrument) of India, and the *oud* (a Middle Eastern lute-type instrument) take on additional metaphorical meaning while producing the sounds that remind people of home. Their exchange and adaptation to the new contexts generate webs of interconnection between the homeland and the diaspora.[18]

16. See Brubaker, "'Diaspora' Diaspora."
17. Bohlman, *World Music*, 115.
18. Bohlman, *World Music*, 117.

As diasporas move into cities, they encounter the music and arts of contrasting diasporas in their new context. Many adapt and seek to assimilate into the new realms of music and the creative arts. Yet others are resistant, preferring the traditions they have always known. As a popular Hindi song in the 1960s and 1970s acknowledges, "My shoes may be Japanese, my trousers may be English, my hat may be Russian, but my heart is still Indian."[19] At the same time, with exposure to multiple cultural musics, cross-fertilization breeds new musical and artistic fusions. Diasporic border crossings produce new fusions, such as *chutney* (Caribbean) and *bhangra* (India).[20] Relational dynamics are taking place in the midst of fusing lives together through music and the arts. These processes frequently lead to forms known as popular music.[21] They reveal what many people are doing with music and the arts in their lives. In addition, they offer Christian witnesses some places of encounter.

Festivals

Festivals of world musics are ubiquitous in cities around the globe. Celebrating diversity, festivals likewise foster encounters in the city. Los Angeles communities, for example, celebrate Greek festivals, Cinco de Mayo, and Chinese New Year annually in locations where communities of diaspora live. Ethnic foods and performances of cultural music and dances showcase diaspora. Beyond the opportunity for public socializing, festivals of world music bring a convergence of many different histories, placing them side by side on the world stage. Musicians and audiences interact with local, ethnic, national, and religious communities. They afford people opportunities to learn about one another in celebratory environments. They give voice to the people we encounter in daily life, who have essential roles in the city but are not commonly acknowledged. This range of festivals offers Christian witnesses arenas of encounter and further engagement in local communities.

Networks

Musical and artistic networks are an emerging phenomenon in our global era. Natural voice movements—such as the Natural Voice Practitioners Network (NVPN) in the United Kingdom—are also emerging in North America,

19. Cited in Ravi Zacharias, "Influence among and through Cultural Influencers," Lausanne Movement, June 20, 2013, https://www.lausanne.org/content/influence-among-and-through-cultural-influencers-lausanne-global-leadership-forum.
20. For a very helpful glossary of diaspora mixes and fusions in world musics, see Bohlman, *World Music*, 126–27.
21. Bohlman, *World Music*, 124.

Australia, South Africa, and the Republic of Georgia.[22] Over the last fifty years, an emerging grassroots choral culture has sat at the intersection of two contemporary developments: (1) a thriving grassroots network of open-access community choirs built on weekend singing workshops and summer camps, and (2) a growing transnational network of amateur, non-Western-trained choral singers participating in community choirs. Across Britain, such networks bring together more than fifty choirs. They have a highly diverse a cappella repertoire. Such networks of choirs regularly join together in combined choral singing at festivals such as the Thames Choral Festival.[23] For example, past Thames Choral Festivals have included folk songs from eastern Europe, a Yoruba song from Nigeria that generates audience participation, a song based on Turkish poetry, an upbeat Zulu song, and in closing, a Motown favorite, "Dancing in the Street."[24]

This network of choirs sings with a purpose: to raise funds for WaterAid, a charity that provides clean water in Africa and Asia.[25] One event raised over half a million British pounds. This unmediated city event brings together people in creative collaborations that speak into third-world concerns, acknowledging and incorporating "invisible" people usually marginalized out of the mainstream. Interconnecting globally through world song, they are changing the agenda from aesthetic performance to performance that makes a difference in the physical lives of people. In singing for a common cause, the movement is generating new collaborations that broaden arts agendas to engaging global concerns. The focus shifts away from song as a product to the processes of creativity: diverse peoples are engaging one another in ways that empower everyone involved. They encourage people to explore different ways of using their voices and of being with one another.

Although the movement does not claim to be Christian, I believe such artistic networking offers a model for effectively engaging with people through their musics and artistic practices. Musicians and artists in the cities and around the nation are extending musical hospitality to the newly arrived nations now living among them. They are breaking down musical walls through their inclusive approach to peoples and their music-cultures. Reading Western staff notation is no longer required as a membership card. Hospitality through the

---

22. For a fascinating and astute ethnography of the emergence of these groups, see Bithell, *A Different Voice*.

23. See Thames Choral Festival songs: "Thames Festival 2010 Choir," https://youtu.be/JVo YIgi_kV4; "Ziymazumekisi—Sing for Water London 2015," https://youtu.be/Q3g3MJBp4fI.

24. Bithell, *A Different Voice*, 12.

25. See "Shona Malanga—Sing for Water 2013," https://youtu.be/lf5ypuf3TdA; "Ide Were," https://youtu.be/O_khgEZ0hJ8.

arts, when integrated with Christ-centered witness, has the potential to take incarnational friendship a step further. I believe that demonstrating God's love, compassion, and dignity to all peoples through their artistic practices takes high priority on God's missional agenda.

Arenas of Engagement

As we have seen above, diasporas, festivals, and networks are core elements in the processes of negotiating new globalizing contexts through music and the creative arts. Numerous groups outside the church already use these elements extensively. With peoples on the move in an interconnected era, we need to ask how we, as a diverse, global church, are engaging with the nations via the music and arts of these diverse peoples. We seem to be falling woefully short. We are unaware of where people are located and where they are hurting. We seem to engage only on superficial levels, oblivious to the array of possibilities for interacting with vast numbers of people seeking deeper spirituality and meaningful relationship with God.

The implications of such networks and diasporas for witnessing to Jesus Christ and making a difference in their lives go unnoticed by us. There is hope, though. Gateways and windows of opportunity stand open for getting involved in the lives of people through cultural musics and arts. In the face of overwhelming need, brave pioneers are doing innovative work. They are entering new fields of artistic engagement. In order to understand some of the deeper cultural issues at hand when addressing the arts in the city, we turn first to hip hop culture, followed by a set of initiatives focused on forging relational bonds of Christ-centered witness through the arts.

Taking It to the Streets: Hip Hop Culture

Initially infamous for its lead artists' criminal lifestyles and their openly defiant, in-your-face messages addressing societal issues of injustice and evil, hip hop has become a youth phenomenon. Arising in the squalor and mess of the inner cities in the United States, first in New York City and then in Los Angeles, hip hop gives voice to ignored youth—the marginalized, the poor, and the downtrodden.[26] It also strives to increase social consciousness and racial and ethnic pride.[27] Its artists play prophetic roles as they speak to those

---

26. See Chang, *Can't Stop, Won't Stop*; Hodge, *Soul of Hip Hop*; and Kitwana, *Hip Hop Generation*.
27. Hodge, "No Church in the Wild."

things that many would rather avoid. The hip hop culture also incorporates multiple art forms, from music to dance to visual art. We see this in the way it incorporates spoken word (rap), graffiti, various dance styles, and samples of different musical genres, primarily rap music, a related movement. These multimedia messages have resonated with the marginalized, poor, and victims worldwide. Daniel White Hodge, a leading scholar in the field, shares hip hop's core dynamics and critical features.

Vignette 9.1

Hip Hop Has Gone Global

Daniel White Hodge
Associate Professor of Intercultural Communication
and Communications Department Chair,
North Park University, Chicago

Hip Hop is a global entity. What started on the margins has evolved into a global cultural expression toward oppression, racial injustice, exclusion, and disenfranchisement; those are core elements to Hip Hop culture. Now . . . we all know the mess that comes on popularized radio stations—and yes, it can be quite horrific. I feel you. I really do! But that is not Hip Hop culture. Hip Hop is an urban subculture that seeks to express a *lifestyle, attitude,* and/ or *urban individuality.* Hip Hop at its core—not the commercialization and commodity it has become in certain respects—*rejects* dominant forms of culture and society and seeks to increase a social consciousness along with a racial/ethnic pride. Thus, Hip Hop uses *rap music, dance, music production, emceeing,* and *allegory* as vehicles to send and fund its message of social, cultural, and political resistance to dominant structures of norms. This is part of what Jesus was about . . . resistance to dominant structures of norms. Jesus *is* Hip Hop! Baby-mama drama, came from the 'hood, officials hated him, and one of his boys did him in? C'mon now, that's Hip Hop! It's time we start seeing Hip Hop beyond the commercialized, hypersexual lens that so often gets portrayed. And while those elements are part of the culture, and they are problematic, they do not represent the core and theological components of Hip Hop culture.

Hodge further maintains that hip hop "engages profound religious themes and has the capacity to provide hope to people who have often been ignored by many Christian churches."[28] Tupac Shakur's lyrics below reveal the religious dynamics at work within much of rap music:

"God"

God
When I was alone, and had nothing
I asked for a friend to help me bear the pain
No one came, except God
When I needed a breath to rise, from my sleep
No one could help me, except God
When all I saw was sadness, and I needed answers
No one heard me, except God
So, when I'm asked, who I give my unconditional love to?
I look for no other name, except God.[29]

Hodge notes five theological components of hip hop that reveal how music and the arts function as forms of social resistance and culture change, meeting life head-on in light of the gospel.

Vignette 9.2

Hip Hop's Five Theological Components

Daniel White Hodge
Associate Professor of Intercultural Communication
and Communications Department Chair,
North Park University, Chicago

Hip Hop has five main theological components: a theology of suffering, a theology of community, a theology of the Hip Hop Jesus, a theology of social action and justice, and a theology of the profane. From a gospel perspective, Hip Hop fits into many narratives in which Jesus encompassed those elements. And with the current shift in Christian theology toward a more intercultural approach, Hip Hop provides a platform by which to engage Christianity from a much more intercultural perspective (e.g., not from white evangelicalism). So, Hip Hop provides the *space, venue, context,* and *freedom* to create a theology of the marginalized, oppressed, and disenfranchised, just like Jesus

28. Hodge, "No Church in the Wild," 102.
29. Tupac Shakur, "God," on *The Rose That Grew from Concrete*, vol. 1, Amaru / Interscope Records, 2000. Used with permission of Amaru Entertainment, Inc.

did, in a post-soul/post–civil rights era. It also creates a theological space for post–civil rights young adults to question, doubt, and push theological boundaries further. For example, rap music is a theological precept when we examine the definition. Rap is the main medium of the Hip Hop culture that brings definition, value, understanding, and appreciation to the social isolation, economic hardship, political demoralization, and cultural exploitation endured by most ghetto and poor white communities. Thus, rap is the musical expression that complements the oral communication of its culture. Rap also captures and esteems the ghetto poor existence as valid and real to all people of color, as well as to many poor whites. The gospel makes such esteem and validation imperative, and it does so for those not approved by the norm. In other words, the music becomes a form of theological expression, identity, and formation, which is something that we in the West do not fully understand because so often we're in our heads rather than in our bodies theologically. Hip Hop gets the full-body experience of God, the Son, and the Spirit![a]

[a] For further discussion on the structure of hip hop theology, see Daniel White Hodge, *Hip Hop's Hostile Gospel: A Post-Soul Exploration*, Studies in Critical Research on Religion 6 (Leiden: Brill, 2017).

What then do witness and ministry in the inner cities of the United States, where hip hop culture is at home, look like? My colleague Jude Tiersma-Watson tells about her experience with two major demographics, African Americans and Latinos, who share the same spaces in the inner city of Los Angeles. African Americans primarily find their voice in rap music, which has arisen out of oral traditions. In addition to rap music, graffiti art appropriates spaces and venues for the local inner-city context. In Los Angeles, graffiti as an art form is especially important to the diverse Latino population, since it draws from their cultural traditions of mural art. Latinos who come to the city and seek to fit into the new setting do not limit themselves to music from their home country. For example, Tiersma-Watson has noticed many Latino Angelinos also identifying with music of the city, including that of hip hop culture.[30] At the same time, however, they maintain and voice their cultural expression by drawing from their heritage of mural art on walls. Spaces for alternative writing become arenas of engagement that witness to the love and compassion of God. In one such situation, urban art has become an integral part of church planting.

30. Jude Tiersma-Watson, email correspondence with author, October 17, 2018.

Vignette 9.3
Writing Alternative Narratives
through Street Art in Los Angeles

Jude Tiersma-Watson
Associate Professor of Urban Mission,
Fuller Theological Seminary

Ruben Nuño describes himself as a missionary church planter masquerading as a pastor. When he returned to his home city of Los Angeles after serving cross-culturally in France and North Africa, he began using the lens of a missiologist. That led to asking new questions: "What might it mean to contextualize the gospel for young people in the neighborhoods of LA—to see the gospel arise from the roots of the neighborhoods, rather than bringing in the dominant culture?"

As Pastor Ruben spent time in the neighborhoods, he realized that the heart language of the young people was neither Spanish nor English but graffiti art, which had been in use since the late 1970s, when it emerged out of the south Bronx. Pastor Ruben helped facilitate the creation of the Belmont Art Space, an expression of a church plant in a specific place that was important to local youth—near the famous Belmont yard. Once home to many revolving graffiti "pieces," this space was lost to gentrification and is now a luxury housing complex. Pastor Ruben created a new space where young artists could express themselves and their aspirations.

The Belmont Art Space began with youth spray painting their names, as was their custom, but then shifted to asking, "What would it mean for God to rename you?" A further shift moved them from painting their own names to representing the local community in their art. Together they were envisioning the good of the city. Here was a new wineskin created from and for a constantly evolving city. Together they created a mural under a local bridge. This mural represented the history and dreams of the local neighborhood, dreams that reflect the desire for shalom, which is core to God's kingdom.

Through this art space, Pastor Ruben witnessed a resilient culture refusing to accept someone else's definition of them. By painting their names on walls, they were not allowing someone else to name them, but were taking their own power and naming themselves. In the shadow of Hollywood, this raw, authentic artistic expression came from the streets. It was a very public and in-your-face expression that gave them a voice and expressed prophetic resilience. Through their writing (graffiti), the youth were creating an alternative narrative in which they were the actors and agents, cocreators with God in the ongoing work of culture creating.[a]

[a] For an overview of LA graffiti, see Susan A. Phillips, *Wallbangin': Graffiti and Gangs in L. A.* (Chicago: University of Chicago Press, 1999). For a historical overview of graffiti, see Troy Lovata and Elizabeth Olton, eds., *Understanding Graffiti: Multidisciplinary Studies from Prehistory to the Present* (New York: Routledge, 2015). For a deeper view of the role of murals in Chicano identity, see Holly Barnett-Sanchez and Tim Drescher, *Give Me Life: Iconography and Identity in East LA Murals* (Albuquerque: University of New Mexico Press, 2016); and Jude Tiersma, "Reading the Writing on the Wall: Missional Transformation through Narrative in Postmodern Los Angeles" (PhD diss., Fuller Theological Seminary, 1999).

Dealing with Dominance and Power: Muted Group Theory

Throughout our hip hop culture discussion, we find a recurring theme of engaging dominant culture through the arts. Giving voice to the voiceless, standing up to injustice, and maintaining identity are all elements that reflect groups of people who have been silenced and/or ignored. Dealing with dominance and power issues is inherent in any multicultural context. Muted Group Theory[31] addresses issues that arise whenever there is "unequal participation in a society in generating ideas and encoding them, when realities and values of sub-dominant groups are inadequately recognized by the dominant group, and [when] the mechanisms . . . limit access to arenas where societal rewards are obtained."[32] Music and the arts, as seen in hip hop culture, unearth and confront deeply embedded issues of injustice in ways that overcome voicelessness.

The dominance of a prevailing culture and its worldview leaves out subdominant groups who express themselves differently, as in cultural art forms. Dominant cultures may force subdominant groups to conform or be excluded, often based on whether those groups are able to accept varied forms of expression. In such scenarios, differences of expression generate pools of misunderstanding that remain unresolved, allowing tension and issues to fester among subdominant groups. Music and the arts vent such tensions. Engaging

31. Muted Group Theory is a helpful intercultural communication theory that addresses issues of power and overcoming voicelessness. Although women's studies, in particular, is one of the major disciplines that has applied it to their field, other disciplines are beginning to apply it to their unique contexts. See Ardener, "Ardener's 'Muted Groups,'" 50; Scott A. Chadwick, "Muted Group Theory," accessed May 17, 2018, http://oregonstate.edu/instruct/theory/mutedgrp.html; Kramarae, "Muted Group Theory and Communication"; and Meares, Torres, Derkacs, Oetzel, and Ginossar, "Employee Mistreatment and Muted Voices."

32. Linda Barkman, "Applying Muted Group Theory to Missiology: Studying Dynamics between Female Prisoners and Prison Ministry Volunteers at the California Institution for Women," paper presented at the annual meeting of the American Society of Missiology, St. Paul, Minnesota, June 16–19, 2016.

people through their heart languages provides arenas for finding identity and belonging that foster witnessing at deeper levels of life among muted groups. It turns off the mute button and frees inner-city youth to be themselves and relate to the God who is for them.

Forging Bonds through Music and Artistic Interaction

While hip hop culture is a global phenomenon, it is only one music-culture that engages peoples within cities worldwide. Many cities are dotted with diasporas living in clusters throughout adjacent neighborhoods and nearby towns. Cultural groups formerly in the minority are moving beyond segmented neighborhoods. Every context increasingly feels the presence of diversity. What is it to follow Christ and give witness to him in emerging hypermulticultural contexts? We need to recognize two new perspectives and approaches that can guide our quest.

First, global shifts are forcing practitioners of the arts in witness to recognize their work not as cultural *products* but rather as *processes* of creativity that create relationship and meaning. Musical practices in South Africa reinforce the notion that "meaning does not reside 'in the music' but is rather 'produced' in the ever-shifting interaction between actors, interpreters, and performers."[33] The processes of music-making and the arts engender dynamic interactions that bridge and bond peoples within and across cultures. That is, social interaction takes place within the processes of musicking[34] and creating art together. It is in the processes surrounding the production of music and art that relational bonding takes place. Performing, creating, experiencing, and expressing culture together provide the cultural glue for bringing people together. The process frees up people groups to move from shallow interactions to deeper levels of identity and life issues, including religious allegiances. Empathy and mutual understanding emerge on more intimate levels. "Aha" moments of breakthrough understandings become pivotal moments that bridge and bond people relationally.

Second, here we suggest an initial model to address the multiple approaches for reaching the nations wherever they are located (see fig. 9.1). It outlines a series of stepping-stones for moving from focusing only on the product to engaging in the processes of musicking and artistic creativity, in order to generate pivotal moments of deeper understandings among peoples.

Figure 9.1 illustrates building webs of relationships among peoples who daily rub shoulders with one another but who otherwise have limited means

33. Erlmann, *Nightsong*, 102, quoted in Bithell, *A Different Voice*, 28.
34. Christopher Small's concept of *musicking* was discussed in chapter 8.

Figure 9.1
Stepping-stones to forging relational bonds: music and the creative arts

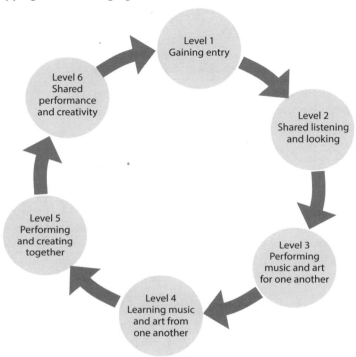

of initiating dialogue and relational interaction. While the end goal and reason for coming together centers on a product—a musical performance, storytelling, creating a public artwork, drama, a church rite, or another arts-based project—the model focuses on the processes of creative interaction that forge bonds of relationship-cum-friendship. Dialogical interaction involved in each of the stepping-stones leads to a series of pivotal moments along the way that bridge and bond musicians and creative artists into dynamic relationships. In the midst of the processing, they move from initially shallow levels of relating to the joy of discovering one another on more intimate levels. A common outcome is the building of sustainable community through pivotal moments that bear testimony to Christ through God-glorifying relationships within local communities. Although the model focuses mainly on music, it does so in the broader sense of music and cultural arts integrated together, not compartmentalized away from each other. Storytelling and song quite naturally arise in combination with other artistic practices, often including feasting together. Such practices of creativity are inclusive rather than exclusive. They allow everyone to participate in some way. Indeed, we see this inclusivity as an emerging reality of the arts in a global world where equity exists among all peoples and their cultural arts.

Vignettes 9.4 through 9.6 demonstrate various new possibilities of witness through the global arts, as outlined in our model. In our twenty-first-century world dealing with so many issues and pressures, each stepping-stone offers dialogical engagement for building sustainable relationships. We begin with the pursuit of cross-cultural understanding wherein some people have not had opportunity to process their own identity, tell their stories, and pursue relating with others around topics that are usually ignored or covered up.

Vignette 9.4

Fuse Music Project: Bonding across Cultures through Music

Sunita Puleo
Founder of Fuse Music Project

What's your heart music? Having grown up in a bicultural family in a New York City neighborhood where people speak more than eight hundred different languages means that my heart music—my cultural home—is not easy to find. I hear snippets of it played by Indian *tabla*, acoustic folk guitar, Peruvian pan flute, Chinese *erhu*, sticks hitting buckets, and so many more. As a professional musician, I keep chasing a sound that will somehow include them all—the sound of home. As an invested, caring citizen of our world, I'm chasing more than just a sound. I'm chasing deep, Spirit-enabled unity between people, and we're seeing it happen in Fuse.

Fuse Music Project began with five professional female performing artists from different cultural backgrounds intending to contribute individual, culturally inspired sounds to create a multicultural blend of sounds. Most of us didn't previously know each other. Our mixed heritages ranged from all over the world: the Philippines, Guatemala, the Bahamas, India, the British Isles, and the African American context within the American South. We spent a month or more easing into collaborating, while fundraising and scheduling a performance. Our process was much like Dr. King's "stepping-stones to forging relational bonds" (fig. 9.1), but in real life the steps are not always ordered: they all happen at different levels all the time.

Gaining entry. In addition to making music, or at least playing with sounds, we talked a lot in the beginning. We drank tea in each other's homes, we took selfies, and we laughed a lot. Members commented that this was un-like some past rehearsal experiences, where they had to leave some or all of their personal lives at the door, or where they had to suppress themselves in deference to someone else's ego. We decided that this group would be a safe place to express anything—emotions, spirituality, controversial thoughts, and life struggles. We became friends.

Shared listening and performing for one another. To find songs that would express our cultural roots, we spent whole-group and individual rehears-als listening to YouTube videos picked out by different members, or listening to each other perform possible repertoire. I went to hear one of the members perform in her context, and it helped me to know her better.

Learning music from each other. We each had to learn songs differently—some by ear, some with written lyrics and chords. Some could improvise Western harmonies; others learned harmonies as alternate melodies. We had to learn to clap on either the second and fourth beat or the first and third, or in different rhythms. We had to learn to sing and understand lyrics in several different languages. We had to take turns leading. Because of our small group, we also had to stretch ourselves to play unfamiliar instruments to help members re-create cultural musics. We were all in this together.

Creating together. Making space for unique, individual contributions to cultural songs also translated into daily life: we began to be affected by one another. One member vocalized short prayers to Jesus as she got ready to sing, and soon others tried that. One member seemed to prayerfully medi-tate as she just breathed, and we followed suit together. Our regular musical warm-ups became sacred time and space: we could weave in and out of different tones and moods and identities without the burden of a song form to anchor us. We all wished for more time in that space, learning to move in sound as a group of unique individuals.

Performing together. There is nothing like performance to bond perform-ers. But this was different; we had been digging into each other's lives through this music, and now we were going to open that intimate space to an audi-ence. We were courageously presenting raw, complicated identities, but as a group. When one woman sang about her experience as an African American mother who feared for her children's safety in a world of racial violence, we sang it with her. We had spent months entering into that song, feeling her pain, letting the song affect us, letting our friend affect us. Together, we ex-pressed her fear, pain, and hope. Despite growing up in a hypermulticultural context, I had never engaged so deeply with this aspect of African American life. We experienced the depth of this shared expression across the team in the songs each member chose.

The final piece of performance is what the audience receives. At our most recent performance, I looked up from our last note to a truly pivotal moment. Our small, mostly Anglo American audience had tearfully stood on their feet to applaud, and they wouldn't stop. Some were weeping openly. After closing, we held people as they wept over how much it meant to them to experience this kind of unity between people of different cultures being expressed through the arts. Some shared their struggles with cultural identity or their hopes for building bridges in their contexts. Some just said, "The world needs more of this right now."

Gaining entry (level 1) into the lives of "strangers" is one of the most difficult steps to take. The ambiguity of creating new pathways for intercultural engagement and witness calls for courage, determination, and persistence. The Fuse Music Project experienced this. It required a vision and determined desire to make a difference in the world on the part of Fuse's founder. Beginning with themselves, the group has seen friendship blossom, understanding develop, and empathy increase for one another's story in context. Spiritual growth and connection have taken place. Fuse performances for audiences have served as experiential metaphors of cross-cultural bonding and fostered pivotal moments as people received glimpses of each performer's cultural history and life concerns. Audiences gained a sense of creating deeper levels of community.

This type of artistic bonding is taking place in other locations around the globe, varying in accordance with historical and cultural sensitivities. In the hypermulticultural context of Australia, for example, more than two hundred languages are spoken. The diasporas come from different ethnic groups from those found in the United States or Europe. Welcoming migrants and various long-term ethnicities to the sacrament of Communion through the sharing of cultural songs and storytelling employed several stepping-stones in our model that made Communion a place of welcome and witnessed to God's embrace of all peoples.

Vignette 9.5

Welcoming the Stranger to Table Fellowship in Australia

Amelia Koh-Butler
Doctor of Missiology

Newcastle, Australia, offers many choices of cuisine. Sunday regularly saw just as many cultures: Aussie, Irish, Scottish, British, Samoan, Fijian, Chinese,

Indonesian, Dutch, South African, Sudanese, Italian, and Greek. Yet it was not until we invited people to share their songs and hospitality stories that chatter started about God's hospitality.

Over six months, people shared songs from their life experience. This led to story sharing and deep listening. People learned about their own identity and the identity of others. Over the ensuing twelve months, as minister, I used those songs and stories to develop a repertoire of styles, songs, and stories to help community members know each other. Every month we introduced the people's music into worship. They blossomed. New people appeared, and more stories were welcomed.

For many, the table of the Lord had previously been hijacked by the dominant culture—a kind of British colonialism that left other cultures silenced and feeling out of place. But now, hearing from different cultures and encouraging new expressions of the sacramental story transformed Communion from an intimate family meal to a multilayered banquet of community interaction. God's table was bigger than any of us first thought!

Learning one another's songs and learning new songs together opened people up to the possibility of a heaven where people of difference could co-exist. Teaching songs to one another also meant people coming to terms with their past and allowing the healing of fellowship to reframe stories. Telling of mourning led to new dancing.

Centered on learning about God's hospitality, different cultural groups in this Australian church were given voice and included in the processes of making music and storytelling. As an inclusive means of artistic engagement, the processes moved toward a practice of Communion where all people could feel recognized, respected, accepted, and at home within their own identities.

Likewise, the cities of Africa experience multiculturalism in yet different configurations, with extremely high percentages of young people. For example, in Lilongwe, the capital of Malawi, 70 percent of the population is under the age of thirty.[35] Youth make up even higher portions of the population in the cities. A country seeking to find its voice and cultural identity, Malawi is also highly in need of development. Creating an event called "Pa

---

35. Dr. Mwerapusa Mawindo, email correspondence with author, August 4, 2017. "That distribution reflects the general national trend; Malawi is a very young nation and with increasingly ongoing urbanization it will soon be a young urban population." Additionally, two out of every three persons in the country is under the age of twenty-five. "Malawi Youth Data Sheet 2014," Population Reference Bureau, 2014, http://www.prb.org/pdf14/malawi-youth-data sheet-2014.pdf.

Moto: Culture in the City," Dr. Mwerapusa Mawindo turned to storytelling and song as a means of linking young urban professionals by drawing from cultural wisdom. Similar to Australian practices, Pa Moto draws from the Malawi tradition of sitting around the fire at night and telling stories—a tradition giving way to modern habits of ignoring ways of coming together. The event showcased eleven stories: six via a mix-and-mingle exercise that had people hunting down stories, and five more that were narrated on two storytelling stages.

The goal of this project—researching cultural stories and songs and then sponsoring an evening of storytelling and song—was to reestablish identity through cultural continuity among young urban professionals as they move into the future. The process engaged multiple stepping-stones from our model.

Vignette 9.6

Something Old, Something New, Something Retold
Kamdothi: A Chewa Folktale

Mwerapusa Mawindo
Founder of Imagine Africa: The Bantu Chapter

Kamdothi sings a modern-day song to us all. It reminds us to refuse to be so swept up by the guile of modernism that we forget the voice of our mother Malawi—our traditions and our identity. (Pa Moto participant)

The storyteller began: "After years of trying, one family in Maravi finally admitted what they had been too afraid to utter: they could not have children. Desperate, they sought the help of a gifted healer, who gave them a beautiful baby girl. As they turned to leave, he said, 'Because this child is from the dust, she must not be touched by rain. The day she is, is the day she returns to the dust.' So, whenever rain clouds gathered, Mum ["Mom" in British English, the national language of Malawi] would sing, 'Kamdothiwe, thawa mvula' [Kamdothi, run away from the rain] and Kamdothi would echo back 'thawa mvula' [run from the rain]. The day came, however, when Kamdothi decided she was having much too much fun to oblige Mum's silly superstitions. Ignoring the darkening sky and her mother's song of warning, she failed to notice until too late that she had lost an ear, followed by her leg and then her hand. Kamdothi was soon washed away by the rain."

Placed in dialogue with critical thought and other forms of orality, this familiar tale on the importance of obedience sparked the imagination of the young professionals and facilitated conversations in a manner that would have been impossible otherwise. For Imagine Africa, an organization that is developing new models of spiritually and culturally oriented development, Kamdothi and the other stories at Pa Moto succeeded in orienting urbanites to their past (something old), discovering new narratives (something new), and affirming the reality of difference and texture in modern Malawian urban identities (something retold)—all of which are fundamental pillars in building a community that is working for progressive and relevant development.

Symbolism contained in the story and song was reinterpreted by the young urban professionals for their contemporary context. Dr. Mawindo explains:

> For us at "Pa Moto: Culture in the City," the complexity of dealing with this story was in the fact that many felt that our sociopolitical elders had made decisions that, rather than placing them in the elder's role, make them *kamdothis*. That is, being enthralled by the promises and wonders of the modern world, they have failed to take heed of the call to strength, integrity, and hard work, and instead chosen the easier path of corruption, stealing, and nepotism to acquire this good life ("We are so busy having fun in the rain we are unaware or uncaring of the consequences of playing in it much longer").[36]

They also applied it to themselves, acknowledging how they are uncritically buying into the media, allowing the "rain" to wash away their strong history of Christian identity and cultural traditions. Dr. Mawindo further points out that "our truth-tellers engaged the stories, poetry, and subjects that we as a society gloss over, run away from discussing, or simply don't know need mentioning. They brought their candor hats and didn't pull any punches. It could have been a difficult dialogue, and yet it was made easier by the fact that it was placed in the powerful form of storytelling."

The vignettes in this chapter give just a sample of initiatives that innovatively employ global arts in Christ-centered witness. Notice how the various approaches involve a range of people, from professional artists to peoples who naturally engage in the participatory arts of their cultural context. Key to each approach is identifying various heart musics and artistic heart languages that are appropriate to diverse, hypermulticultural contexts. These artistic languages can then be a part of forging relationships and expressing their devotion to Christ.

36. Dr. Mwerapusa Mawindo, email correspondence with author, July 19, 2017.

Conclusion: Engaging Global Arts in Hypermulticultural Contexts

Globalization is generating growing crescendos of nations and peoples migrating worldwide, especially toward the Western world. The psalmist's call to "let the far ends of the earth honor him" (Ps. 67:7 CEB) is becoming a reality in ways not previously imagined. The church has access to people groups previously cut off from contact.

As people bring their portable practices with them, all the world is relating through music and the arts. Celebration of diversity and shifts in the way we perceive music and the arts are taking place outside the contexts of Christian witness and worship. Diaspora, festivals, and networks form three major tributaries that feed into the converging streams of the cultural arts actively feeding into globalization processes. Music and the arts foster enhanced interaction, enhanced interconnection, and enhanced configurations of collaboration. It is striking that groups in the secular music world, such as the Thames Choral Festival, are seeking to help others alleviate poverty and provide safe water, traditionally a part of mission and Christ-centered witness. The secular world of music and the arts is engaging peoples worldwide, and their work challenges Christian witness to new dimensions of dialogical engagement that make a difference in today's world.

We need to acknowledge that music and the arts offer dialogical ways of encountering and engaging with diverse peoples in Christ-centered witness. Giving voice to muted groups through the arts cuts through multiple barriers of communication and works toward positive social interaction. Identifying, acknowledging, and engaging with people's heart musics and artistic languages—from writing on walls to *bhangra* music-cum-dance—provides profound opportunities to engage people on deeper levels within their worlds and to build incarnational friendships. Shifting our focus from art products to the processes of creating art and music provides stepping-stones for forging relational bonds that engender pivotal moments, ultimately demonstrating Christ's love—in us and for all peoples. Peoples move toward him, God is glorified, and the psalmist's call, "May all the peoples praise you" (Ps. 67:3), becomes a living reality.

But how do we begin to incorporate what we have learned throughout our journey in the global arts? What will we take into our practices of witness and worship? Our concluding postlude invites us to reassess and reimagine ways to extend our approaches of dynamic witness through the global arts. We engage with two questions: How do we move beyond conventional boundaries and preconceptions for engaging the arts? What are the essential elements that form a road map to guide us along the way? We turn to theological imperatives, shifts in perspectives, and action points to ignite us to move out among the nations, wherever the peoples are found.

Questions for Discussion

1. What shifts are taking place in relation to the global arts in the twenty-first century?
2. How is the secular world employing the global arts to make a difference in the lives of worldwide movements of people?
3. How can we initiate incarnational friendships via the arts in ways that break through multiple barriers of communication? Give one or two examples (see fig. 9.1).

Postlude

Revealing God's Glory and Salvation via Global Arts

Worship services typically conclude with a musical postlude to send believers out into the world as faithful witnesses. Similarly, in this book we as art makers and appreciators have journeyed together from worship to witness. The bookends of worship and witness are essential for God's interaction in the world today; they contain all the means through which God makes himself known and relates with us. However, discussions regarding art and following Christ often only engage with the realm of worship. This book has focused on the arts-in-witness—the bookend that completes and facilitates our dynamic interactions with the living God, pushing us out of our comfortable worship settings into a needy world. Without both bookends, the books fall over.

The critical need for the arts in both witness and worship recently came home to me in an amazing way. While at a missions dinner, as I was completing this book, I heard a surprising update on the work I had done with the Maasai people of East Africa back in 1999.

My Story: Worshiping as Witness in Our Global World

It had become something of a ritual. Every Sunday, the young Maasai *moran* (warrior) found himself drawing close to the church building as the local Maasai faith community gathered to sing their praise and adoration to God on the plains of East Africa. Leaning against a nearby tree, he listened avidly to hear the good news the songs were proclaiming about this God he did not know. He loved what he heard and kept returning for more. Eventually, he found himself wanting to follow Jesus. His father and family members fought against him. But he knew he wanted what the believers were singing about. Finally, he made the difficult decision, against his family's wishes. He decided to follow Jesus and joined the community of believers in singing of God's glory and salvation. Today, the transformed *moran*-turned-believer is not only a faithful worshiper but is training to become a missionary himself. Worship and witness had joined hands to draw this Maasai warrior to follow Christ.

I sat there dumbfounded as I listened to this story of the *moran*-turned-believer at a dinner in a Southern California home, attended by members of a local faith community with varying degrees of global reach—from local businesspeople to Tommy Walker, an internationally renowned worship leader and composer. I was delighted and amazed to hear of the growth that had been taking place among the Maasai church in Kenya and Tanzania over the last eighteen years, since I had last visited a fledgling community of Maasai believers.[1] The missionary couple further explained to the guests the pivotal role that our 1999 workshop, "New Songs for Worship," had played in church planting. Centered on engaging the Scriptures via a people's spoken and musical heart languages, the workshop's group-composing process and the resulting worship songs had contributed significantly to triggering a movement of Maasai peoples coming to faith in Christ. Right next to me that evening sat a Maasai Anglican priest, a recent master of divinity graduate from Fuller Theological Seminary. I had invited him to come and hear of the work among his people back home. At the end, the Maasai priest felt compelled to stand and extend thanks on behalf of his people for the local-global church's collaboration in God's work. In this one setting, a local faith community out of East Africa was speaking into a local Southern California context, a sample of interaction that makes up our globalized world. Worship and witness through relevant song forms and the arts had played pivotal roles in revealing God's glory and salvation in two strikingly different settings in each community. God is at work among all peoples, in both local and global-city contexts.

This story teaches an additional striking lesson. We often do not immediately see how God is at work in drawing peoples to himself. This is especially true when it comes to the global arts. Sometimes we do not realize their effect until many years later. When I had done the Maasai New Song workshop in 1999, I knew something special was happening, but I had no idea how pivotal that missional arts project would become. In the task of effective witness,

1. One of my last New Song workshops in 1999 was among the Maasai since they longed to learn about making songs for worshiping God in their vernacular language. It was a highlight of my time in Africa.

contextualization of the arts for witness and worship had played a pivotal role in making Jesus Christ known and followed. The evening brought into focus what the psalmist declared centuries ago:

> All the nations you have made
>   will come and worship before you, Lord;
>   they will bring glory to your name. (Ps. 86:9)

Now we come to the conclusion of our journey in addressing the former lack of missiological focus on the arts-in-witness. Two questions have been constantly at the forefront: If witness is both dialogical and relational, how then do the arts excel in expressive dialogue and relational bonding in profound and persuasive ways? What then are the arts' implications for mission? As we conclude, I invite you to reconsider and reimagine the global arts in relation to witness in ways that expand our horizons.

Expanding Horizons

It is a new day for the global arts and Christ-centered witness. Much is already taking place. It is emerging in widening circles of kingdom expansion. And it is invading our own local communities without our ever leaving home. As the dynamics of globalization continue to confront us on a daily basis, we need broadening arenas of engagement through the arts. The task of missions is expanding in much more inclusive ways. Our approaches need continuity *and* change. Pioneer missions, like those of earlier years, seeking to reach the unreached—those who have never heard the gospel message in relevant ways in order to make intelligent responses to Christ—are on the rise. For example, 81 percent of the world's Hindus, Muslims, and Buddhists do not personally know a Christian, and they make up the largest unreached people groups in the twenty-first century.[2] With current population growth rates, the need to reach out continues to grow unabated.[3] At the same time, however, as we have previously noted, peoples are moving into new parts of the world and rubbing shoulders with peoples they have never had opportunities to meet before. The nations are living among each other in new configurations. Neither pioneer mission nor global mission should be ignored. Rather, both need to be intentionally pursued.

2. See "Mission Trends and Facts," *Joshua Project*, accessed May 17, 2018, https://joshua project.net/assets/media/handouts/mission-trends-facts.pdf.
3. Hiebert, *Gospel in Human Contexts*, 179.

In today's local-global reality, definitions and conceptions of the arts keep shifting and taking new shapes. Music and the arts travel with the people who interact with them. As a result, "everyone is a scattering, everyone is displaced, . . . left without a stable home or identity."[4] Global displacement does not automatically change a people's heart language merely because they find themselves in a new place.[5] Both heart languages and newly encountered cultural arts form and influence people and their interactions with one another. Rubbing shoulders with new peoples puts us on the road and in contact with one another in ways that can enhance our approaches for making Christ known and worshiped. Recognizing that music and the arts are culturally defined requires broadening definitions of the arts that include all peoples. Culturally determined aesthetic standards and expectations also bring different and emerging artistic considerations to the table. Expanding and changing definitions of music and the arts are taking place at especially rapid rates in urban centers worldwide, from Berlin to Montreal, Mexico City, Chicago, and Hong Kong.[6]

In global Christian circles, we see a growing use of the term "creative arts." This term fosters inclusion and integration of cultural art forms in witness and worship. Parts of the church in Asia, for example, are searching to move beyond the rigid religious expression first introduced in the days of colonialism, predominantly Western classical music. For many Asian churches, according to Joseph Lee of Singapore, "any undefined area or genre of artistic expression which could aid in Christian worship, discipleship, or evangelism would then be parked under the label *creative arts*."[7] A vast continuum of arts is available for witness and worship. Thus, "creative arts," as a term, is a possible beginning point for seeking to find ways of embracing all peoples through their culturally defined art forms.

I invite you to reassess and reimagine ways to extend and engage in dynamic witness through the global arts. Here I gather together essential elements that create a road map for making God's salvation and glory known among all the nations (Ps. 67:2), from the "ends of the earth" (Ps. 67:7) to the globalizing cities of the world. This invitation to engage the arts extends to us all, breaking conventional boundaries and preconceptions of relegating the arts to professional artists.

4. Taylor, *Global Pop*, 181.

5. Traditional art forms are still valued in a global world, sometimes even increasing in value as a means of maintaining identity. See "Keepers of the Arts," *Novica*, accessed May 17, 2018, https://www.novica.com/keepers-of-the-arts.

6. Tessa Wegert, "The New Creative Cities: 5 Urban Centers Influencing Art and Design," *Shutterstock* (blog), June 13, 2017, https://www.shutterstock.com/blog/global-creative-cities.

7. Joseph Lee, email correspondence with author, July 17, 2018.

Lifeline of global arts and witness: three strands braided together

We often see the road map for Christian witness as a group of pathways with different ways of experiencing and expressing our relationship with Christ. In order to effectively embrace the global arts in mission, we need to push the analogy further. We need to ask what it takes to navigate these pathways as we foster people's movement toward Christ. We need a strong lifeline that helps us stay on the path. We need a lifeline that keeps us focused on reaching the summit of coming into relationship with Jesus Christ and bowing in reverent worship before him as Lord and Savior. A lifeline is a braided rope that weaves together three smaller strands of rope in ways that strengthen and support people as they move out into new regions and territories. Each of these strands is inextricably bound up with the others as the three intertwine; each is critical and essential. In order to proceed toward Christ, we need to be clear about what we think about God (theological perspectives), what we think about the world (worldview perspectives), and how we practice or do life (emerging practices). These three all work together in an interwoven lifeline rope.

Theological Imperatives

Dialogue lies at the heart of the two great commandments. In the first commandment, loving God with our whole heart, soul, and mind is, in essence, a call to enter into relational dialogue with the living God (Matt. 22:37). Through worship, both formal and informal, we continue in relationship on a daily basis. Worship takes many forms, many of which are informed and facilitated by the arts. God does not, however, allow us to love only him, or even to love only our most immediate circle of relationships. We are also to love our neighbors as ourselves (Matt. 22:39). Out of our love relationship with God, he calls us into further dialogue with our neighbors, even those who force us to cross cultural boundaries, as in the good Samaritan story (Luke 10:25–37). As we enter into dialogue with our neighbors, we come into relationships where we extend hands of friendship, concern, care, and compassion, and, in the process, we witness to those around us and throughout the world. In this way we flesh out the two great commandments in relational dialogue. The expressive arts contribute to this dialogue by fostering interactive relationships among and between peoples. They are effective means for following the two greatest commandments.

The Great Commission (Matt. 28:16–20) then brings the two greatest commandments into even sharper focus. Not only are God's people to love God and to love their neighbors, but they are also to go, to baptize, and to make disciples of all peoples. Music and the global arts as expressive languages excel in accessing both the cognitive and affective levels of human communication and trigger the transformation of lives. Above all, they foster further allegiance and faithfulness in following Jesus as Lord.

Throughout our journey together, I have focused mainly on the book of Psalms for learning how God and his people interact with one another via the arts. I have sought to show through an art form, poetry, that God does communicate his goodness, his awareness of injustices, his displeasure when his people are going against him, and his desire for all nations to sing his praise. The psalms themselves model dialogue between God and his people, where the people come to him in prayer, in times of distress, and in exuberant adoration of the one who saves them. The parameters of the psalms and their dialogical interactions between God and his people encompass both worship and witness.

Other biblical precedents throughout the Scriptures further demonstrate the importance of the arts for both worshiping and witnessing to the glory and salvation of God. I find it significant that at pivotal moments the arts summarize, reflect on, and historically document God's interventions among his people. Take Exodus, for example, and the way it makes a case for multidimensional communication. The narrative of salvation in Exodus is embedded in a story, remembered in a meal, and told in song. Eugene Peterson cautions and forcefully argues that "the story, the meal, and the song turn like gears in a transmission—one off the other, to keep our understanding of and participation in salvation entire and healthy. Each part is essential to the others. It is God's work in history in 'ways past finding out.' The story, the meal, and the song keep us in living touch with what God is doing in history."[8] Peterson is pointing out the multisensory approaches to creating understanding. We need a broader conceptualization of witness and the means of doing mission. This implies that we need to intentionally read the Scriptures with an awareness of differing arts naturally embedded within the sacred text, looking in particular for the places where we see God interacting and relating with his peoples. Once we turn our attention there, we find that encountering and engaging with God and the nations through the global arts is modeled for

8. Peterson, *Christ Plays in Ten Thousand Places*, 170.

us throughout the Scriptures.[9] How then do we put into practice what the Scriptures are modeling for us? We turn first to new ways of thinking about the global arts.

Shifts in Perspectives

Shifting times call for shifts in perspectives, more expansive definitions, and emerging practices. Music and the arts, employed to honor and declare God's greatness and salvation, need to move out beyond the walls of the church into daily life in ways that bring about kingdom values. Not only do the Scriptures give insight to this, but it also seems that the secular world, particularly the globalizing world, has already shifted in perspectives and practices regarding the role of the arts.[10] Frankly, we in the Christian community are scrambling to catch up. I highlight here ten of the numerous changes currently taking place. When it comes to global arts and Christ-centered witness (and worship), we need to consider making the following shifts in our thinking:

1. *Shift from depending only on spoken and printed languages to embracing the full extent of expressive languages for communicating Christ.* This requires a turn from perceiving witness and evangelism as only proclaiming God's Word in spoken or written formats to including the holistic range of multiple artistic formats. The new perspective fosters embracing all cultural peoples and their artistic languages, when discerningly appropriated, and redeeming them for making the gospel known and faithfully lived out. A people's expressive languages offer a resource of culturally defined signal systems that contribute to bringing peoples to see the glory of God and know his salvation.

2. *Shift from assuming that the arts constitute one universal language to identifying what is universal and what is not.* We cannot justifiably assume that what effectively speaks to people in one context will function in exactly the same way in another place. Nor will it mean the same thing. Assuming that there is just one template of communication via the global arts adds up to matrices of miscommunication on multiple levels. What *is* universal is that each language group has a cluster of arts that are culturally defined and appropriated. We need to research the

9. Best, "Worship and Witness."

10. For example, ethnomusicologists assert that music and the arts function in society in multiple ways that affect lives. This often contrasts with the way music is limited to certain roles within the Western church. See Bohlman, *World Music*; Rice, *Ethnomusicology*.

definitions and theoretical frameworks of people's cultural art forms
and incorporate them into our ministry approaches.[11]

3. *Shift from assuming that music and other global arts function in isolation from one another to embracing multidisciplinary and integrative
   art forms.* Using the global arts in witness does not mean preferring one
   art form over any other. It is not an either-or choice but rather a matter
   of both-and, selecting which art forms speak most appropriately within
   the cultural context and the role they will play in communicating Christ.
   Global arts are not intended to be compartmentalized away from one
   another but rather are meant to be integrated, working interdependently
   and in tandem with one another.

4. *Shift from viewing the arts as mere cultural commodities to seeing them
   as cultural texts that carry significant content requiring translation for
   deeper communicative impact.* There is more to music and the arts
   than merely meets the eyes and ears of the beholders. They are not
   devoid of content, nor are they merely entertainment that leads up to
   spoken communication. Rather, they are cultural resources available
   for translating the most important message the world needs to hear.
   Many cultures expect to receive significant information through music
   and the arts. The arts engage people in processing their lives, bringing
   coherence to their societies.

5. *Shift from seeing the arts as separate entities apart from people to realizing that the arts are directly linked to people: music and the arts
   shape identity.* Music-cultures and their related art forms are intimately
   linked to a people and provide the cultural milieu within which they
   interact socially and build their identity. These identities differ among
   and between people. We need to expect cultural differences rather than
   uniformity. We need to revel in the diversity and creativity each people
   has to offer in worship and praise to God. All peoples are called to offer
   their best to God in ways that honor him. This requires our moving
   from expecting only one style or genre of art as the accepted form for
   worship and praise to embracing the deeply ingrained, identifying art
   forms of all people as potential conduits for engaging with God.

6. *Shift from working in spite of culture to working with culture.* We need
   to follow the incarnational approach of Jesus during his sojourn on earth:
   making himself known by engaging in the local spoken and expressive

---

11. See Stone, *The World's Music*. Also see McGann, *Exploring Music as Worship and
Theology*. McGann applies ethnomusicological research methods to liturgical studies in a very
accessible way that is also relevant to music and the arts in witness.

languages of a people. Naturally, this needs to be done with discernment and to focus on bringing God honor and glory that reveals his nature and character. We need to turn from noncritical contextualization to critical contextualization with the purpose of creating transformed lives.

7. *Shift from engaging cultural musics only when moving outside national borders to embracing the nations and their cultural arts living within our local contexts.* Local and global arts are present and accessible as peoples are moving throughout the world. The nations now live among all of us. This new reality requires shifting the dynamics of witness through the arts by engaging both local and global arts.

8. *Shift from focusing solely on presentational art forms to recognizing the value of participatory art forms.* Participatory art forms excel in engaging people through direct interaction with one another, building relationships, forming community, and processing differences. They allow people to move into safe spaces for renegotiating life and renewing our common humanity.

9. *Shift from focusing on product and performance to focusing on process and pivotal moments.* We need to loosen our fixation on products and performance only and intentionally recognize what lies behind the product and performance. The creative processes involved in collaborative music-making—musicking—and collaboration in other arts, such as drama, are roadways to dialogical engagement that forges relationships. Thomas Turino's concepts of "presentational" and "participatory" arts provide a broader range of possibilities for interacting with people worldwide. The arts in witness excel at engaging people with one another. Inclusivity rather than exclusivity becomes a hallmark of membership, acceptance, and recognition of other peoples around us and throughout the world. This serves as a foundational means for extending the love of God via the heart languages contained within peoples' art forms.

10. *Shift from professional artists only to laity, ministers, missionaries, and professional artists collaboratively witnessing through the arts.* This shift points to a running thread throughout all nine shifts in perspectives. That is, laypeople, missionaries, ministers, and professional artists are all called to bear witness to Christ through culturally relevant art forms. It is time to recognize that the call to witness goes out to all peoples. At the same time, the arts in witness are for all people. Music and the arts—the creative arts—are available resources for declaring God's glory and salvation. They should no longer be restricted to professional musicians and artists, although professional musicians and artists still have

critical roles to play. This work must be done by nonprofessionals and professional artists, missionaries and ministers of the gospel, all collaboratively engaging with the arts in witness with cultural sensitivity, discernment, and appropriateness.

Based on the above theological imperatives and shifts in perspective, how do we then put into practice their implications? In the following, I suggest essential practices and action points for engaging in the journey of witness through the global arts.

Emerging Practices

There is no one cultural arts template for witnessing to the good news of Jesus Christ. Such approaches have historically created major impediments in speaking into the lives of people in persuasive and transformative ways. The fact that peoples live in a plethora of diverse contexts requires flexibility in configuring and reconfiguring how we approach ministry and witness. We must know the foundational faith and cultural issues when approaching witness via the arts. We must first know God's Word and do our cultural exegesis of the arts of the peoples with whom we are interacting. Following on that, we must then be able to adjust and adapt our approaches according to a people's context, life situations, and generation. Just as teachers must be flexible in their lesson planning, adjusting their method according to language, skill set, learning style, and motivation, so we need to adjust and contextualize our methods for bearing witness to God's glory and salvation to diverse peoples.

The following five emerging practices are interlinked and based on the multivocal nature of the arts. These practices emerge from recognizing the significant interactional dynamics within creative processes. For each practice, I also include here an action point to be taken for initiating that particular practice.

Active Theologizing of God's Word

Active theologizing needs to be practiced in both local and globalized contexts. Theological reflection begins by asking what it means to follow Jesus in my local context and in light of the Scriptures. God's Word needs to be brought into the lives of local worshiping communities and translated into the expressive arts available within each context. Songs and creative arts resulting from believers' encounters with the living God become enduring products for ever-expanding audiences. They are transportable, beginning first with small groups in their immediate surroundings, and then being offered to larger regional groups, to national ones, and finally to global audiences. Authenticity of engagement with God through the Scriptures will be most effective when done at the local, heart-language level of the individuals or groups in the creative processes. Such theologizing then needs to be "evaluated in the light of global theologizing" and needs to contribute to the building up of concrete manifestations of everyday life, rich with practical implications[12] for faithful witness. This practice is central and key to all witness and worship.

Action point for active theologizing. Intentionally foster the regular meeting together of musicians, artists, practitioners, believers, and Christian leaders around the Word of God with the goal of creating new songs, dramas, poetry, and other creative arts. Ideally, local faith communities can encourage, motivate, and support knowing God more fully through the processes of creativity.

Contextualizing the Gospel for Living Christianly

This practice requires moving out of our comfortable religious boxes into expanded visions for bringing God into everyday life, into spiritual formation, and into public arenas where people are hurting, suffering, experiencing trauma, and in need of education related to health issues (e.g., malaria and HIV/AIDS). This practice includes ministry among the poor and other development issues. It entails a huge undertaking, and the arts can be instrumental in educating, healing, and reconciling, among other things. We must seek to bring relief to the suffering and sick and to visibly reveal God's compassion at work among a people.

Action point for contextualizing the gospel. Do intentional research into the needs of particular societies and communities. When working cross-culturally, this practice requires exegeting local art cultures, building collegial relationships with local leaders, and interacting with the people in the community. Listening, learning, and collaborating together for creating culturally relevant music and art that emerges from within the group lies at the core of transformative interaction.[13]

Proclaiming God's Story among People Who Prefer Oral Learning Styles

Telling God's story via oral forms has become an evangelistic method focused mainly on oral learners, nonreaders who either cannot or choose not

12. Hiebert, *Gospel in Human Contexts*, 180.
13. For a very complete approach to contextualizing for daily life, see Schrag, *Creating Local Arts Together*.

to read. In a very real sense, all peoples are oral learners. Everybody loves a good story. Storytelling easily confronts deeply embedded worldview values and causes people to internally wrestle with issues they have been trying to avoid. When designed to speak to particular cultural groups, stories allow people to hear and relate with the characters in a story on topics they would not otherwise have opportunity or desire to engage.

Action point for proclaiming God's story. Focus in particular on cultural forms that foster telling the gospel story. Then also look for forms and genres wherein peoples are freed up to tell their own stories of God at work in their lives and their particular life concerns. When working cross-culturally, be open to forms other than what you expect to use in telling the good news of Jesus Christ. Storytelling can include a combination of story, song, proverbs, painting, dance, or other art forms. It will vary according to age group, ethnicity, and/or professional status when practiced in the city. Be especially aware of the multiple dimensions of any context.

Dialoguing toward Peace

Musicking and creative arts processes foster loving our neighbors. While I have focused especially on loving our religious neighbors, the dialogues of beauty and art bridge broken relationships and foster reconciled relationships among all peoples. In particular, they provide accessible opportunities for mediating between cultures and peoples of differing faith allegiances. Where interfaith dialogue is often confined to high theological debates, global arts and their multiple arenas of dialogue generate common points of connection and joyous delight through the arts. People experience and are reminded of the common humanity they share. Building trust through the arts plays a dynamic role in incarnational witness.

Action point for dialoguing toward peace. Identify peoples of different faith traditions with whom you can interact and build bridges of friendship. Consider people who have been displaced or recently moved into your area. Or search for opportunities to work among groups in disagreement where musicking and the creative arts can serve as mediators and bonding agents. Showing respect and offering joy creates an atmosphere that frees people up to participate, interact, and share.

Forging Bonds for Sustainable Relationships

In the midst of high levels of diversity in our globalized era, heightened misunderstandings take place as people rub shoulders in their daily pursuit of life. The processes involved in musicking and artistic creativity offer a series of stepping-stones by which peoples can come together, especially around a common project. In the midst of each activity, bonding between the engaged people takes place. The process creates space to work through issues, dialoguing back and forth for understanding, and growing in relationship with one another. Musicking and the creative arts provide arenas for voicing identity, being recognized and heard, airing injustices, and venting deeper life issues. Sustainable relationships require committed, long-term interaction. The processes of intentional creativity on a regular basis make that possible.

Action point for forging bonds for sustainable relationships. Remember that initiative, patience, and perseverance in pursuing relational bonding through the arts are essential. Pursue a performance event such as an informal gathering, celebration, or festival that brings together diaspora peoples located within multicultural settings, and create definite goals around which people will interact over a sustained period of time. Starting small, ultimately a network of performing groups can be brought together that can enhance further engagement and form sustainable community.

A Concluding Note

Finally, I cannot help but return to Psalm 67 with its recurring refrain,

> May the peoples praise you, God;
>   may all the peoples praise you. (vv. 3, 5)

The refrain, sung twice, responds to God's work in the world. Its goal is for God's ways to be known throughout the world and his saving power to be experienced among peoples everywhere, from the cities to the far ends of the earth. Knowing God and his ways of justice gives impetus to joyful song and creative delight. I leave you with a benediction:

> May the global arts join in the dialogue of worship and witness.
> May they reveal God's glory and declare his salvation every day
>   throughout all the earth.
> May all nations, with magnificent diversity, join in the grand procession of praise to God!
> May the peoples' worship crescendo in glorious witness to God's glory
>   and salvation!

Questions for Discussion

1. Discuss the significance of the three major strands that create a lifeline for witnessing to Christ via the global arts.
2. Identify five of the most important shifts in perspectives for employing the global arts in Christian witness. Reflect on the impact of not recognizing these shifts and how to implement new perspectives.
3. Based on one or two of the five emerging practices, develop a collaborative plan for employing the global arts in Christian witness.

Webography

In an era of social media and the internet, our access to a vast range of resources is staggering. The following websites, blogs, and YouTube links provide a sampling of where and how to begin connecting with the global arts. These focus on organizations that are leading the way in promoting and engaging with global arts in contextualized worship and witness. Links to some creative, innovative, and powerful musical performances from around the world are also provided. This is certainly not an exhaustive collection, but it is intended to launch you on a journey of pursuing contextualized arts in witness and worship worldwide.

Artists in Christian Testimony
https://actinternational.org
> A.C.T. International "exists to mobilize and equip artistic and innovative ministries and missionaries for Christian work around the world."

Calvin Institute of Christian Worship: Multicultural Worship
https://worship.calvin.edu/resources/resource-library/listing.html?search=multi cultural%20worship&type=tag
> This resource focuses on the study and renewal of worship and is currently exploring multicultural worship that engages with the global arts.
>
> *Sample post:* Listen to Professor Jean Kidula (University of Georgia), ethnomusicologist from Kenya, on the history of worship music coming into Kenya: https://worship.calvin.edu/resources/resource-library/jubilation -awe-penitence-and-petition-in-corporate-worship-in-kenya.

Center for Excellence in World Arts

http://www.gial.edu/world-arts-center

> The center is "a collaborative space where best practices, resources, and strategies for arts and cross-cultural service are developed and disseminated through innovative courses, conferences, and artistic events."

Christians in the Arts Network of Japan

http://www.japancan.com

> The vision of Japan CAN (Christians in the Arts Network) is to build the church in Japan through culturally appropriate projects while equipping and encouraging arts specialists to affect the world for Christ.

Ethnodramatology

http://www.ethnodrama.com

> Ethnodramatology explores the different types of theater and drama around the world. The participants' goal is not to come up with universal principles that apply everywhere, but to seek ways to understand the unique qualities of each kind of drama. They also seek ways to encourage different forms of theater and find ways to communicate within those established forms. Also see www.ethnodramatology.blogspot.com.

Fuller Theological Seminary, Global Arts and World Religions

https://www.fuller.edu/academics/areas-of-interest/global-arts-and-world-religions

> This area of interest available to Fuller students offers "opportunities to investigate world religions as they are practiced, reflect on perceptions toward one another, and develop hands-on tools for engagement with peoples of differing faiths via the arts. Cultural and religious studies challenge students to think missiologically and theologically and learn practical ways to minister within local, regional, and global contexts." Courses also deal with global Christian worship and witness.

Global Christian Worship

http://globalworship.tumblr.com

> This is one of the most helpful resources in global Christian worship, with relevant posts for the church calendar and fascinating updates almost daily. The blog states that it is a "guided tour through music and arts coming from various Christian worship traditions around the world, plus a few other things of related interest such as multicultural musics."
>
> *Sample posts:* "Haiti: Prayers, Art & Song" (http://globalworship.tumblr.com/post/151476992850/haiti-prayers-art-song); "'Rise India' song" (http://globalworship.tumblr.com/post/158257203180/rise-india-song); "He Is

Carrying the Burden for Our Sins and Walking Forward" (Good Friday song in Hindi, India) (http://globalworship.tumblr.com/post/171900608700/he-is -carrying-the-burden-for-our-sins-and).

Global Consultation on Music and Missions (GCoMM)

http://www.gcommhome.org

The purpose of the Global Consultation on Music and Missions is to explore how God is drawing the nations to himself through music and related arts. The events call together mission and music leaders from around the world to (1) dialogue about the roles and foundations of heart music in the lives of all Christians; (2) connect and form personal friendships and organizational partnerships; (3) share resources, strategies, and models that have proved useful in a variety of contexts; (4) identify current challenges and opportunities; and (5) encourage further communication and networking (e.g., journals, databases, websites).

Hearts Sounds International (A Ministry of OM Arts)

http://heart-sounds.org

Heart Sounds International exists to help ignite biblically appropriate and culturally relevant heart worship in places where Christ followers are restricted, persecuted, or unknown.

International Council of Ethnodoxologists (ICE)

https://www.worldofworship.org

ICE envisions a future in which communities of Jesus followers in every culture engage with God and the world through their own artistic expressions. They offer networking, training, and resources for the flourishing of biblical and culturally appropriate arts.

International Orality Network (ION)

https://orality.net

The International Orality Network is an affiliation of agencies and organizations working together with the common goal of making God's Word available to oral learners in culturally appropriate ways that enable church-planting movements everywhere.

Lausanne Arts Issues Network

https://www.lausanne.org/networks/issues/arts

This network "exists to catalyze and connect artistic Christians and evangelical influencers concerning the role of artists and the arts for global mission—through gatherings focused on biblical prayer, reflection, training, and ministry action."

Liberty University Master of Arts in Ethnomusicology

https://www.liberty.edu/online/masters/ethnomusicology

As multicultural issues continue to emerge worldwide, ethnomusicology has become an important field of study in music education, music performance, and other areas of cross-cultural service. This ethnomusicology program aims to provide a strong foundation in scholarship and research, non-Western music theory, and application of resources to the field.

SIL Ethnomusicology and Arts

http://www.sil.org/arts/ethnomusicology.htm

Ethnomusicology and Arts within SIL focuses on research, documentation, and promotion of artistic forms of communication around the world in order to help communities meet their needs and goals.

(un)Common Sounds: Songs of Peace and Reconciliation among Muslims and Christians

http://www.songsforpeaceproject.org

This site provides resources and materials reporting on the (un)Common Sounds project, which explored the contribution of music and the arts in fostering sustainable peacebuilding among Muslims and Christians. Research and concerts were held in Beirut, Lebanon, and in Yogyakarta and Bandung, Indonesia.

Wild Hope International (Tanzania)

http://wildhopeinternational.org/who-we-are/#vision

Wild Hope's mission is to adventurously empower emerging leaders through Christian discipleship to step into their destiny as children of God who will transform their communities and the world. Wild Hope includes an emphasis on worship and is the group with whom Roberta King facilitated a 1999 workshop on New Songs for Worship. The newly created contextualized worship songs played a pivotal role in bringing Maasai people to faith, ultimately contributing to planting twenty-two churches in Tanzania.

The following list of online videos focuses on people and groups mentioned in the text.

China

Canaan Hymns
https://youtu.be/xa1saiWejjo

Xiao Min, "The Lord and I"
https://youtu.be/L8xqRkQ38wQ

Côte d'Ivoire

Harris Church 44th Anniversary at Adwumakase-Kese (January 2013)
https://youtu.be/hbg8nV3A-ps

Nyarafolo Baptism After-Celebration in Tiepogovogo (April 2018)
https://youtu.be/kxw1iXVDM68

Nyarafolo Baptism in Village of Tiepogovogo (April 2018)
https://youtu.be/PPdFwPpqe4E

Nyarafolo Bible Translation and Songs
https://vimeo.com/119493538

Senufo Art of Weaving
https://youtu.be/wCey7toVZ30

Egypt

Mustafa Said on the Oud
https://youtu.be/AsRa8utsG7U

Ethiopia

Tesfaye Gabbiso
https://youtu.be/EAWC6ZDXVB8
https://youtu.be/EM_TMWWSJs8

Indonesia

Children's Dance Group Performance—Yogyakarta
http://www.songsforpeaceproject.org/multimedia/childrens-dance-group
-performance

Suarasama—Isa Alaihissalam
http://www.songsforpeaceproject.org/multimedia/745

Rock the Peace Concert—Bandung
http://www.songsforpeaceproject.org/multimedia/test

Kenya

Afrizo singing group, Daystar University
https://youtu.be/AIKY3kEdJfs
https://youtu.be/KbKN5TEGqMM
https://youtu.be/rh-C6lTftAk

Japheth Kasanga
https://youtu.be/Wk7NY-Ra1ss

Reuben Kigame and Sifa Voices
https://youtu.be/Oa8m3N2gu6A

Lebanon

Songs of Divine Love Concert: Ritornello Al-Awadil
http://www.songsforpeaceproject.org/multimedia/songs-of-divine-love-concert
   -ritornello-al-awadil

(un)Common Sounds Trailer
http://www.songsforpeaceproject.org/multimedia/uncommon-sounds-trailer-1

Malawi

Storytelling
https://youtu.be/w_k1rb_mxc8

Morocco

Fez Festival of World Sacred Music
https://youtu.be/fTCCBLMnX9g
https://youtu.be/UFlRiWzJrcs

Mozambique

Megan Meyers on Ethnomusicology, Mission, and Hip Hop in Mozambique
https://youtu.be/mdMotso-TYQ

Pakistan

Eric Sarwar
https://youtu.be/0vEENjm0kwE

Tehillim Worship Symposium and Psalm Fest 2018—Pakistan
https://youtu.be/HkCHz71yQqk

Southern Sudan

Dinka
https://youtu.be/W3oYUDfjC3s

Tanzania

Munishi Wanamwabudu Nani
https://youtu.be/ubk_EecbGjA

Turkey

Sibel Üçal on Kanal Hayat—Istanbul
https://youtu.be/iuabOolrkQM

Uganda

Adungu Harps
https://youtu.be/Yj7swiCiUWU

United States

Tupak Shakur, "God"
https://youtu.be/qM6RVloJ3Fk

Ukulele in Prison Ministry: "This Little Light of Mine" performed at
Oregon State Penitentiary
https://youtu.be/FPwfWQiw4J0

Bibliography

Aasland, Erik. "Two Heads Are Better Than One: Using Conceptual Mapping to Analyze Proverb Meaning." *Proverbium: Yearbook of Annual Proverb Scholarship* 16, no. 3 (2009): 1–18.

Adeyamo, Tokunboh, ed. *Africa Bible Commentary: A One-Volume Commentary Written by 70 African Scholars*. Nairobi: WordAlive, 2006.

Anderson, Benedict. *Imagined Communities: Reflections on the Origin and Spread of Nationalism*. New York: Verso, 2006.

Ardener, Shirley. "Ardener's 'Muted Groups': The Genesis of an Idea and Its Praxis." *Women and Language* 28, no. 2 (2005): 50–54.

Bailey, Kenneth. *Finding the Lost: Cultural Keys to Luke 15*. St. Louis: Concordia, 1992.

Balisky, Lila W., compiler. *Songs of Tesfaye Gabbiso*. Translated by Haile Jenai. Addis Ababa, Ethiopia: SIM Press, 2012.

———. "Theology in Song: Ethiopia's Tesfaye Gabbiso." *Missiology: An International Review* 25, no. 4 (1997): 447–56.

Barnett-Sanchez, Holly, and Tim Drescher. *Give Me Life: Iconography and Identity in East LA Murals*. Albuquerque: University of New Mexico Press, 2016.

Bavinck, J. H., and David Hugh Freeman. *An Introduction to the Science of Missions*. Philadelphia: P&R, 1964.

Bediako, Kwame. "Scripture as the Interpreter of Culture and Tradition." In Adeyemo, *Africa Bible Commentary*, 3–4.

Best, Harold M. "Worship and Witness: The Indivisible Task of Continuous Outpouring." In *Unceasing Worship: Biblical Perspectives on Worship and the Arts*, 77–93. Downers Grove, IL: InterVarsity, 2003.

Bevans, Stephen B., SVD, and Roger P. Schroeder, SVD. *Constants in Context: A Theology of Mission for Today*. Maryknoll, NY: Orbis, 2004.

Bithell, Caroline. *A Different Voice, a Different Song*. Oxford: Oxford University Press, 2014.

Bohlman, Philip V. *World Music: A Very Short Introduction*. Oxford: Oxford University Press, 2002.

Bowden, Ross. *Creative Spirits: Bark Painting in the Washkuk Hills of North New Guinea*. Melbourne: Oceanic Art Pty Ltd, 2006.

Brubaker, Rogers. "The 'Diaspora' Diaspora." *Ethnic and Racial Studies* 28, no. 1 (January 2005): 1–19.

Brueggemann, Walter. *The Message of the Psalms: A Theological Commentary*. Minneapolis: Augsburg, 1984.

———. *Praying the Psalms: Engaging Scripture and the Life of the Spirit*. 2nd ed. Eugene, OR: Cascade, 2007.

Brueggemann, Walter, and William H. Bellinger Jr. *Psalms*. New Cambridge Bible Commentary. New York: Cambridge University Press, 2014.

Campbell, Karen. "How Can We Sing Songs in a Strange Land? The Experience of Dinka Episcopal Christians in Kakuma Refugee Camp, Kenya." Paper presented at the Global Consultation on Music and Mission, Fort Worth, Texas, 2003.

Chang, Jeff. *Can't Stop, Won't Stop: A History of the Hip Hop Generation*. New York: St. Martin's Press, 2005.

Charles, Mark. "A Laughing Party and Contextualized Worship." In Krabill, Fortunato, Harris, and Schrag, *Worship and Mission for the Global Church*, 267–69.

Clapp, Rodney R. *A Peculiar People: The Church as Culture in a Post-Christian Society*. Downers Grove, IL: InterVarsity, 1996.

Csordas, Thomas J. "Introduction: Modalities of Transnational Transcendence." *Anthropological Theory* 7, no. 3 (2007): 259–72.

DeNora, Tia. *Music in Everyday Life*. Cambridge: Cambridge University Press, 2000.

Downes, Stan, Robert J. Oehrig, and John Shane. *Summary of the Nairobi Church Survey*. Nairobi: Daystar University College, 1989.

Erlmann, Veit. *Nightsong: Performance, Power, and Practice in South Africa*. Chicago: University of Chicago Press, 1996.

Finnegan, Ruth. *The Hidden Musicians: Music-Making in an English Town*. 2nd ed. Middletown, CT: Wesleyan University Press, 2007.

———. *Oral Literature in Africa*. Nairobi: Oxford University Press, 1998. Original publication, London: Clarendon, 1970.

Geany, Jane. *On the Epistemology of the Senses in Early Chinese Thought*. Honolulu: University of Hawaii Press, 2002.

Glaze, Anita J. *Art and Death in a Senufo Village*. Bloomington: Indiana University Press, 1981.

Goldingay, John. *Psalms 1–41*. Vol. 1 of *Psalms*. Baker Commentary on the Old Testament Wisdom and Psalms. Grand Rapids: Baker Academic, 2006.

————. *Psalms 42–89*. Vol. 2 of *Psalms*. Baker Commentary on the Old Testament Wisdom and Psalms. Grand Rapids: Baker Academic, 2007.

————. *Psalms 90–150*. Vol. 3 of *Psalms*. Baker Commentary on the Old Testament Wisdom and Psalms. Grand Rapids: Baker Academic, 2008.

Hall, Edward T. *The Silent Language*. Greenwich, CT: Fawcett, 1959.

Hanna, Judith Lynn. "Dance Movement and the Communication of Sociocultural Patterns." In *To Dance Is Human: A Theory of Nonverbal Communication*, 83–100. Chicago: University of Chicago Press, 1987.

Hatcher, Mark J. "Poetry, Singing, and Contextualization." *Missiology: An International Review* 29 (2001): 475–88.

Healey, Joseph, and Donald Sybertz. *Towards an African Narrative Theology*. Nairobi: Paulines Publications Africa, 1996.

Held, David, Anthony McGrew, David Goldblatt, and Jonathan Perraton. *Global Transformations: Politics, Economics and Culture*. Stanford, CA: Stanford University Press, 1999.

Hiebert, Paul G. *Anthropological Reflections on Missiological Issues*. Grand Rapids: Baker, 1994.

————. "Critical Contextualization." *Missiology: An International Review* 12, no. 3 (July 1984): 287–96.

————. *The Gospel in Human Contexts: Anthropological Explorations for Contemporary Missions*. Grand Rapids: Baker Academic, 2009.

————. "Metatheology: The Step beyond Contextualization." In Hiebert, *Anthropological Reflections*, 93–105.

————. "The Missionary as Mediator of Global Theologizing." In *Globalizing Theology: Belief and Practice in an Era of World Christianity*, edited by Craig Ott and Harold A. Netland, 288–308. Grand Rapids: Baker Academic, 2006.

Hill, Harriet. "The Arts and Trauma Healing in Situations of Violence and Conflict." In Krabill, Fortunato, Harris, and Schrag, *Worship and Mission for the Global Church*, 177–78.

Hodge, Daniel White. *Hip Hop's Hostile Gospel: A Post-Soul Exploration*. Studies in Critical Research on Religion 6. Leiden: Brill, 2017.

————. "No Church in the Wild: Hip Hop Theology and Mission." *Missiology: An International Review* 41, no. 1 (2013): 97–109. https://doi.org/10.1177/0091829612467157.

————. *The Soul of Hip Hop: Rims, Timbs and a Cultural Theology*. Downers Grove, IL: InterVarsity, 2010.

Hollinger, David A. *Postethnic America: Beyond Multiculturalism*. New York: Basic Books, 2000.

Holton, Jared. "Performing toward Peace." In King and Tan, *(un)Common Sounds*, 158–77.

Jewell, Dawn Herzog. "Winning the Oral Majority." *Christianity Today*, March 2006, 56–58. https://www.christianitytoday.com/ct/2006/march/30.56.html.

Johnson, Vivien. *Lives of the Papunya Tula Artists*. Alice Springs, Australia: IAD Press, 2008.

Kaiser, Walter C., Jr. "God's Purpose for Mission in the Psalter of Israel." In *Mission in the Old Testament: Israel as a Light to the Nations*, 27–36. Grand Rapids: Baker Academic, 2012.

Kidula, Jean Ngoya. "Music Culture: African Life." In King, Kidula, Krabill, and Oduro, *Music in the Life of the African Church*, 37–56.

——. *Music in Kenyan Christianity: Logooli Religious Song*. Bloomington: Indiana University Press, 2013.

——. "Polishing the Luster of the Stars: Music Professionalism Made Workable in Kenya." *Ethnomusicology* 44 (2000): 408–28.

King, Roberta R. "Bible: *Lex Canendi, Lex Credendi*." In King, Kidula, Krabill, and Oduro, *Music in the Life of the African Church*, 117–32.

——. "Encountering Abraham in Africa." In *Conversations at the Edges of Things: Reflections for the Church in Honor of John Goldingay*, 142–53. Eugene, OR: Pickwick, 2012.

——. *Pathways in Christian Music Communication: The Case of the Senufo of Côte d'Ivoire*. American Society of Missiology Monograph Series. Eugene, OR: Pickwick, 2009.

——. "Stepping Stones toward Senufo Christian Songs." In King, *Pathways in Christian Music Communication*, 63–77.

——. *A Time to Sing: A Manual for the African Church*. Nairobi: Evangel Publishing House, 1999.

——. "Toward a Discipline of Christian Ethnomusicology: A Missiological Paradigm." *Missiology: An International Review* 32 (2004): 293–307.

King, Roberta R., Jean Ngoya Kidula, James Krabill, and Thomas Oduro, eds. *Music in the Life of the African Church*. Waco: Baylor University Press, 2008.

King, Roberta R., and Sooi Ling Tan, eds. *(un)Common Sounds: Songs of Peace and Reconciliation among Muslims and Christians*. Eugene, OR: Cascade, 2014.

Kitwana, Bakari. *The Hip Hop Generation: Young Blacks and the Crisis in African-American Culture*. New York: Basic Civitas, 2003.

Krabill, James R. *The Hymnody of the Harrist Church among the Dida of South-Central Ivory Coast (1913–1949)*. Frankfurt am Main: Peter Lang, 1995.

Krabill, James R., Frank Fortunato, Robin P. Harris, and Brian Schrag, eds. *Worship and Mission for the Global Church: An Ethnodoxology Handbook*. Pasadena, CA: William Carey Library, 2013.

Kraft, Charles H. *Communication Theory for Christian Witness*. Maryknoll, NY: Orbis, 1991.

Kramarae, Cheris. "Muted Group Theory and Communication: Asking Dangerous Questions." *Women and Language* 28, no. 2 (2005): 55–61.

Labberton, Mark. *The Dangerous Act of Loving Your Neighbor*. Downers Grove, IL: InterVarsity, 2010.

Lederach, John Paul. *The Little Book of Conflict Transformation*. Intercourse, PA: Good Books, 2003.

———. *The Moral Imagination: The Art and Soul of Building Peace*. Oxford: Oxford University Press, 2005.

Lingenfelter, Sherwood G. *Transforming Culture: A Challenge for Christian Mission*. Grand Rapids: Baker, 1998.

Lovata, Troy, and Elizabeth Olton, eds. *Understanding Graffiti: Multidisciplinary Studies from Prehistory to the Present*. New York: Routledge, 2015.

Marcus, Scott L. *Music in Egypt: Experiencing Music, Expressing Culture*. New York: Oxford University Press, 2007.

Mbiti, John S. "'Children Confer Glory on a Home': Introduction to the African Proverbs Series." In *The Voice of the People: Proverbs of the Basotho*, vol. 4, edited by Makali Isabella Mokitimi, i–xx. Pretoria, South Africa: Unisa Press, 1997.

———. *Introduction to African Religion*. 2nd ed. Long Grove, IL: Waveland, 2015.

McGann, Mary E. *Exploring Music as Worship and Theology: Research in Liturgical Practice*. Collegeville, MN: Liturgical Press, 2002.

Meares, Mary, Annette Torres, Denise Derkacs, John Oetzel, and Tamar Ginossar. "Employee Mistreatment and Muted Voices in the Culturally Diverse Workplace." *Journal of Applied Communication Research* 32, no. 1 (2004): 4–27.

Meyers, Megan. "Songs of Life: Music, Mission, and Medicine." *Evangelical Missions Quarterly* 53 (January 2017): 41–47. https://s3.amazonaws.com/missio-emq/EMQ _Volume_53_Issue_1.pdf.

Miller, Terry E., and Andrew Shahriari. *World Music: A Global Journey*. New York: Routledge, 2006.

Moon, Jay. *African Proverbs Reveal Christianity in Culture: A Narrative Portrayal of Builsa Proverbs Contextualizing Christianity in Ghana*. American Society of Missiology Monograph Series 5. Eugene, OR: Pickwick, 2009.

Myers, Bryant L. *Engaging Globalization: The Poor, Christian Mission, and Our Hyperconnected World*. Grand Rapids: Baker Academic, 2017.

Nelson, Kristina. *The Art of Reciting the Qur'an*. Austin: University of Texas Press, 1985.

Netland, Harold A. Introduction to *Globalizing Theology: Belief and Practice in an Era of World Christianity*, by Craig Ott and Harold A. Netland. Grand Rapids: Baker Academic, 2006.

Nettl, Bruno. *The Study of Ethnomusicology: Thirty-One Issues and Concepts*. 2nd ed. Urbana: University of Illinois Press, 2005.

Neuliep, James W. *Intercultural Communication: A Contextual Approach*. Los Angeles: Sage, 2015.

Okullu, Henry. *Church and Politics in East Africa*. Nairobi: Uzima Publishing House, 1974.

Okwepo, Isidore. *African Oral Literature: Backgrounds, Character, and Continuity*. Bloomington: Indiana University Press, 1992.

Ong, Walter J. *Orality and Literacy: The Technologizing of the Word*. London: Methuen, 1982.

Osborne, Grant R. *The Hermeneutical Spiral: A Comprehensive Introduction to Biblical Interpretation*. 2nd ed. Downers Grove, IL: IVP Academic, 2006.

Ott, Craig, and Stephen J. Strauss, with Timothy C. Tennent. *Encountering Theology of Mission: Biblical Foundations, Historical Developments, and Contemporary Issues*. Grand Rapids: Baker Academic, 2010.

Peterson, Eugene H. *Answering God: The Psalms as Tools for Prayer*. San Francisco: Harper & Row, 1991.

———. *Christ Plays in Ten Thousand Places: A Conversation in Spiritual Theology*. Grand Rapids: Eerdmans, 2005.

Phillips, Susan A. *Wallbangin': Graffiti and Gangs in L. A.* Chicago: University of Chicago Press, 1999.

Piper, John. *Let the Nations Be Glad! The Supremacy of God in Missions*. 3rd ed. Grand Rapids: Baker, 2010.

Pocock, Michael, Gailyn Van Rheenen, and Douglas McConnell. *The Changing Face of World Missions: Engaging Contemporary Issues and Trends*. Grand Rapids: Baker Academic, 2005.

Racy, A. J. *Making Music in the Arab World: The Culture and Artistry of Tarab*. Cambridge: Cambridge University Press, 2003.

Reisacher, Evelyne. *Joyful Witness in the Muslim World: Sharing the Gospel in Everyday Encounters*. Mission in Global Community. Grand Rapids: Baker Academic, 2016.

Rice, Timothy. *Ethnomusicology: A Very Short Introduction*. New York: Oxford University Press, 2014.

Roseman, Marina. "A Fourfold Framework for Cross-Cultural, Integrative Research on Music and Medicine." In *The Oxford Handbook of Medical Ethnomusicology*, edited by Benjamin Koen, 18–45. New York: Oxford University Press, 2008.

Sadie, Stanley, ed. *The New Grove Dictionary of Music and Musicians*. 2nd ed. 29 vols. New York: Oxford University Press, 2001.

Sanneh, Lamin O. *Translating the Message: The Missionary Impact on Culture*. 2nd ed. American Society of Missiology 42. Maryknoll, NY: Orbis, 2009.

———. *Whose Religion Is Christianity? The Gospel beyond the West*. Grand Rapids: Eerdmans, 2003.

Schrag, Brian. *Creating Local Arts Together: A Manual to Help Communities Reach Their Kingdom Goals*. Edited by James R. Krabill. Pasadena, CA: William Carey Library, 2013.

Scott, Joyce. *Moving into African Music*. Claremont, South Africa: Pretext Publishers, 2009.

Shaw, Susan Maxine. *Storytelling in Religious Education*. Birmingham, AL: Religious Education Press, 1991.

Shelemay, Kay Kaufman. *Soundscapes: Exploring Music in a Changing World*. 2nd ed. New York: Norton, 2006.

Shiloah, Amnon. *Music in the World of Islam: A Socio-Cultural Study*. Detroit: Wayne State University Press, 1995.

Small, Christopher. *Musicking: The Meanings of Performing and Listening (Music Culture)*. Middletown, CT: Wesleyan University Press, 1998.

Smith, Alex G. "Communication and Continuity through Oral Transmission." In *Communicating Christ through Story and Song: Orality in Buddhist Contexts*, edited by Paul H. De Neui, 2–26. Pasadena, CA: William Carey Library, 2008.

Smith, Donald K. *Creating Understanding: A Handbook for Christian Communication across Cultural Landscapes*. Grand Rapids: Zondervan, 1992.

Steffen, Tom. *Worldview-Based Storying: The Integration of Symbol, Story, and Ritual in the Orality Movement*. Richmond, VA: Orality Resources International, 2018.

Steger, Manfred B. *Globalization: A Very Short Introduction*. Oxford: Oxford University Press, 2009.

Stinton, Diane B. *Jesus of Africa: Voices of Contemporary African Christology*. Maryknoll, NY: Orbis, 2004.

Stone, Ruth M. *Theory for Ethnomusicology*. New York: Pearson, 2008.

———, ed. *The World's Music: General Perspectives and Reference Tools*. Vol. 10 of *The Garland Encyclopedia of World Music*. New York: Routledge, 2002.

Storr, Anthony. *Music and the Mind*. New York: Ballantine Books, 1992.

Sun, Irene Ai-Ling. "Songs of Canaan: Hymnody of the House-Church Christians in China." *EthnoDoxology* 4, no. 3 (2010): 1–10.

Sunquist, Scott W. "Church: The Community of Worship and Witness." In Sunquist, *Understanding Christian Mission*, 281–310.

———. "A Historian's Hunches: Eight Future Trends in Mission." In *The State of Missiology Today: Global Innovations in Christian Witness*, edited by Charles E. Van Engen, 285–98 (chap. 8). Downers Grove, IL: IVP Academic, 2016.

———. *Understanding Christian Mission: Participation in Suffering and Glory*. Grand Rapids: Baker Academic, 2013.

Taylor, Timothy D. *Global Pop: World Music, World Markets*. New York: Routledge, 1997.

Titon, Jeff Todd, ed. *Worlds of Music: An Introduction to the Music of the World's Peoples.* 5th ed. Belmont, CA: Schirmer Cengage Learning, 2009.

Titon, Jeff Todd, and David B. Reck. "Discovering and Documenting a World of Music." In *Worlds of Music: An Introduction to the Music of the World's Peoples, Shorter Version,* 3rd ed., edited by Jeff Titon, 355–81. Belmont, CA: Schirmer Cengage Learning, 2009.

Turino, Thomas. *Music as Social Life: The Politics of Participation.* Chicago: University of Chicago Press, 2008.

Van Engen, Charles E. "Toward a Contextually Appropriate Methodology in Mission Theology." In *Appropriate Christianity,* edited by Charles E. Van Engen, 203–25. Pasadena, CA: William Carey Library, 2006.

Vogler, Christopher. *The Writer's Journey: Mythic Structure for Writers.* 2nd ed. Studio City, CA: M. Wiese Productions, 1998.

Wade, Bonnie C. *Thinking Musically: Experiencing Music, Expressing Culture.* New York: Oxford University Press, 2004.

Walls, Andrew F. *The Missionary Movement in Christian History: Studies in the Transmission of Faith.* Maryknoll, NY: Orbis, 1996.

———. "The Western Discovery of Non-Western Christian Art." In Walls, *Missionary Movement in Christian History,* 173–86.

Wheeler, Andrew C. *Land of Promise—Church Growth in a Sudan at War.* Nairobi: Paulines Publications, 1997.

Wright, N. T. *The New Testament and the People of God.* Minneapolis: Fortress, 1992.

Yamamori, T., and C. R. Taber, eds. *Christopaganism or Indigenous Christianity?* Pasadena, CA: William Carey Library, 1975.

Index